Methodism and Society
in
Theological Perspective

METHODISM AND SOCIETY

Volume III

Methodism and Society in Theological Perspective

S. Paul Schilling

Edited by the Board of Social and Economic Relations
of The Methodist Church and Published by

Abingdon Press

NEW YORK   •   NASHVILLE

METHODISM AND SOCIETY IN THEOLOGICAL PERSPECTIVE

Copyright © 1960 by Abingdon Press

Library of Congress Catalog Card Number: 60-11221

SET UP, PRINTED, AND BOUND BY THE
PARTHENON PRESS, AT NASHVILLE,
TENNESSEE, UNITED STATES OF AMERICA

Introduction

IN THE CONCLUSION OF HIS CLASSICAL STUDY OF *The Social Teaching of the Christian Churches*, Ernst Troeltsch made the remark: "Faith is the source of energy in the struggle of life, but life still remains a battle which is continually renewed upon ever new fronts." If Troeltsch were alive today, he would find ample confirmation of this statement in the upheavals of the twentieth century. The arena of the social struggle has become global. Myriads of human beings in Asia, Africa, and Latin America have seen a glimpse of a better life and are rising to claim their share in the resources of the earth. Revolutions in expectations are breeding revolutions of the social order. Changes which once took centuries are now telescoped into decades. Modern science and technology are providing unprecedented opportunities for the enhancement of life or for totalitarian regimentation of human ants. The entire globe is an explosive "area of rapid social change" from which no country is exempt. In an interdependent world, the battle for freedom from hunger and misery, from diseases and illiteracy, from injustice and tyranny, from the threat of atomic annihilation, is everybody's concern and everybody's responsibility.

Does the Christian faith furnish a "source of energy" and a sense of urgency and direction in this new battle for the dignity and welfare, no longer of particular groups of underprivileged alone, but of every member of the human race? It must frankly be acknowledged that the churches, as often in the past, are disappointingly slow in their response to swiftly changing situations and weak and divided in

5

their social witness. For many Christians, the world-transforming power of the gospel is reduced to the virtue of social respectability.

Yet, in the longer perspectives of history, it must also gratefully be recognized that this century has witnessed an almost miraculous upsurge of social concern in widening Christian circles. The labors of the pioneers of the American social gospel movement and related endeavors in Europe, though often decried by advocates of a theological and economic status quo, have not been without fruit. From an irritant, the movement has turned into a ferment. From an act of prophetic revolt, it has developed into an impressive range of official and unofficial program activities of the churches—largely reformist and educational, it is true, yet not insensitive to the urgings of the prophets to translate "social creeds" into bolder and more costly deeds.

Acceptance of social responsibility on the part of the churches, however variously conceived, has to such an extent become a part of American culture that it is easy to overlook its comparative novelty. A glance at the international scene furnishes an even more telling indication of the truly amazing growth of social awareness within the short span of a few decades. When the Methodist Episcopal Church and the Federal Council of the Churches of Christ in America in 1908 adopted the "Social Creed," such a step would have been unacceptable to most Protestant and Eastern Orthodox bodies on other continents. The first ecumenical world conference on Practical Christianity, held in Stockholm 1925, was above all a stirring confession of the failure of the Christian churches to live up to their mission in society. But one needs to have only the slightest acquaintance with the program of the World Council of Churches, a generation later, to become aware of the extent to which the struggle for a responsible society has become a commonly accepted obligation. The huge project currently undertaken by the World Council on "The Common Christian Responsibility Toward Areas of Rapid Social Change" is a very instructive illustration of this change of mind.

The progressive leavening of the life of the denominations and the growth in sensitivity and professional expertness, which characterize the movement of social Christianity at home and abroad today, are doubtless in part a response to the pervasive pressures of history. But they also reflect profound changes in the Church's understanding of

6

its own life and mission. A few of these changing emphases may be listed in summary fashion:

(1) There is a new emphasis on the Church—the people of God, the body of Christ—as a corporate agent of social criticism and redemption. Its primary impact on society does not reside in its social teachings and program activities. Its impact derives above all from its very existence in the world as a community of believers and from the redemptive radiance of their life in prayer and worship, in Christian self-discipline, and in care for the neighbor near and afar. (2) The gospel of salvation is the opposite of religious individualism; it is social because it is personal. Its concern is not with disembodied souls nor with material progress without soul, but with the wholeness of man-in-community. (3) The Christian social witness becomes relevant and effective in the myriads of decisions and actions of laymen and lay women as they seek to live out their faith in the rough-and-tumble of everyday life. The Evanston Assembly of the World Council of Churches in 1954 offered a pointed formulation of this view: "The real battles of the faith today are being fought in factories, shops, offices, and farms, in political parties and government agencies, in countless homes, in the press, radio and television, in the relationship of nations." (4) There is also a growing recognition that social prophecy, in order not to remain a pious but ineffectual gesture, must be instrumented by social and political realism and translated into strategic planning. In the complexities of an increasingly organized and technicized society, the scattered efforts of individuals and small groups in immediate situations do not suffice. Christian efforts need to be co-ordinated in an all-inclusive strategy—a strategy which rests on an incisive diagnosis of national values and evils, which projects Christian imperatives into captivating and realizable goals, and which knows how to utilize the decision-making processes in an organized society.

The last point is worth stressing. Despite its flourishing busyness, the Christian social witness is caught up in a grave though mostly unavowed crisis. The root cause of the crisis lies, no doubt, in the fact that the "source of energy in the struggle of life" (to quote again Troeltsch's phrase) for many Christians has lost its transforming dynamism. But there is also a disturbing feeling that much of the Christian social witness is "beating the air"—not only because it is

7

often hesitant and weak but because it has become uncertain of its target. Hampered by social and ethical myopia, Christian groups are slow to recognize that the battlefield of social responsibility has become vastly expanded and more complex. A missionary strategist once remarked: "The devil never laughs so heartily as when he succeeds in luring devout Christians to concentrate their efforts on secondary fronts. For then he has the central front, unguarded, all to himself." Though some may take exception to the language, no one can deny the pertinency of this observation in a time when the configuration of the battle is undergoing such swift and extraordinary changes.

It is not without reason, therefore, that Christian leaders are paying increasing attention to broader questions of aims and goals and the attendant problems of long-range planning. What are the purposes of this nation? What are the purposes of the Christian Church in and beyond the nation? To be sure, there is a legitimate place for particular "causes" and "emphases." But, in the opinion of many, the present situation calls for an imaginative attempt to rethink larger priorities. To take an illustration, are those right who suggest that the overriding Christian social concerns in the years ahead should be world peace under law, a more equitable partnership in utilizing the abundant material and technological resources of the earth, and the population explosion?

It is in this world context that the project on *Methodism and Society* is set. Like other Christian bodies, Methodism is challenged to ponder the lessons of its heritage, to redefine its social motivations and ideals, to assess its present activities and resources, and to project adequate strategies for more vigorous advance. The MESTA[1] study is an exploratory contribution to this task. Although it is chiefly concerned with the interaction of Methodism and American society, its broad Protestant approach, it is hoped, will commend it to the attention of social-minded Christians in other denominations as well.

Following the invitation from the Board of Social and Economic Relations, the committee appointed by the Boston University School of Theology faculty prepared a prospectus which was approved by the Board in September 1957. The committee has worked as a team in the general planning and in the definition and constant review of

[1] The term "MESTA," frequently used in these volumes, is an abbreviation of the original working title, "Methodist Social Thought and Action."

scope and research procedures. While the designated authors have carried primary responsibility for the writing of the individual volumes, these also include, in varying degrees, contributions of other members.

The preliminary survey of source materials indicated that such a study, to fulfill its purpose, would require a far greater amount of primary research than had been originally anticipated. Hence the committee carried out a series of specialized projects covering such sources as Annual Conference Journals and regional periodicals, files of boards and agencies of The Methodist Church, educational curriculum materials, and personal records. Limitations of time and resources have prevented more than a sampling of representative periods, regions, and types of data. The largest single project—on "The Beliefs of Methodists" (designated MR [2])—is described in Appendix B of the present volume, p. 275. A full account of this particular inquiry is given in a mimeographed monograph by Herbert E. Stotts.

The findings of the whole project have been condensed in a series of four volumes appearing under the general title of *Methodism and Society*.

Volume I, *Methodism and Society in Historical Perspective*, traces the social history of Methodism up to 1908, when the adoption of the "Social Creed" by the Methodist Episcopal Church and subsequently by the Federal Council of Churches of Christ in America opened up a new period. Beginning with a consideration of British Methodism from John Wesley to 1850, it recounts the checkered history of Methodism's interaction with the American environment.

Volume II, *Methodism and Society in the Twentieth Century*, brings the story up to the present time, correlating the growth of social concerns with major developments in national life. In further parts, the volume examines the contributions of specific agencies and groups, both official and unofficial, and gives a topical presentation of Methodism's stand on major issues.

The present volume, *Methodism and Society in Theological Perspective*, pursues a two-fold aim. After analyzing the social implications of John Wesley's thought, it discusses major trends and emphases in relating religious convictions and social conduct as they appear in twentieth-century Methodism in the United States. The constructive part suggests in broad outline a theology of society which is both rooted in the truths of the Christian faith and relevant to the contemporary social scene.

The fourth volume, *Methodism and Society: Guidelines for Strategy*, relates the findings of the preceding studies to the insights of social science into the processes of decision-making and planning. Against this background it seeks to develop a framework of principles and considerations which may serve as guidelines for a realistic strategy of social education, leadership, and action.

Some of the general features, and limitations, of the project should be pointed out. As the reader of the volumes will notice, the study pays major attention to the institutional manifestations of Methodist social concern. Such an approach may tend to create the one-sided impression that the social witness of Methodism is to be seen chiefly in its institutional activities and in deliberate efforts of clergy and lay professionals to promote social change. The committee was, of course, aware of the fact that the social radiation of a church is an expression of its total life as it interacts with the environing culture, and especially of the countless decisions of individual Christians in the run of everyday life. It has therefore sought to probe also these elusive realities at certain points—particularly through the inquiry into the actual religious beliefs and social attitudes of Methodists, referred to above as MR[2].

The fact is often overlooked that The Methodist Church as a denomination is not limited to America alone. It is world-wide in structure and polity, as evidenced by the composition of its top legislative and executive organs, the General Conference and the Council of Bishops. A study of the varied relations existing between Methodism and society around the globe would be of great benefit in fostering a deeper sense of fellowship and a mutual understanding of the widely differing conditions under which Methodists are called to bear their social witness. The present volumes, however, are focused on the religious and social scene of the United States, with some notable exceptions. Thus Volume I includes an account of the social history of British Methodism from Wesley to 1850. The narrative of twentieth-century developments in Volume II suggests the influence of international perspectives on General Conference resolutions and Board actions. The deliberative parts of Volumes III and IV possess, in the nature of the case, a transcultural reference.

The ecumenical aspirations and affiliations of Methodism pose a somewhat similar problem, especially with respect to Volumes III and IV. It would have been theoretically possible to attempt to define a distinctive Methodist theology of society and a corresponding social strategy. Both theological and pragmatic reasons led the committee to adopt a different course. Methodism is officially committed to the cause of Christian unity. Methodist pronouncements and attitudes today are more expressive of the common outlook of social-minded Protestantism than of a separate tradition. Moreover, in the realm of strategy and action, it would clearly be self-defeating to seek to do in isolation what can be accomplished more effectively by a pooling of resources. Guided by such considerations, the committee has deliberately chosen to place its discussion of Methodist social responsibility in the broader framework of co-operative Christianity. Especially in the constructive parts, emphases of the Methodist heritage have been freely combined with the experiences and insights of the ecumenical community. It is hoped that this approach not only will be recognized as congenial to Methodism, but also will enhance the contribution of the project to a common task.

As previously indicated, the research phase of the project has been a co-operative venture of high order. It has benefited from the assistance of hundreds of correspondents, collaborators, and advisers across the country—denominational and interdenominational executives, liaison persons with the boards of The Methodist Church, ministers and laymen engaged in social work, academic scholars, social researchers, theological students, and so forth. Altogether over six thousand persons participated in the inquiry on "The Beliefs of Methodists." Drafts of the manuscripts were reviewed by members of the subcommittee of the Board of Social and Economic Relations as well as by outside experts.

Substantial reviews of the manuscript of the present volume on *Methodism and Society in Theological Perspective* were contributed by Waldo Beach, L. Harold DeWolf, Georgia Harkness, Gerald O. McCulloh, Gordon E. Michaelson, J. Robert Nelson, and Mack B. Stokes.

Of the faculty members of the Boston University School of Theology, William C. Moore did substantial research on church school materials, and Donald T. Rowlingson assisted in the reading of

Southern periodicals. Members of the committee have used the opportunity of exploring aspects of the project in seminars. The following students of the School furnished resource materials in the form of term papers, research memoranda, and, in a few instances, doctoral dissertations on related topics: Donald W. Anderson, C. Phillip Bosserman, John C. Campbell, John H. Cartwright, Lloyd E. Chorpenning, Ivan N. Clark, John T. Dahlquist, James B. Darcy, Richard L. Deats, Dewey R. Findley, Harold W. Garman, Ronald H. Goetz, John H. Graham, Hugh E. Haggard, Richard L. Hamilton, Donald H. James, Pierre M. Kempf, C. Travis Kendall, C. Eric Lincoln, Robert Paul Lisensky, Robert C. Mezoff, Leslie H. McKown, Orloff W. Miller, Ralph T. Mirse, Charles H. Moore, Robert W. Musil, Joseph A. Perez, Charles M. Prestwood, F. Warren Rempel, C. Ollyn Russell, Robert L. Shelton, John J. Shephard, James A. Smith, Robert E. Snyder, Henry J. Stonie, Duane F. Stroman, Harry G. Swanhart, Alfred H. Tracy, Mark C. Trotter, John G. Wall, Douglas E. Wingeier, and J. Philip Wogaman.

The voluminous material thus assembled is deposited in the library of Boston University School of Theology, which has established a repository of documents and publications on Methodism and society. A portion of the data has also been transcribed and coded in a punched-card file.

The committee wishes to express its deep gratitude to all those, named and unnamed, who in various ways so generously contributed to this undertaking. A special thanks is due to Mrs. S. Paul Schilling for her continued collaboration with the author in preparing the present volume for the press; and to the librarian of Boston University School of Theology, Jannette E. Newhall, who, with her staff, not only unsparingly assisted the committee in its researches but also provided office space in a congenial atmosphere.

NILS EHRENSTROM
PROJECT DIRECTOR

Foreword

THIS VOLUME IS PART OF A LARGER STUDY OF "METHODISM and Society" undertaken by the Board of Social and Economic Relations of The Methodist Church in co-operation with the faculty of the Boston University School of Theology.

It is the hope of the Board that the four volumes of the project will serve as a foundation for study and action in the church, with the aid of forthcoming study guides and interpretive materials, and that it will be used extensively by professors and students in colleges, universities, and seminaries, and by scholars doing independent study. The volumes should find their place as a significant contribution to ecumenical interests and research in the broader reaches of the total Christian impact upon society.

The interest of The Methodist Church in social matters goes back to its founder, John Wesley. It was an integral part of the thought, life, and activity of early Methodism. This interest in the welfare of people and the direction which society takes has been of increasing concern to The Methodist Church in the United States of America.

"The Social Creed" of the Methodist Church was adopted by the General Conference of the Methodist Episcopal Church in 1908. This was a turning point in the life of Methodism and for all the churches associated together in the Federal Council of the Churches of Christ in America. For it was the "Social Creed" of The Methodist Church which was adopted with little change as the social ideals of the Federal Council of Churches in 1908.

The Board of Social and Economic Relations was established by the General Conference of The Methodist Church in 1952 and received as its mandate the implementation of the "Social Creed."

As the new board began its work in race relations, economic life, and social and civic welfare, it soon became apparent that there was no systematic, objective survey and evaluation of the historical involvement of Methodism in the United States in social issues and the realization of social justice by the society.

Such questions as the following seemed to require answers:

Has The Methodist Church actually been a determining factor in the achievement of social justice in the United States?

Has The Methodist Church largely reflected advances made by secular and political institutions or has it actually been a pioneer for social justice which is the assumption that most Methodists make?

What has been the relationship of Methodist social action to Methodist theological beliefs?

Is there a well-defined Methodist theology for social action?

What has been the relationship of Methodist social action to that of other churches?

What have been the special social action emphases characteristic of Methodism in the United States?

What should Methodist social action be and do in the future?

The board decided to undertake a study of Methodism and the social scene in the United States of America and applied to the Fund for the Republic for a grant to undertake the project. The fund made a grant which has been supplemented by the board's own funds and by a research grant from Boston University to bring the project to conclusion. We are grateful to the fund for its support.

The board consulted with various educational institutions of our connection and decided that the project would be well done at the Boston University School of Theology. We are especially glad that Nils Ehrenstrom, Professor of Ecumenics at Boston, and for many years the director of studies for the World Council of Churches, consented to become the chairman of the committee and project director. The other members, appointed by the faculty, were Dean Walter G. Muelder; Paul Deats, Jr., Associate Professor of Social Ethics (secretary of the committee) Richard M. Cameron, Professor of Church History; Allan K. Chalmers, Professor of Preaching and Applied

Christianity; S. Paul Schilling, Professor of Systematic Theology; and Herbert E. Stotts, Professor of Church and Community. They have discharged their responsibilities with imagination and diligence and have worked in the closest co-operation with the board and its subcommittee for the project.

The board's own committee consisted of:

> MR. SAMUEL W. WITWER, CHAIRMAN
> MR. JOHN C. SATTERFIELD, VICE CHAIRMAN
> MRS. T. J. COTTINGHAM, SECRETARY
> BISHOP LLOYD C. WICKE
> BISHOP WILLIS J. KING
> DR. GEORGIA HARKNESS
> THE REVEREND FRANK M. TEMPLIN

They were the responsible representatives of the board in the formulation, organization, and carrying out of the undertaking.

The board extends its deepest thanks to each member of the committee for doing so well a task which consumed many hours of detailed and hard work. We are especially grateful for the work of Mr. Witwer and Mr. Satterfield, who spent many days with the faculty committee to bring the project into formulation and fruition.

The books were written by members of the faculty committee as follows:

Volume I   *Methodism and Society in Historical Perspective*— Richard M. Cameron

Volume II   *Methodism and Society in the Twentieth Century*— Walter G. Muerder

Volume III *Methodism and Society in Theological Perspective*— S. Paul Schilling

Volume IV *Methodism and Society: Guidelines for Strategy*— Herbert E. Stotts and Paul Deats, Jr.

To these authors we express our thanks and commend their work to the church.

Another group of persons actively participated in the undertaking. These were the expert critics who reviewed the books. At least four critics were chosen for each book (including one non-Methodist).

These critics examined and evaluated the books carefully from the vantage point of their own specialized technical skills. To these critics we are indebted for incisive, objective, and constructive suggestions which improved the early drafts of the manuscripts greatly.

We are especially happy to acknowledge the work of Charles H. Seaver of White Plains, New York, who for many years has worked in similar projects and who in this connection edited for style and content, and prepared the indexes.

All concerned with the project are conscious of the special responsibility which the office staff, both in Boston and in Chicago, assumed in bringing the entire undertaking to completion.

The board and the faculty of Boston join in hoping that this project will be a forerunner of other larger and more penetrating analyses of the total social scene and the part of Methodism in it.

Above all, it is the earnest desire of all those who participated in any way in the project that the work will be an honor to the Lord whom we serve and be one of his instruments to sharpen the social witness of his Church in the world.

The project has been a co-operative one. The gathering and selection of the material, the interpretations and evaluations, and the method of presentation have been the primary responsibility of the faculty committee and the individual authors to whom the board extended great freedom. In no sense, therefore, can or should any statement in the books of this project (except direct quotations from official actions) be regarded as an official declaration of The Methodist Church or of the Board of Social and Economic Relations.

Alfred Dudley Ward

General Secretary
Board of Social & Economic Relations
and General Editor of the Project

16

Contents

17

PART TWO: PROPOSALS

C. The Ministry of the Laity in Society

PART ONE

The Record

CHAPTER ONE

Methodists and Theology

SOCIAL THOUGHT AND ACTION MAY BE CALLED CHRISTIAN when they are inspired and informed by Christian faith—man's trustful commitment to God as he is uniquely and supremely revealed in Jesus Christ. Such faith implies distinctive views of God, of the basic structure of existence, and of the meaning for human life of God's creative and redemptive activity. That is, it implies a theology. This theology may be coherently formulated by systematic theologians, or it may remain the largely unexpressed living convictions of ordinary believers. But in one form or another it underlies and permeates the worship, thought, and life of all members of the Christian community. Hence any true understanding of Christian social thought and action necessarily involves theological reflection.

The significance of theology in this area is frequently denied or misunderstood. This may be sometimes due to a misconception of what theology is. It is partly traceable to the seeming irrelevance to daily life of some theological discussions. It also springs to some degree from the fact that theologians themselves often differ widely in both their interpretations of Christian belief and their accounts of the relation between such belief and ethical and social thought. The result is that many laymen are left bewildered, strongly inclined to depreciate the importance of theology in general. Our problem in this book is therefore to discover what relation has actually prevailed between theology and Christian social thought and action; and, against this background, what the content of sound theology is as it relates to society.

In this context we are concerned primarily with The Methodist

23

Church. The prevalent misunderstandings make it imperative that we begin with an estimate of the place of theology itself in Methodist faith and life.[1]

According to a widespread opinion Methodists have only a marginal interest in doctrine. In a recent essay Wilhelm Pauck remarks that "no denomination has shaped the untheological character of American Protestantism as decisively as the Methodists have done." This low estimate of theology he ascribes historically partly to Methodism's hostility to Calvinism and partly to its stress on practical rather than doctrinal Christianity. Methodists, he finds,

are primarily concerned with developing among their members a personal commitment to the gospel and to the life of moral perfection which they see implied in it. They regard Christianity as a social movement which through its organization endeavors to bring about a Christian transformation of the whole of human life. They are not hostile to theology but they relegate theological responsibility to a minor place in the life of both the Church and the individual Christian.[2]

In 1947 an editorial in *Life* contrasted John Wesley's "small attention to the fine points of theology" with the Wesleyan stress on regularity in religious practices which gave Methodism its name. The writer then declared: "Though methodicalness is no longer distinctive of the Methodist Church, a casual approach to theology still is."[3] If theology is really so unimportant for Methodists, it cannot affect their social attitudes very significantly, and what small bearing it may have will be almost impossible to discover. It is therefore necessary to investigate the actual status of doctrinal concern among Methodists.

---

[1] The term *theology* may denote a body of thought or a process of thinking. Thus Christian theology may designate a system or collection of beliefs held by Christians, or it may refer to the thoughtful inquiry into and exposition of the meaning and truth of the faith of Christian people. The term will be used in both senses in this book; the context will normally indicate which is implied. *Doctrine* means simply teaching or instruction, particularly beliefs which are taught because they are held to be true. *Dogma* is doctrine authoritatively determined, usually by some official church body, and often formulated in an approved creed or confession of faith.

[2] "Theology in the Life of Contemporary American Protestantism," *Religion and Culture: Essays in Honor of Paul Tillich*, ed. Walter Leibrecht (New York: Harper and Brothers, 1959), pp. 273, 280.

[3] *Life*, Nov. 10, 1947, p. 113.

A. Subordination of Doctrine to Life

Admittedly some of the most frequently quoted statements of Wesley himself suggest a low estimate of theology. The sole condition of membership in the societies he organized was the desire in those seeking admission "to flee from the wrath to come, and to be saved from their sins." [4] When this was present, Methodists did not impose "any opinions whatever" as a basis of admission. They asked only: "Is thy heart herein as my heart? If it be, give me thy hand." [5] In 1749 Wesley wrote: "Orthodoxy, or right opinions, is, at best, but a very slender part of religion, if it can be allowed to be any part of it at all." [6] What, then, is central in religion? "I will not quarrel with you about any opinion. Only see that your heart be right toward God, that you know and love the Lord Jesus Christ; that you love your neighbor, and walk as your Master walked. . . . Give me an humble, gentle lover of God and man." [7]

As we shall see, such passages are far from providing an accurate picture of Wesley's total view. Nevertheless, they have been very influential, and they represent an early expression of a strong tendency throughout Methodist history to subordinate doctrine to life. Three manifestations of this tendency may be noted.

1. Various corporate utterances and the statements of representative individuals reveal a Methodism concerned more with the living relation of men to God than with the doctrines that interpret that relation. "The insistent Methodist emphasis," writes Harris Franklin Rall, "has been on Christianity as a gospel and a way of life. . . . Doctrinal formulation, like church order, has been distinctly secondary." [8] Supporting this judgment, the Episcopal Address to the

---

[4] "The General Rules."

[5] "Thoughts upon a Late Phenomenon," 9. *The Works of John Wesley* (Grand Rapids, Michigan: Zondervan Publishing House, 1958-59), XIII, 266. This edition of Wesley's works is a photo offset reproduction of the authorized edition published by the Wesleyan Conference Office in London in 1872, which is in turn a reprint of the third edition of Wesley's *Works*, edited by Thomas Jackson and published in London by the Wesleyan-Methodist Book-Room in 1829-31. All later references to Wesley's *Works* in this book will designate this edition.

[6] "A Plain Account of the People Called Methodists," I, 2. *Works*, VIII, 249.

[7] "A Farther Appeal to Men of Reason and Religion," Part III, IV, 10. *Works*, VIII, 244.

[8] R. Newton Flew (ed.), *The Nature of the Church* (London: S.C.M. Press, 1952), pp. 329-330.

General Conference of The Methodist Church in 1944 declared:

The Methodist insistence has not been so much upon opinion as upon life. Its distinguishing mark is not so much what men believe, as what they are, what they experience, how they act. The unique traditions of Methodism are, therefore, to be sought in patterns of action rather than systems of dogma.[9]

Sometimes this emphasis has been expressed in terms of a primary concern for persons rather than correct beliefs. In 1927 Bishop Adna W. Leonard wrote that if the Methodist Episcopal Church ever allowed her interest in orthodoxy to surpass her interest in men, "it would be a tragedy unspeakable." [10] In similar vein the editor of Together introduces a pictorial story of a Methodist family by noting the Church's "emphasis on people—rather than, say, theology or liturgy." [11]

At the Methodist Episcopal General Conference at Des Moines in 1920 the address of the bishops related this practical interest to the mission of the church:

In other centuries, creedmaking periods in history, men of ability gave themselves to the doctrinal task of reconciling the attributes of God. To-day the church of God must give itself to the human task of reconciling the sons of God. It must repeat the atoning ministry of its Master in mediating between men estranged, bitter, and hostile.[12]

Bishop John Wesley Lord has related this emphasis specifically to social action. Methodists, he observed in May 1959, "are people who believe in a way of life," which is, however, "not so much a way of believing as it is of acting." "We take a stand," he continued, "because of our responsibility to society . . . because we are people of the way. . . . You can get us on these great social issues," but not on doctrinal issues. "Nothing can split the world wide open so much as allegiance to doctrine and dogma." [13]

[9] Journal, 1944, p. 155.
[10] "Essentialist," Northwestern Christian Advocate, Feb. 2, 1927, p. 372.
[11] Jan., 1959, p. 19.
[12] Journal, 1920, p. 168.
[13] A press preview of the 163rd session of the New England Annual Conference, Springfield, Massachusetts. Christian Science Monitor, May 12, 1959.

On occasion this practical concern has reflected an obvious impatience with much theological discussion. Reminiscing on his experience at the Lausanne Conference on Faith and Order, Bishop Francis J. McConnell observed that the first question was "that old abomination as to which was the true church," while in one session the conference attempted the "hopeless task of framing a definition of the church." In contrast, Bishop McConnell rejoiced that at the Jerusalem Conference "the aim was not so much to get together on a doctrinal basis or on a liturgical basis. The aim was to get together." [14] In similar vein, Bishop G. Bromley Oxnam, one of the first presidents of the World Council of Churches, pictures millions worshiping in church on a given Sunday and going forth inspired. "Inspired to do what? Enter debate concerning the nature of the Church? I hope not. If they are inspired to worship and love God, to love and serve their fellows and to do so in the name of Jesus Christ our Lord, I have reason to believe in the Church." Bishop Oxnam also questions the value of "abstruse" discussion of Christology. "If Jesus is God incarnate, would we not do better to consider His way, in fact? His Truth? His Life?" [15]

Another active participant in the ecumenical movement, Albert C. Outler, manifests full respect for the necessity and importance of contemporary conversations on "faith and order"; yet in this context he also voices something of the traditional Methodist emphasis by insisting on the derivative nature of doctrine. Discussing the problem of Christian unity, he writes:

Christian community is primary; Christian doctrines are explicative. A doctrinal system, a developed liturgy, a settled policy, all these are achievements possible only within a community that has its life and power from another originating source than these. . . . The quest for unity between the divided Christians must begin with the mutual recognition of their actual community in Jesus Christ. For it is only in the atmosphere of acknowledged community that the quest for doctrinal consensus has any lively hope of succeeding.[16]

[14] By the Way; an Autobiography (Nashville: Abingdon Press, 1952), pp. 189, 191, 193.
[15] A Testament of Faith (Boston: Little, Brown and Company, 1958), pp. 130, 129.
[16] The Christian Tradition and the Unity We Seek (New York: Oxford University Press, 1957), p. 66.

27

2. Indirect evidence of a tendency to view formal statements of doctrine as more or less incidental is found in the ambiguity which prevails regarding Methodist doctrinal standards. The Church's sole official statement of doctrine is of course the twenty-five Articles of Religion.[17] Twenty-four of these were selected from the Thirty-nine Articles of the Church of England and modified by John Wesley. With the addition of one article regarding the "rulers of the United States," they were adopted by the Christmas Conference of 1784 as a doctrinal basis for the new Methodist Episcopal Church. Maintained by each of the three resultant Methodist bodies which reunited in 1939, they were continued in The Methodist Church. They are thoroughly Protestant in flavor, asserting emphatically that men are justified by grace through faith. Since Wesley's editing removed the predestinarian elements which appear in the Thirty-nine Articles, the Twenty-five reflect negatively and indirectly his belief that salvation is open to all. But one looks in them in vain for a positive statement of most of the historic Methodist emphases.

Few would maintain that these disciplinary materials are adequate guides to Methodist teaching or that they alone are pertinent. In fact, the Constitution of The Methodist Church itself suggests other sources. The first "Restrictive Rule," adopted originally in 1808, provides: "The General Conference shall not revoke, alter, or change our Articles of Religion, or establish any new standards or rules of doctrine contrary to our present existing and established standards of doctrine." The distinction made between Articles of Religion and "established standards of doctrine" implies the existence of other standards than the Articles. But what are they? The issue has been long and widely discussed, but there is no authoritative answer.

The original framers of the rule may have had in mind the doctrines taught by John Wesley in his *Notes on the New Testament* and in the first fifty-three of his published *Sermons*. These are specifically listed as doctrinal bases by the British Methodist Church. On the other hand, between 1784 and 1808 six different doctrinal tracts, mostly by Wesley, appeared in various editions of *The Doctrines and Discipline of the Methodist Episcopal Church*. Dealing with predesti-

---

[17] There are doctrinal implications also in the "General Rules." However, these are primarily a code of conduct, dealing with the fruits of faith rather than the nature of it.

nation, the perseverance of the faithful, Christian perfection, baptism, and antinomianism, they occupied the bulk of the space in the *Disciplines* of those years. These doctrinal sections were omitted in 1812, and have never reappeared. Were they the standards which the framers of the first Restrictive Rule had in mind? It seems quite possible, but we do not know. This we do know: for the typical American Methodist of 1960 "present existing and established standards of doctrine" mean neither the doctrinal tracts nor Wesley's *Sermons* and New Testament *Notes.* As Bishop John J. Tigert declared in 1908, since 1812 no definite content has been assigned to the phrase.

The Methodist Church is thus in the anomalous position of prohibiting changes in standards of doctrine which are supposedly established but the nature of which no one knows! The fact that the Church is not at all embarrassed by this situation is strong evidence that it regards precise doctrinal statements as relatively unimportant. A similar conclusion can be drawn from the circumstance that the official publication which is still entitled *Doctrines and Discipline* contains far more discipline than doctrine. In the 1956 edition only seven pages out of 780—those containing the Articles of Religion—are specifically devoted to doctrinal material as such.

Clearly it would be inaccurate to leave the matter here. There are important and convincing indications that the major beliefs of ecumenical Christianity are normative for Methodists. This is clear, for example, from Methodist responses to World Conferences on Faith and Order held at Lausanne (1927), Edinburgh (1937), and Lund (1952). Though adherence to the Apostles' Creed is not required by The Methodist Church, it is deeply cherished and widely used; and two recent affirmations of faith, given semi-official approval by inclusion in *The Book of Worship* and *The Methodist Hymnal,* are also frequently employed. The prescribed ritual of the Church, occupying 136 pages in the *Discipline,* is grounded in and expressive of great theological convictions. The same is true of Methodist hymnody. Nevertheless, Methodists apparently do not deem it necessary or desirable anywhere to state definitely and officially the theology which is everywhere assumed.

In this respect The Methodist Church differs markedly from confessional bodies like Lutherans and Presbyterians; and is historically in basic agreement with communions like the Baptists, Congregationalists, Disciples, and Friends, which share its insistence on the primacy of Christian experience. As W. A. Visser 't Hooft has pointed out, all of these latter groups demand the "largest possible liberty of interpretation of the meaning of creeds, sacraments, and ministry, rather than uniformity of order or the adoption of the same confessions." For them the church is "essentially a community of believers rather than a community of belief or of corporate faith." [18]

3. A further intimation that theological factors are relatively secondary for Methodists is found in the absence of any "doctrinal test" for admission to church membership. In 1864, when the Methodist Episcopal Church first provided a definite form for use in the reception of members, one question prescribed was: "Do you believe in the doctrines of Holy Scripture, as set forth in the Articles of Religion of the Methodist Episcopal Church?" In 1924 this question was changed to read: "Do you receive and profess the Christian Faith as contained in the New Testament of our Lord Jesus Christ?" However, belief in the Apostles' Creed continued to be required after 1924, as before, since it was included in the baptismal covenant which new members were expected to ratify and confirm. This requirement was dropped in 1932.

The ritual approved in 1938 by the last General Conference of the Methodist Episcopal Church, South, required the Apostles' Creed by way of the baptismal covenant, but contained no other doctrinal

[18] W. A. Visser 't Hooft and J. H. Oldham, *The Church and Its Function in Society* (London: George Allen and Unwin, 1937), p. 53. In contrast, the majority of Lutherans ascribe decisive doctrinal authority to the Book of Concord (1580), consisting of the Apostles', Nicene, and "Athanasian" Creeds, the Augsburg Confession and the Apology related to it, Luther's Large and Small Catechisms, the Smalkald Articles, and the Formula of Concord. The constitution of the recently formed United Presbyterian Church in the U. S. A. includes a thirty-page Confession of Faith (a modification of the Westminster Confession of 1649), the Larger Catechism, the Smaller Catechism, and the Statements of Faith of the two bodies which merged to form the new church. These materials, totaling one hundred pages, or 45 per cent of the contents of the constitution, are regarded as expressing the teaching of Scripture, the faith of the ecumenical creeds, and the distinctive doctrines of the Reformed faith.

A significant attempt to synthesize the creedal and noncreedal positions is found in the recently formed United Church of Christ, the General Synod of which approved in 1959 a new Statement of Faith which is now being considered by the various synods, conferences, and associations. This statement aims to declare "in words of our time" the faith set forth in Scripture, the ecumenical creeds, and the confessions of the Reformation. However, it is viewed "as a testimony, and not as a test, of faith," and its use by local congregations in worship will be optional.

prescription. New members were not even specifically required to affirm the faith contained in the New Testament.

In accord with the ritual adopted by The Methodist Church formed in 1939, persons uniting with the Church are called upon to renew the vow made when they were baptized (which contains no reference to the Apostles' Creed), to confess Jesus Christ as Savior and Lord and pledge their allegiance to his kingdom, and to "receive and profess the Christian faith as contained in the New Testament of our Lord Jesus Christ." In addition, they are required to affirm their loyalty to The Methodist Church, and to promise to uphold it by their attendance, prayers, gifts, and service.

These provisions are doctrinally much less specific and permit much greater breadth of theological interpretation than the membership requirements of Lutheran and Presbyterian churches, while they have much in common with those of Congregationalists, Disciples, and Baptists. They are also quite similar to those of the Protestant Episcopal Church, except that this communion requires adults receiving baptism to affirm the declarations of the Apostles' Creed. In their requirements for admission, therefore, as in their attitude toward creedal statements, Methodists are aligned with the Protestant groups which allow considerable freedom of interpretation within the bounds of relatively simple doctrinal affirmations which are regarded as central. Methodists are thus predisposed, from the time when they first undertake membership in the church, to regard correctness of doctrine as secondary to other aspects of their Christian commitment.

B. Recognition of the Importance of Theology

On the whole, we have discovered in both John Wesley and later Methodism a subordination of doctrine to Christian experience and life, some suspicion of the exploration of doctrinal questions as a possible threat to effective Christian action, a relative lack of concern for exact theological formulations, and an extension of wide freedom to the individual believer in interpreting his faith. If seen in isolation, these characteristics could easily lead to the conclusion that Methodists are indifferent to theology. However, other weighty factors must be taken into account before a verdict is reached.

John Wesley himself was anything but antitheological. He specifically repudiated "speculative latitudinarianism." "Indifference to

all opinions" is "the spawn of hell. . . . A man of truly catholic spirit
. . . is fixed as the sun in his judgment concerning the main branches
of Christian doctrine." The genuine Christian is not a man of "muddy
understanding," whose mind is "all in a mist"; rather, "he is steadily
fixed in his religious principles, in what he believes to be the truth
as it is in Jesus." [19]

The clue to an understanding of Wesley is the distinction he made,
not always consistently, between "opinions" and "essential doctrines."
Opinions have to do with forms of church government, modes of
worship, and those doctrinal positions which, however objectionable
they may be intellectually, are held by persons with "real Christian
experience" and thus "are clearly compatible with a love to Christ
and a work of grace." [20] In relation to such views, "which do not strike
at the root of Christianity, we think and let think." [21] The Christian
is free to accept or reject any belief which does not hamper the grace
of God or the human love which this grace calls forth.

But by the same token there are beliefs which are central and
necessary. Some of them are implicit in the single condition which
Wesley imposed for membership in the early Methodist societies—
a desire "to flee from the wrath to come," and to be saved from sin.
Actually these words presuppose a whole theology—of God's sovereignty and judgment, man's sinfulness, and the divine grace which
alone can save him.

In other passages Wesley is quite explicit. Among convictions
which do strike at the root of Christianity he mentions belief in the
inspiration of the Scriptures, in the Bible as the "only and sufficient
rule both of Christian faith and practice," and in Christ as "the
eternal, supreme God." [22] Even the "right heart" turns out on definition to include doctrinal elements. It involves not only love toward

[19] Sermon, "Catholic Spirit," III, 1, 4. *Wesley's Standard Sermons*, ed. Edward H.
Sugden (London: Epworth, 1921), II, 142-3. This two-volume set contains the
forty-four sermons selected by Wesley himself as doctrinal norms, and nine additional
sermons of the edition of 1771. Sermon III is the work of Charles Wesley. These
sermons also appear in Vol. V of the Zondervan edition of Wesley's *Works*. Wesley's
other collected sermons, totaling eighty-eight, appear in Vols. VI and VII of the
Works. Hereafter the *Standard Sermons* will be designated simply by the name of the
editor.
[20] "To John Newton," May 14, 1765. *The Letters of the Rev. John Wesley, A.M.*,
ed. John Telford (London: Epworth Press, 1931), IV, 298.
[21] "The Character of a Methodist." *Works*, VIII, 341.
[22] *Ibid.* Cf. "Thoughts upon Methodism," *Works*, XIII, 258.

God and neighbor and other deeply personal aspects of the Christian life, but also belief in God "and his perfections"—"his eternity, immensity, wisdom, power; his justice, mercy, and truth"—belief in Jesus Christ, and submission to the righteousness of God through faith in Christ, with renunciation of all trust in one's own goodness.[23]

So important did Wesley deem right doctrine that he sought to safeguard conformity to his conception of it even in the provisions governing the purchase of "preaching houses." Each deed was to include the clause: "In case the doctrine or practice of any preacher should, in the opinion of the major part of the trustees, be not conformable to Mr. W[esley]'s *Sermons,* and *Notes on the New Testament,* on representing this another preacher shall be sent within three months." [24] He also sought doctrinal as well as disciplinary soundness in his American preachers. "Let all of you," he wrote, "be determined to abide by the Methodist doctrine and discipline published in the four volumes of *Sermons* and the *Notes upon the New Testament,* together with the *Large Minutes* of the Conference." [25]

On one occasion several members of the Methodist society in Yorkshire, troubled because the "false doctrines" preached by the minister of their parish church were weakening their religious zeal, inquired whether they should continue to attend services. The Conference—no doubt guided by Wesley—replied:

First, that it was highly expedient, all the Methodists (so called) who had been bred therein should attend the service of the Church as often as possible: But that, secondly, if the Minister began either to preach the absolute decrees, or to rail at and ridicule Christian perfection, they should quietly and silently go out of the church; yet attend it again the next opportunity.[26]

Clearly Wesley was not unconcerned about doctrine. He did distinguish between peripheral opinions and essential beliefs, and he sharply opposed controversy over fine points and nonessentials, mainly

[23] Sermon, "Catholic Spirit," I, 12, 13. Sugden, II, 136-37. Cf. letter to John Newton, May 14, 1765. *Letters,* IV, 298.

[24] *The Journal of the Rev. John Wesley, A.M.,* ed. Nehemiah Curnock (New York: Eaton and Mains, n. d.), Sept. 5, 1783, VI, 444-45.

[25] "To the Preachers in America," Oct. 3, 1783. *Letters,* VII, 191.

[26] "On Hearing Ministers Who Oppose the Truth," 3. *Works,* XIII, 246. Paradoxically, this advice illustrates both concern for sound doctrine and antipathy to a particular kind of doctrine which Pauck rightly regards as partly responsible for Methodist subordination of theology.

because such argumentation set up false barriers between Christians and retarded the work of Christ. He also deprecated rigidity in creedal formulations, and allowed broad freedom in the interpretation of Christian doctrine. Nevertheless, his admonition to his followers to "let think" did not relieve them of the obligation to think, or of responsibility for commitment to the great central affirmations of the Christian faith. Yet he saw the acceptance of these truths not as an end in itself, but always as contributory to man's experience of the saving grace of God, newness of life in Christ, and growth in love, through the indwelling of the Holy Spirit.

The Methodist Church in its recent history has not been so emphatic as was Wesley in insisting on clarity of belief, nor has it usually expected even of its ministers quite the degree of conformity that he demanded of his preachers. Nevertheless, the total record reveals a real and deepening theological concern. There are many evidences of individual and corporate recognition of the importance of meaningful beliefs.

Among such evidences, indeed, are some of the considerations previously cited to indicate Methodist freedom from rigidity in theology. The membership vows, for example, though broadly formulated, involve momentous affirmations concerning the heart of our Christian faith. Seriously undertaken, they require nothing less than the opening of one's life to the forgiving grace of God in Christ and complete commitment to his will and way.

The Episcopal Address to the Southern Methodist General Conference held in Memphis in 1926 not only stressed the importance of doctrine, but insisted on adherence by ministers to particular doctrinal standards.

There is no proper place among us for those who do not believe our authoritative standards. This action is not due to a certain narrowness, certainly not to the denial of the right of any man who possesses the ability to think for himself, and bearing his own responsibility to God to reach his own conclusions. Liberty to think is allowed. . . . The question with us is totally different. Can the man who seeks admission into our ministry that he may preach another gospel find among us a fruitful field of service? . . . In our ministry there is no place for the man who denies our faith.[27]

[27] *Journal*, 1926, pp. 213-14.

The final General Conference of the Methodist Protestant Church manifested a similar mood. It adopted a report on the State of the Church which added to a plea for doctrinal clarity an insistence on adherence to Biblical truth:

> To have no stable religious convictions is to have a religion of soft senti-ments. There is a great need for sound clear thinking with our Bibles before us and our hearts before God . . . Our people need to have their faith established in the fundamental doctrines of the Word of God. We have been toying with a thousand speculative opinions, when there is need to believe the truth and know why we believe it.[28]

When Bishop Edwin Holt Hughes of the Methodist Episcopal Church addressed the Southern Methodist General Conference of 1938, discussing four great unities of the three Methodist bodies which were soon to unite, he thought a shared theology important enough to list along with a shared history, a shared character, and a shared government.[29] It is also noteworthy that Bishop McConnell, in spite of his aspersions against doctrinal hair-splitting, was himself an eminent leader among Methodist religious thinkers, and made distinguished contributions to the theological literature of his time.[30]

In 1948 the General Conference of The Methodist Church, desiring to stimulate in the rank and file of its members a deeper understanding of their faith, included a year's study of "Our Faith" in the program adopted for the ensuing quadrennium. The result was the publication and wide use, in 1950 and afterward, of eight popularly written booklets exploring the meaning of Christian belief in God, Christ, the Bible, love, prayer, immortality, the Holy Spirit, and the kingdom of God.

A similar concern, carried out on a deeper level, was manifest in the statement, *Educational Principles in the Curriculum*, approved on January 3, 1952, by the Curriculum Committee of the Methodist General Board of Education. The result of two years of study, the report devotes the first of its four sections, comprising almost half

[28] *Journal*, 1936, pp. 73-74.
[29] *Daily Christian Advocate*, 23 (1938), 75-78.
[30] See, for example, *The Christlike God: A Survey of the Divine Attributes from the Christian Point of View* (New York and Cincinnati: Abingdon Press, 1927), and *The Diviner Immanence* (New York: Eaton and Mains, 1910), also *Is God Limited?* (New York and Cincinnati: Abingdon Press, 1924).

of its total length, to an examination of the "basic Christian beliefs from which the principles of Christian education are derived." This statement was partly a response to a growing volume of criticism from Methodists themselves that their church-school literature had no clear theological orientation. It has done much to make church school leaders more aware of the significance of theological issues in Christian teaching. In 1957 the Curriculum Committee undertook the careful revision of this document, enlisting the help of the faculties of all of the Methodist theological seminaries. The result of three years of work is not simply a revision, but a thoroughly new statement, *Foundations of Christian Teaching in Methodist Churches*, published in 1960. Four of the six chapters of this booklet, comprising about two-thirds of its length, deal with theological issues.

The bishops as a body contributed significantly to this deepening theological emphasis in the Episcopal Address to the General Conference of 1952, written by Bishop Paul B. Kern. Methodism, said the bishops,

is not indifferent to the intellectual basis of the faith it proclaims. There are great Christian doctrines which we most surely hold and most firmly believe. Our religious belief . . . rests . . . upon the revealed Word of God perceived and attested by the enlightened conscience of man.

They then went on to state succinctly but carefully twelve "central doctrines of the people called Methodists." [31] Since these were not adopted by the General Conference and do not appear in the *Discipline* of either 1952 or 1956, they fall short of full official status. Nevertheless, they have exerted wide influence, and represent the most authentic summary of Methodist theology now available.

Convincing evidence of current theological concern appeared at the Institute of Theological Studies held at Oxford, England, July 19-29, 1958, under the sponsorship of the World Methodist Council. Many American Methodists were among the approximately one hundred delegates whose theme was "Biblical Theology and Meth-

[31] *Journal*, 1952, pp. 155-59. A service of worship, "The Song of Methodism," which was prepared by James R. Houghton, and provided an appropriate musical setting for each of the twelve affirmations, was a highlight of the 1952 General Conference, and was later used in Methodist gatherings throughout the country. The statement has been included in a booklet, *What Methodists Believe*, circulated by the Methodist Board of Education.

odist Doctrine." Significantly, the group included laymen as well as ministers, and was composed of teachers, pastors, housewives, and students. Papers read and discussed dealt with such subjects as justification, conversion, grace, assurance, the Holy Spirit, the people of God, faith in the Old Testament, the New Testament message and man's response, and faith and order in the New Testament. The Institute stressed the need for a re-examination of the Wesleyan doctrines of sin and redemption and the recovery of the whole gospel, partly through utilizing the resources of biblical theology. A similar institute is planned for 1962.

To such evidences of corporate concern must be added the fact that many individual Methodists have stressed the need for clear theological understanding and registered disapproval when they have found it lacking. In 1933 Edwin Lewis decried the "fatal apostasy" of the church, which he saw illustrated in both poverty of belief and shallowness of religion. "The church," he wrote, "is becoming creedless as fast as the innovators can have their way," with neither the Apostles' Creed nor any other fully Christian confession of faith used in many worship services. "The Social Creed," he pointed out, is no adequate substitute for a religious creed; without the latter "the church as such will cease to exist long before it has had time to make its 'social' creed effective in the life of the world." Admitting that the social creed is itself religious, he questioned whether its religion was sufficiently dynamic. "The church has set itself to do more at the very time that it is lessening its power to do anything." [32]

Equally emphatic opposition has been expressed, even in the most non-theological periods, to the uncritical tendency of some Methodists to contrast belief and action at the expense of the former. Ernest Fremont Tittle, noted exponent of the social gospel, declared in 1917,

It is a matter of very considerable importance what a man's creed is. . . . For what a man believes will eventually influence what he does. His creed will determine his deed. . . . Men do not always act in accordance with their professed beliefs. . . . But what one really believes will influence his whole life.[33]

[32] "The Fatal Apostasy of the Modern Church," *Religion in Life*, 2 (1933), 490-91.
[33] "The Use and Abuse of Creeds," *Methodist Review*, 99 (1917), 866.

Forty years later Bishop Gerald Kennedy dismissed as nonsense the claim that a man's beliefs do not matter as long as he is a good man.

When any person says, "I believe this," or "I believe that," the issues of eternity hang in the balance. Christians who claim that right thinking about God is not important are too simple-minded to be allowed loose. They are the people who are helpless in the face of rascals with crude but vital faith. The only answer to an evil idea is a good idea.[34]

A comparable concern for sound doctrine, though in a much different context, is manifested by Albert C. Outler, whose insistence on the primacy of Christian community in doctrinal discussions we have previously noticed. He concludes from a study of nineteenth-century Christianity that "care for community without a corresponding care for apostolic doctrine is as one-sided as its Scholastic opposite." [35]

Recent years have also seen a growing interest among the laity in theological questions. Samuel W. Witwer illustrates this in his message for Laymen's Day, 1958, when he calls for deeper conviction and clearer understanding of the meaning of the faith as essential to an effective Christian witness. Pointing out that most laymen try to keep informed about their jobs and study regularly the literature of their businesses, professions, and other occupations, he adds that

if the Kingdom is really as important as Christians profess, then we should find time for the daily study of the Scriptures and other literature of our faith. As we increase in knowledge and understanding of the basic Christian affirmations, we shall gain deep conviction.[36]

There is a live demand for explanations of theology expressed in language intelligible to thoughtful laymen. One book which effectively met this condition elicited a memorable comment from a lay preacher in a School for Approved Supply Pastors. "This author," observed the student, "writes so that he can be understood by people as well as by professors and theologians"! When theology is presented in these terms, people respond.

The reason is not hard to discover. Theology deals with the ultimate questions which every man must face, and which in the long

---

[34] *I Believe* (Nashville: Abingdon Press, 1958), p. 91.
[35] *The Christian Tradition and the Unity We Seek,* p. 95.
[36] *Laymen's Day, Sunday, October 19, 1958* (Chicago: General Board of Lay Activities, The Methodist Church), p. 20.

run are the most important questions he can ask. "Who am I? What is the purpose of my life? Who is God? Why does he allow so much suffering? What is the difference between right and wrong? How can I meet temptation and find power to become what God wants me to become? What is the meaning of Jesus Christ? What does he have to say to our day? Is there hope for society, faced by the threat of atomic destruction? What can the Christian faith contribute to a better society? What is the ultimate destiny of mankind?" These are but a few of the basic questions which press for answers. Christians believe that greatest light is shed upon them when they are answered within the perspective of the Christian gospel. The effort to find and state such answers is theology.

Considerations like these lead Georgia Harkness to the judgment that

theology is basic to religion, for while it is not the whole of religion, an emotional experience has no firm rootage without it. There can be no Christian faith without belief in something. If one believes the wrong things, his entire life can be distorted, for the world is so made that a firm structure of personal living can rest only on true foundations.[37]

She also makes plain that "lack of clear understanding of the Christian faith stands in the way of an effective attack on the evils of our society." [38] Since laymen in religion make the vast majority of the social, political, and economic decisions which affect human well-being, it is imperative that Christian laymen be able clearly to relate their thinking in these areas to the things they really believe as Christians. Otherwise, as so often happens, their policies will represent an uncritical adoption of purely secular programs, and their action will be plagued by weakness, uncertainty, and vacillation. Theology is therefore essential to informed and effective Christian social action.

C. Conclusions

With evidence as mixed as that disclosed by our survey, no fair-minded jury could return an unqualified verdict. We have seen a church attempting, with great difficulty and sometimes faltering steps, to avoid the perils of both creedalism and theological indifferentism;

[37] *Understanding the Christian Faith* (Nashville: Abingdon Press, 1950), p. 11.
[38] *Ibid.*, p. 12.

or, positively, trying to walk at the same time two diverging paths—that which asserts the priority of experience and life, and that which affirms the necessity for depth and clarity of religious belief.

Actually, the divergence is more apparent than real. It is true that some Methodists, suspicious of doctrine as they have known it, draw a sharp contrast between belief and life at the expense of the former. But this extreme emphasis on life is itself a theology, implying a doctrine about the ultimate nature of things, hence not really a rejection of all theology. Moreover, some opposition to dogma is at heart an objection to a particular system of belief with which the critic disagrees, and which he identifies with theology in general.

However, most of the reservations concerning theology are cast in relative terms. They reflect not opposition to doctrine itself, but rather a concern lest insistence on the fine points of doctrinal correctness take precedence over the life transformed by the power and love of God. Methodists, in short, are looking for a relevant theology, one which is integrally related to the demands of everyday Christian living in society. Their quarrel is not with religious beliefs as such, but with doctrine which sets up shop for itself, and is irrelevant and unrelated to the life of the Christian in the world.

The characteristic Methodist attitude toward theology can be accurately summarized in a series of paired statements. The Methodist Church accords primacy to the personal experience of the reconciling, transforming power of God and the life of loving service to God and man. Yet it recognizes that belief in God as he is revealed in Christ is not extraneous to but inseparable from such an experience and such a life. It insists that no assent to creedal formulas, however true or precisely wrought, can take the place of a living embodiment of the spirit of Christ. Just as surely it knows that Christian conduct roots in great Christian convictions. Within broad limits it allows and encourages in its members freedom to interpret for themselves the meaning of Christian truth. Yet such freedom does not carry with it liberty to reject the Lordship and Saviorhood of Jesus Christ or other essentials of the New Testament witness. It is wary of doctrinal tests, of creeds used as fences or walls. But it welcomes doctrinal testimonies, and cherishes expressions of belief which serve as platforms for Christians to stand on, and especially to launch out from in proclaiming and living the good news of Christ.

From the standpoint of the present inquiry it is important to note several by-products of the attitudes toward theology which have characterized Methodists.

1. The *content* of theology itself has been strongly affected. It is no accident that a tradition which views Christian experience as more important than doctrinal correctness should emphasize that God can be personally known, that the experience of his redeeming love is open to all who freely turn to him, and that the transformed life of love and true holiness is really possible through the empowerment of the divine Spirit.

2. Methodism has been relatively free from the doctrinal strife and the heresy hunts which have sometimes torn more creedaly oriented communions. With but few exceptions, such as the removal of Hinckley G. Mitchell from the faculty of Boston University School of Theology in 1905, it has found in its stress on the Spirit-filled life a ground of unity and fellowship more powerful than doctrinal differences.

3. Its avoidance of meticulous doctrinal distinctions and its emphasis on practical Christianity have given it a ready appeal to ordinary people in democratic, utilitarian America, accounting partly for its numerical extension and hence a broad opportunity for influence. On the other hand, its doctrinal indefiniteness has sometimes encouraged shallowness. Critical and constructive thinking is hard work, and any suggestion that it is less important than Christian living is readily taken by some as an excuse for avoiding it. Too frequently Methodists, content to let theology remain obscure to them, do not know what they really believe, and quality of life as well as thought has been impaired. Or they unwittingly embrace a "theology" very different from that represented officially by their church. Lacking clear guidance, many laymen have equated the life of the Christian with a conventional moral life, or fallen easy prey to such doctrines as "happiness," "peace of mind," "togetherness," or other popular substitutes for genuine Christian faith, to the great impoverishment of their Christian experience and witness.

4. The conviction of Methodism that the surest mark of Christian discipleship is the life of righteousness and love has often extended to concern for social righteousness. Yet this practical emphasis has also opened the way to programs of social action inadequately related

to any basic structure of Christian conviction, hence vague in purpose and weak in power.

The weaknesses mentioned are not inherent in the Methodist position. Freedom in belief need not mean either freedom from belief or indifference to belief. Wisely and reverently used, it can lead to that depth of understanding which is open only to the free, and which in turn illuminates all the thought and action of the Christian man. Actually, the two paths mentioned earlier are only one. Truly Christian living and thinking are inseparable. To be a Christian one must walk the Christian way, but this he cannot do unless he observes the guideposts along the way. The guideposts, in turn, are there to help those who are actually walking—to aid them in "doing the truth." As Georgia Harkness has shown:

> The Christian faith is both something to be believed and something to be lived. It is, primarily, not a body of dogmas to which the mind gives assent, but a conviction or body of convictions to which the whole person gives himself in the daily decisions of life.[39]

Phillips Brooks, eminent Episcopalian, spoke eloquently in the spirit of that synthesis when he counseled the divinity students at Yale: "Preach doctrine, preach all the doctrine that you know, and learn forever more and more; but preach it always, not that men may believe it, but that men may be saved by believing it." [40] His words are singularly appropriate for Methodists today—clergy and laity alike.

Against the background of this survey of the place of theology in Methodism, we turn now to examine the actual content of Methodist theology as related to social thought and action. Here it will be useful to distinguish between the doctrinal emphases associated with John Wesley and the early Methodist tradition and the broad context of Protestant or universally Christian belief in which these emphases appear.

It must be remembered, however, that the distinction is relative and somewhat artificial, involving much overlapping. The doctrines

[39] The Modern Rival of Christian Faith; an Analysis of Secularism (Nashville: Abingdon Press, 1952), p. 29.
[40] Lectures on Preaching (London: Griffith, Farrar, Okeden, and Welsh, 1886), p. 129.

stressed by Wesley and his followers were not uniquely or distinctively theirs, but aspects of the totality of Christian conviction which they regarded as central, but which they felt were being largely overlooked.

Chapters Two and Three will consider respectively the theology of John Wesley and the status of the historic Methodist emphases today, in each case paying particular attention to the social significance of the doctrines held. Chapters Four and Five will broaden the focus to investigate the total structure of Christian belief which Methodists in the twentieth century find relevant to social thought and action.

CHAPTER TWO

John Wesley's Theology of Salvation

ALTHOUGH TWENTIETH-CENTURY METHODIST THEOLOGY IS BY no means identical with the theology of John Wesley, it cannot be adequately understood apart from his thought. We therefore begin this examination of the social implications of Methodist doctrinal emphases with a sketch of the doctrines which Wesley himself regarded as central.

A. Central Emphases of John Wesley

We have already seen in Chapter One that Wesley distinguished between marginal opinions and essential beliefs, and found the primary significance of the latter in their contribution to the life transformed and empowered by God. This conception of the relation between theology and life offers an important clue to the content of Wesley's theology. Christianity to him was primarily the *gospel*, the good news of the forgiving, life-changing love of God manifest in Jesus Christ and continuously active through the Holy Spirit. Determinative of his theological emphasis was his practical concern for the salvation of men. His central theme, therefore, was salvation, and all the other elements in his theology revolved around this. He was interested in and frequently discussed all the main branches of Christian doctrine, but so decisive and extensive was his attention to the doctrine of redemption that his developed theology could be quite accurately termed a soteriology, or theory of salvation.

As Henry Bett has shown, the main doctrinal emphases of Wesley and his early followers are rooted in this soteriological interest.

It was because the early Methodists were primarily concerned with the

44

salvation of men that they came to stress the fact of a personal experience and a personal certainty of redemption. It was for the same reason that they passionately opposed a doctrine which denied salvation to the larger part of mankind. It was for the same reason, again, that they emphasized the fact and explored the nature of holiness, since that is both the un-failing result and the undeniable evidence of a real and sure experience of salvation.[1]

This dominant interest appears plainly in Wesley's explanation of "the principles of a Methodist," which is valuable also for its evidence that he regarded his beliefs not as distinctive, but as ecu-menically Christian.

I have again and again, with all the plainness I could, declared what our constant doctrines are; whereby we are distinguished only from Heathens, or nominal Christians; not from any that worship God in spirit and in truth. Our main doctrines, which include all the rest, are three—that of repent-ance, of faith, and of holiness. The first of these we account, as it were, the porch of religion; the next, the door; the third, religion itself.[2]

In another passage Wesley stated that salvation by faith was the "standing topic" of his preachers, and that this implied three things: "(1) That men are all, by nature, 'dead in sin,' and consequently, 'children of wrath.' (2) That they are 'justified by faith alone.' (3) That faith produces inward and outward holiness."[3] It is clear that the first of these elements is only superficially different from "the porch of religion" in the preceding passage, since man's need of re-pentance arises from his sinfulness.

This three-point exposition provides a valuable approach to a true understanding of Wesley's theology, not only because it comes from Wesley himself, but also because all of his major emphases can be grouped naturally under these three headings. Their meaning appears more clearly when they are so related and organized than it would if they were simply considered one after the other, as beads on a string. It is apparent that justification by grace through faith is the door to salvation. But two other major emphases of Wesley, the universal availability of salvation and the witness of the Spirit, or Christian assurance, also belong initially here. Put very simply, these doctrines

---

[1] *The Spirit of Methodism* (London: The Epworth Press, 1937), p. 93.
[2] "The Principles of a Methodist Father Explained," VI, 4. *Works*, VIII, 472.
[3] "A Short History of Methodism," 10. *Works*, VIII, 349.

mean that the door is open to all, and that God lets us know when we cross the threshold into our Father's house. However, Christian experience obviously does not cease when we enter; instead, it takes increasingly the form of growth in holiness. This is the heart of two other closely related teachings of Wesley—sanctification and perfection.

On this basis we may without distortion present Wesley's major theological emphases in the form of a chart, as follows:

WESLEY'S THEOLOGY OF SALVATION

	Characteristic Emphasis	Salvation as
The Porch:	Human sinfulness, and resultant need of repentance	Necessary
The Door:	Faith	
	Forgiveness (justification) by grace through faith	Free, unmerited
	Universal availability of God's redemptive grace and possibility of answering faith	Open to all
	Experience of forgiveness and reconciliation, witness of the Spirit, Christian assurance	Personal, consciously experienced
The House:	Holiness of heart and life—sanctification and perfection	Whole, all-inclusive

We turn now to a brief examination of these characteristic teachings.

B. Sin and Repentance

First of all, men stand in need of salvation. Apart from the emancipating grace of God received in faith, men are in bondage to sin. This is why repentance is necessary. "It is only sinners that have any occasion for pardon: it is sin alone which admits of being forgiven. . . . It is our *unrighteousness* to which the pardoning God is *merciful:* it is our *iniquity* which He 'remembereth no more.' " [4] As sinners we have no claim on the divine mercy, no merit of our own to offer. "We are utterly insolvent; we have nothing to pay; we have

[4] Sermon, "Justification by Faith," III, 1. Sugden, I, 122.

wasted all our substance. . . . We are already bound hand and foot by the chains of our own sins." [5]

Wesley distinguishes two kinds of repentance, legal and evangelical. The former is "a thorough conviction of sin," a sense of "our utter sinfulness and helplessness." The latter is "a change of heart (and consequently of life) from all sin to all holiness." [6] The sinner becomes convinced by bitter experience of his inability either to fulfill the law of God or to remove the guilt and burden of his wrongdoing. He therefore replaces trust in his own righteousness with complete trust in the grace of God revealed in Christ. Combined with this evangelical repentance are "fruits meet for repentance"—a repudiation of evil and a joyous turning toward the good.

C. Justification by Faith

Though repentance and its fruits are necessary for forgiveness, they are only indirectly or "remotely" so, because without them faith is impossible. The porch affords access to the door, but only by the door can we enter the house. Faith alone is immediately or directly necessary to justification; it is the sole human condition of the divine pardon.[7]

Salvation through faith is regarded by Wesley as "the fundamental doctrine of the Church," [8] "that important truth, which is the foundation of all real religion." [9] For him, as for Luther, justification is not being made just or righteous,[10] but is rather pardon or forgiveness of sins. To be justified means to be treated by God as though we were righteous, even though we are not; it means to be accepted in spite of our actual unacceptability.

Objectively there are two grounds for forgiveness, the mercy and grace of God and the atoning work of Christ. Subjectively it is

[5] Sermon, "Upon Our Lord's Sermon on the Mount: VI," III, 13. Sugden, I, 441-42.
[6] Explanatory Notes upon the New Testament (London: William Bowyer, 1818), Matthew 3:8; Journal, June 28, 1740, II, 362.
[7] Sermons, "The Scripture Way of Salvation," III, 2; "Justification by Faith," IV, 5, 6; Sugden, II, 451-52; I, 126-127. "Minutes of Some Late Conversations," Aug. 1, 1745, Works, VIII, 281.
[8] "An Earnest Appeal to Men of Reason and Religion," 84. Works, VIII, 35.
[9] "Thoughts on Salvation by Faith," Works, XI, 492.
[10] This Wesley believes possible, but he includes it in sanctification rather than justification.

occasioned by "true and living faith in the merits of Jesus Christ." [11] Such faith is far more than "a train of ideas in the head"; it is "a disposition of the heart." [12] It is not mere intellectual assent, even to the truth of the gospel, but personal trust in Christ and his redeeming life, death, and resurrection. "It is a sure confidence which a man hath in God, that through the merits of Christ, his sins are forgiven, and he reconciled to the favor of God." [13]

Wesley clearly insists that man can claim no credit for either his forgiveness or his faith. Both root in the unmerited grace of God. "Of yourselves cometh neither your faith nor your salvation: 'It is the gift of God'; the free, undeserved gift. . . . That ye believe, is one instance of his grace; that believing ye are saved, another." [14] Salvation is wrought not by faith and works, either ceremonial or ethical, but purely by grace through faith. In this position Wesley is obviously at one with Reformation Protestantism. "Wherein," he asks, "may we come to the very edge of Calvinism?" His reply may sound strange to many present-day Methodists:" (1) In ascribing all good to the free grace of God. (2) In denying all natural free-will, and all power antecedent to grace. And (3) in excluding all merit from man, even for what he has or does by the grace of God." [15] Man must choose to be saved, but the very power by which he turns to God is a divine gift.

This does not mean, however, that righteousness has no relation to salvation. "Good works" cannot save, but they are the inevitable fruit of saving faith. The faith of which Wesley speaks is "necessarily productive of all good works, and all holiness." [16] Some of his sharpest criticisms are directed against antinomianism, the doctrine that those who are saved by grace may ignore the ethical demands of the law of God. "To turn the grace of God into an encouragement to sin, is the sure way to the nethermost hell!" [17] Those who have really experienced the forgiving love of God want to express their gratitude in lives devoted to his service.

[11] "The Principles of a Methodist," 3. Works, VIII, 361-62.
[12] Sermon, "Salvation by Faith," I, 4. Sugden, I, 40.
[13] Ibid., I, 5. Sugden, I, 41.
[14] Ibid., III, 3. Sugden, I, 47-48.
[15] "Minutes of Some Late Conversions," Aug. 1, 1745. Works, VIII, 281.
[16] Sermon, "Salvation by Faith," III, 1. Sugden, I, 46.
[17] Sermon, "A Call to Backsliders," V, 10 (6). Works, VI, 527.

D. Universal Availability of Salvation

Although Wesley's extreme stress on divine grace and his denial of all "natural free-will" brought him to the verge of Calvinism, in decisive respects he stood at the opposite pole from the Calvinists. Salvation and the faith which conditions its acceptance are available to all men. There is no lock or secret combination on the door leading to life eternal; it swings open readily to all who knock.

Hardly any other doctrine was the subject of more vehement and indignant attack by Wesley than predestination. In his sermons, treatises, and letters he repeatedly exposes its defects with a logic which is as vigorously pursued as it is closely reasoned. Even when he affirms most emphatically that God is the source of all human good, and that grace does not depend on any power or merit in man, he labors with the greatest care to show the untenability of any view which restricts salvation to the few who are elected by the unsearchable decrees of an arbitrary God. "The grace or love of God," he writes, "whence cometh our salvation, is FREE IN ALL, and FREE FOR ALL." [18]

Significantly, when Wesley revised the Thirty-nine Articles and sent them to America as a doctrinal basis for the new Methodist Episcopal Church, he eliminated the most extremely Calvinistic passages of Articles IX (Methodist Article VIII), deleted the qualifying adverb *necessarily* from the passage in Article XII (Methodist Article X) which asserts that good works "spring out necessarily of a true and lively faith," and completely omitted the long Article XVII which is an unqualified declaration of predestination.

Of the various arguments which Wesley develops against predestination, five of the most important may be summarized here. (1) The doctrine makes vain the preaching of the gospel—which God himself has commanded—since the aim of preaching is to save souls, but the elect will be saved without preaching, and the nonelect cannot be saved with it. (2) Predestination tends to overthrow and make unnecessary the whole Christian revelation, since men who are saved or damned according to eternal, unchangeable decrees cannot be affected by the gospel. But a gospel which is not necessary is not true, and thus the whole Christian cause is sacrificed. (3) The doc-

[18] Sermon, "Free Grace," 2. Works, VII, 373.

trine destroys zeal for good works, since it tends to lessen our love for the majority of men—"the evil and the unthankful"—and our concern for their spiritual and material needs. (4) It is based on an interpretation of a limited number of Biblical texts which contradict other passages and "the whole scope and tenor of Scripture." (5) It blasphemes and dishonors God, undermining his truth, justice, and love. The God implied by this doctrine is more false, unjust, and cruel than the devil: contrary to what he has said in the Scriptures, he is not willing that all men should be saved; he condemns multitudes for the sin which the withholding of his grace makes inevitable; and he dooms to perdition many of his creatures who earnestly desire salvation. Hence Wesley "abhors" the doctrine.[19]

It is noteworthy that most of the considerations cited by Wesley reflect his practical concern for the salvation of men. Christ came, he was convinced, to seek and to save the lost, and the Christian church is commissioned to preach the gospel of redemption. But if predestination is true, the coming of Christ was in vain and the whole task of evangelism is an empty sham, for there is neither need for it nor value in it. Multitudes are completely beyond the love of God and man, and nothing can be done to help them. This was to Wesley a repudiation of the central meaning of the Christian faith.

It should be noted also that Wesley, like Arminius, believed in election, but election conditioned on the response of men to God's offer of salvation. There is a "decree" which is both unchangeable and unavoidable: "I will set before the sons of men, 'life and death, blessing and cursing.' And the soul that chooseth life shall live, as the soul that chooseth death shall die." [20] "He that believeth shall be saved; he that believeth not shall be damned." The elect are those who truly believe, while the reprobate, the "unapproved of God," are those who continue in unbelief.[21] When the Lord says, "I will have mercy on whom I will have mercy," he means, "on him who believeth on Jesus." [22] In Wesley's mind this interpretation preserves the character of God and provides a firm foundation for human hope.

[19] Ibid., 9-26. Works, VII, 375-83.
[20] Ibid., 29. Works, VII, 385.
[21] "Predestination Calmly Considered," 17. Works, X, 210.
[22] Sermon, "Justification by Faith," IV, 7. Sugden, I, 128.

In the determination of men's destinies "not sovereignty alone, but justice, mercy, and truth hold the reins." [23]

Obviously, man as Wesley sees him has the capacity of free choice: he can either accept or reject the divine grace. But this power is nothing that is inherent in man or that belongs to him by right; it is rather a gift of God. On the surface it is hard to reconcile this assumption of freedom with some of Wesley's descriptions of sinful man, which bear a striking similarity to those of John Calvin himself. He portrays man as "corrupted in every power, in every faculty." His will is "utterly perverse and distorted, averse from all good . . . and prone to all evil." [24] The natural man is "a willing servant of sin, content with the bondage of corruption," boastful of his powers but ignorant of his true state.[25] "Since the fall, no child of man has a natural power to choose anything that is truly good." [26]

We can reconcile this seeming contradiction between human incapacity and freedom only by recognizing that, strictly speaking, the "natural man" has for Wesley no real existence. He is purely an abstraction, but highly useful to set forth the depth and universality of sin and the absence in man of any claim to God's favor. Actually,

there is no man that is in a state of mere nature; there is no man, unless he has quenched the Spirit, that is wholly void of the grace of God. No man living is entirely destitute of what is vulgarly called *natural conscience*. But this is not natural; it is more properly termed, *preventing grace*. Every man has a greater or less measure of this. . . . So that no man sins because he has not grace, but because he does not use the grace which he hath.[27]

In this context Wesley's conception of freedom becomes understandable. Free will in his thought is not the exercise of man's undamaged, unaided natural powers. It is itself a divine gift, the result of that grace of God which works in all men to make possible, though not necessary, their turning to him for redemption.

Although I have not an absolute power over my own mind, because of |

[23] "Predestination Calmly Considered," 54. *Works*, X, 235.
[24] "Upon Our Lord's Sermon on the Mount: I," I, 5. Sugden, I, 324.
[25] Sermon, "The Spirit of Bondage and Adoption," I, 1-8. Sugden, I, 181-85.
[26] "Some Remarks on 'A Defense of the Preface to the Edinburgh Edition of Aspasia Vindicated,' " 5. *Works*, X, 350.
[27] Sermon, "On Working Out Our Own Salvation," III, 4. *Works*, VI, 512.

the corruption of my own nature; yet, through the grace of God assisting me, I have a power to choose and do good, as well as evil. I am free to choose whom I will serve; and if I choose the better part, to continue therein even unto death.[28]

Every man, says Wesley, has such a choice set before him, and he "has in himself the casting voice." [29]

E. The Witness of the Spirit

Those who exercise their God-given freedom to enter the door need be in no doubt as to where they are. They may rightly expect to receive an "inward consciousness" of their acceptance by God. The justifying faith which is open to all is not only the individual's belief that he is forgiven, but a deeply personal *assurance* of forgiveness. This is that "momentous truth" of the witness of the Spirit which Wesley regarded as "one grand part of the testimony" which God has given [the Methodists] to bear to all mankind." Following Paul in Romans 8:16, he affirms that the Spirit of God, through "an inward impression on the soul," "immediately and directly witnesses to my spirit, that I am a child of God; that Jesus Christ hath loved me, and given Himself for me; that all my sins are blotted out, and I, even I, am reconciled to God." [30] To this testimony is added that of our own spirits—our consciousness of strength from God enabling us to keep his commandments and to live as his adopted children in love toward God and man.[31]

In stressing Christian assurance Wesley did not exaggerate the role of emotion. He explicitly sought to avoid "the wildness of enthusiasm" as well as "mere formality" without power. Moreover, he warned against "any supposed testimony of the Spirit which is separate from the fruit of it." He who really experiences the living God, rather than merely a passing emotion, will evidence the appropriate fruits: "love, joy, peace, patience, kindness, goodness, faithfulness, gentleness, self-control—all inward and outward holiness." Roots and fruits go together, and both should be the joyous possession of the Christian believer.[32]

---

[28] Sermon, "On What Is Man?" 11. Works, VII, 228-29.
[29] Sermon, "The General Spread of the Gospel," 12. Works, VI, 281.
[30] Sermon, "The Witness of the Spirit: II," I, 4; II, 2. Sugden, II, 343-45.
[31] Sermon, "The Witness of the Spirit: I," I, 1-6. Sugden, I, 204-7.
[32] Sermon, "The Witness of the Spirit: II," I, 2; V, 3, 4. Sugden, II, 358-59.

The witness of the Spirit was the central expression of Wesley's profound emphasis on religious experience in the broader sense. Appearing repeatedly in his writings are phrases like "we experimentally know," "experience shows," and "the experimental knowledge of Christ." Such expressions clearly reflect his firm conviction that God can be directly and personally known—that God's righteousness and love may be *lived through* by each individual rather than merely believed in on the testimony of others. However, this immediate awareness of God's presence also provides powerful evidence for the truth of the Christian message. Wrote Wesley: "I now am assured that these things are so: I experience them in my own breast." [33] In his Sixth University Sermon he spoke of "the sure test of experience."

Though this emphasis might easily lead the individual to mistake for truth his own pious imaginings, Wesley successfully avoided the pitfalls of subjectivism by combining personal experience with other tests. "Scripture, reason, and experience" were his norms of religious truth.[34] He continually checked his findings with the historic revelation of God recorded in the Scriptures, the writings of the Fathers of the early church, the experience of the Christian community, past and present, his own critical intelligence, and the lives of those who claimed an experience of the Spirit's witness.

Yet experience remained indispensable. Though Wesley admitted that "experience is not sufficient to prove a doctrine unsupported by Scripture," he insisted that it "is sufficient to confirm a doctrine which is grounded on Scripture." [35] It is true that the intimations of experience are suspect if they stand alone. Nevertheless, no religious teaching means very much unless its claims are experimentally validated. Theoretical truth, however strong its support in tradition or external authority, is powerless and dead if it remains theoretical. It must become realized truth for particular men and women. The truth that saves and transforms is the truth that is personally appropriated. "The image of God impressed on a created spirit"—this is "the strongest evidence of the truth of Christianity." [36]

[33] "To Dr. Conyers Middleton," Jan. 4, 1749, II, 12. *Letters*, II, 383.
[34] Sermon, "The Repentance of Believers," I, 2. Sugden, II, 381.
[35] Sermon, "The Witness of the Spirit: II," V, 2. Sugden, II, 357-58.
[36] "To Dr. Conyers Middleton," Jan. 4, 1749, III, 1. *Letters*, II, 383.

F. Holiness of Heart and Life

A doorway fails to serve its purpose if we only stand in it instead of passing through it. So for Wesley even the most vivid experience of God's pardoning love received in faith falls short of fulfillment if it does not lead to holiness of heart and life. Salvation is to be lived. Faith must bear fruit in righteousness.

The fundamental doctrine of the people called Methodists is: Whosoever will be saved, before all things it is necessary that he hold the true faith; the faith which works by love; which, by means of the love of God and our neighbour, produces both inward and outward holiness.[37]

Thus Wesley held what might be termed today a dynamic as opposed to a static conception of faith and salvation. For him it meant not a formal change of legal status before God or a guarantee of heaven, but newness of life. In one sermon he declared that however strong our faith "it will never save us from hell, unless it now save us from all unholy tempers; from pride, passion, impatience; from all arrogance of spirit, all haughtiness and over-bearing; from wrath, anger, bitterness; from discontent, murmuring, fretfulness, peevishness." [38] "We are all indeed called to be saints, and the very name of Christian means no less." [39]

In a day when many believed that God's pardon only *canceled* sin, Charles Wesley sang:

> He breaks the power of canceled sin,
> He sets the prisoner free.

John Wesley heartily agreed. God saves us not only *in* our sins, but *from* our sins.[40] The *Conference Minutes* for 1746 declared: "In asserting salvation by faith, we mean this: (1) That pardon (salvation begun) is received in faith, producing works. (2) That holiness (salvation continued) is faith working by love. (3) That heaven (salvation finished) is the reward of this faith." The Christian's ex-

---

[37] "To the Editor of Lloyd's Evening Post," Nov. 17, 1760. *Journal*, IV, 419. Cf. "Thoughts on Salvation by Faith," 11. *Works*, XI, 493.
[38] "On Charity," III, 7. *Works*, VII, 54.
[39] Sermon, "True Christianity Defended," II, 1. *Works*, VII, 457.
[40] Sermon, "The Spirit of Bondage and Adoption," I, 2. Sugden, I, 182-83.

perience on earth therefore includes both justification and sanctification. In the former we are saved from the guilt of sin and restored to the divine favor by what God does for us through his Son. In the latter we are saved from the power of sin and restored to the divine image by what God does in us by his Spirit.[41] A whole gospel would not proclaim one aspect and forget the other.

Wesley's position is clearly summed up in his description of a true "gospel-minister." Such a preacher declares "the whole counsel of God"; he preaches "the whole Gospel, even justification and sanctification preparatory to glory"; he "does not put asunder what God hath joined; but publishes alike *Christ dying for us* and *Christ living in us*." [42] In thus uniting two divergent emphases of sixteenth-century Protestantism—justification by faith and holiness of life—Wesley rendered a notable service to ecumenical Christianity.

In defining sanctification or holiness he makes plain that it is much more than conformity through human effort to certain prescribed rules or practices—as apparently he believed in his pre-Aldersgate period. The Christian is expected, indeed, to do no harm, to do good, and to use the ordinances of God. But true holiness is an inward reality, rooted, like forgiveness, in the grace of God. It is "the life of God in the soul of man; a participation of the divine nature; the mind that was in Christ; or the renewal of our heart after the image of Him that created us." [43] It is "nothing short of holy tempers": long-suffering, gentleness, lowliness, and the like, but chiefly love; from these outward works spring.[44]

To use one of Wesley's favorite expressions, holiness is the experience of one who is "not almost only, but altogether a Christian." Having the faith which works by love, he loves God with his whole being, and he loves all men, even his enemies, as himself.[45] In constant fellowship with God, he lives the "life which is hid with Christ in God." [46]

[41] "Explanatory Notes upon the New Testament," Matthew 11:28; sermons, "On Working Out Our Own Salvation," II, 1, Works, VI, 509; "Justification by Faith," II, 1, Sugden, I, 119; "The New Birth," Introduction, 1, Sugden, II, 227.
[42] "Thoughts concerning Gospel-Ministers," 4. Works, X, 456.
[43] Journal, Sept. 13, 1739, II, 275. Cf. Journal, Oct. 14, 1738, II, 89-90.
[44] Sermon, "On Charity," III, 12. Works, VII, 56.
[45] Sermon, "The Almost Christian," II, 1-11. Works, V, 18.
[46] "An Answer to an Important Question." Works XIII, 263.

In this connection Wesley devotes considerable attention to the new birth, which he sees as the gateway to holiness. The new birth is thus closely related to justification, the door to salvation. Chronologically, neither precedes the other, but logically—"in the order of thinking"—justification comes first. But whereas justification is largely negative, removing the blot of sin and restoring the divine favor, the new birth is more positive, involving a new creation, "a change from the love of the creature to the love of the Creator; from earthly and sensual to heavenly and holy affections." Through the power of God passion becomes meekness, and hatred, envy, and malice are replaced by "a sincere, tender, disinterested love for all mankind." [47]

Once entered, the holy life is not a static thing, but a deepening, enlarging process. Wesley writes of "a gradual sanctification, a growing in grace, a daily advance in the knowledge and love of God" which normally continues through most of the earthly life of the believer. However, it is often punctuated by lapses. Hence repentance and faith are necessary not only when the divine grace is initially accepted, but "in every subsequent stage of our Christian course." Even though we know ourselves as children of God we also know that we are still sinners, marked by pride, self-will, uncharitable words and actions, and lack of love toward God and man. Our conviction of the continuation of such sins and our inability to free ourselves from them constitutes a form of repentance. Indeed, the Christian who is really advancing in the knowledge and love of God is all the more sensitively aware of his alienation from God. But such repentance is not accompanied by the sense of condemnation, the tormenting fear, or the consciousness of the divine wrath which preceded the experience of forgiveness, nor does it imply any doubt of the favor of God. It combines a conviction of our own helplessness with an assurance of God's abiding grace. Thus, while sin remains, it does not reign.[48]

Wesley believed, moreover, on the basis of the New Testament,[49] that growth in grace should culminate in what he called "entire sanctification." "If sin cease before death, there must, in the nature of the

---

[47] Sermon, "The New Birth," Introduction, 1; II, 5; Sugden, II, 227, 234. Journal, Sept. 13, 1739, II, 276.

[48] Sermons, "The Repentance of Believers," Introduction, 2; I, 4, 16-18; "The Scripture Way of Salvation," III, 6-8; "Upon Our Lord's Sermon on the Mount: I," I, 13. Sugden, II, 379-81, 388-90, 454-55; I, 329.

[49] Matt. 22:37; John 17:20-23; Rom. 12:1-2; II Cor. 7:1; Eph. 3:14, 16-19; II Thess. 5:23.

thing, be an instantaneous change; there must be a last moment wherein it does exist, and a first moment wherein it does not." [50] He mentions knowing "a large number of persons" who exhibited all the evidences of having reached this freedom from sin.[51] Nevertheless, he also affirmed the real possibility of backsliding, and of a new turn to God thereafter. His interpretation of the Christian life allowed no room for either complacency or despair.

Inseparable from Wesley's doctrine of sanctification was his teaching concerning Christian perfection. In fact, he typically used the terms holiness and perfection interchangeably. "Perfection is only another term for holiness, or the image of God in man. 'God made man perfect,' I think is just the same as 'he made him holy,' or 'in his own image.' " [52] Sanctification refers mainly to the activity of the Holy Spirit through which man is led toward holiness or perfection, while these terms denote the quality of life which results when the sanctifying action of God arouses a trustful, obedient response. Perfection therefore signifies the ideal norm of the Christian life, the goal which all are called to seek; its fulfillment is the consequence of entire sanctification.

Wesley makes clear that perfection means neither absolute perfection, which belongs to God alone, nor angelic or "Adamic" perfection, in which original faculties remain unimpaired. It does not involve freedom from ignorance, error, physical or mental infirmities, temptation, or involuntary violations of the divine will. It does involve freedom from (1) the commission of sin, viewed as the voluntary transgression of a known law, and (2) evil thoughts and tempers.[53] Less precisely, Wesley defines the essence of perfection simply as "perfect love" (I John 4:18).[54] "They that love God with all their heart and all men as themselves are scripturally perfect." [55] In his "Answer to the Rev. Mr. Dodd," after referring to the freedom from intentional sinning of those "born of God," he continues:

[50] "Minutes of Several Conversations," 1744-1789. Works, VII, 329.

[51] Sermon, "A Call to Backsliders," II, 10(3). Works, VI, 526. It is significant that Wesley never claimed this for himself.

[52] "An Answer to the Rev. Mr. Dodd," 3. Works, XI, 451.

[53] Sermons, "On Perfection," I, 1-2 (Works, VI, 412); "Christian Perfection," I, 1, 4, 7-9, 20-21, 24 (Sugden, II, 152-56, 168-71).

[54] "A Plain Account of Christian Perfection," 26. Works, XI, 442.

[55] "To Miss March," April 7, 1763. Letters, IV, 208.

All this, with abundantly more than this, is contained in that single expression, "the loving God with all our heart, and serving him with all our strength." Nor did I ever say or mean any more by perfection, than thus loving and serving God. But I dare not say less than this.[56]

This view of perfection as centering in love opens the way for Wesley to view it as capable of growth. "It is improvable. It is so far from lying in an indivisible point, from being incapable of increase, that one perfected in love may grow in grace far swifter than he did before. . . . It is constantly both preceded and followed by a gradual work." [57] As Charles Wesley wrote,

> Yet when the work is done,
> The work is but begun.

Difficulties in Wesley's doctrines of perfection and entire sanctification are readily apparent. He finds Biblical support by resorting to an uncritical method of proof-texting, using about thirty selected passages. His limitation of sin here to conscious violation of a known law fails to do justice to the full range and reality of sin for Christian faith—or to the depth of his own conception elsewhere. In asserting that God replaces the sinful heart with a heart of love he seems to envisage a kind of impersonal subconscious process which contradicts his volitional notion of sin. Further, there is no basis in Paul's writings for the expectation of an instantaneous destruction of sin in the believer.

Nevertheless, none of these defects invalidates the central import of Wesley's stress on holiness. He insists that salvation involves not only the forgiveness but the spiritual renewal and transformation of the sinner through divine power. God calls the Christian to the attainment of "mature manhood," "the measure of the stature of Christ" (Eph. 4:13), and his indwelling presence makes such fulfillment possible. The faith that saves bears fruit in a life permeated by love toward God and man. This is the "religion of love" which Wesley finds "beautifully summed up in that one comprehensive petition: 'Cleanse the thoughts of our hearts by the inspiration of

[56] Works, XI, 451.
[57] "A Plain Account of Christian Perfection," 26. Works, XI, 442.

thy Holy Spirit, that we may perfectly love thee, and worthily magnify thy holy name.' " [58]

Clearly this is no sectarian doctrine. Its ecumenical character is demonstrated not only by the prominent place of the Collect for Purity in the treasury of Christian devotion, but also by the almost universal use among Protestants of hymns like Charles Wesley's "Love divine, all loves excelling." Not Methodist only, but authentically Christian is the prayer:

> Finish, then, Thy new creation;
> Pure and spotless let us be;
> Let us see Thy great salvation
> Perfectly restored in Thee.

G. Social Implications of Wesley's Theology

John Wesley never worked out a social philosophy on the basis of his theological views, nor was he involved very directly in action to change social structures. He remained throughout his life primarily an evangelist, seeking to bring persons of all sorts and conditions under the power of the redemptive love of God. Nevertheless, there are unmistakable social implications in his theology of salvation.

1. God has acted to redeem all men; we are therefore called upon to love all men and to seek their highest spiritual and material welfare. No human being, no matter how unworthy or disreputable, stands outside the circle of Christian responsibility, because no human being is excluded from the redemptive concern of God.

A poor wretch cries to me for an alms: I look, and see him covered with dirt and rags. But through these I see one that has an immortal spirit, made to know, and love, and dwell with God to eternity. I honour him for his Creator's sake. . . . I love him for the sake of his Redeemer. The courtesy, therefore, which I feel and show toward him is a mixture of the honour and love which I bear to the offspring of God; the purchase of his Son's blood, and the candidate for immortality. This courtesy let us feel and show toward all men; and we shall please all men to their edification.[59]

2. Salvation is realized in proportion as the faith which inaugurates

---

[58] Sermon, "On Laying the Foundation of the New Chapel, near the City-Road, London" (April 21, 1777), II, 4. Works, VII, 424-25. Cf. sermon, "True Christianity Defended," I, 7. Ibid., 455-56.

[59] Sermon, "On Pleasing All Men," II, 5. Works, VII, 145-46.

it is expressed in love. The witness of the Spirit is confirmed by the fruits of the Spirit, and he who really trusts in Christ for redemption is marked by an "inward and outward holiness" which centers in a "sincere, tender, disinterested love toward God and man." Growth in holiness necessarily involves good works, which include not only devotional practices but acts of mercy aimed at meeting both bodily and spiritual needs.

This religion we long to see established in the world, a religion of love, and joy, and peace, having its seat in the inmost soul, but ever showing itself by its fruits, continually springing forth, not only in all innocence (for love worketh no ill to his neighbour), but likewise in every kind of beneficence, spreading virtue and happiness all around it.[60]

3. Salvation is throughout ethical—though not only ethical. It is necessary because men have departed from God's righteous will; it is given by God according to "justice, mercy, and truth"; and it is fulfilled in the life of Christlike character. Thirteen of Wesley's fifty-three standard sermons expound with penetrating insight the Sermon on the Mount, which he calls "the sum of true religion."

4. Salvation is not only future, but relates to the life of men here and now. It includes present experience of freedom from "unholy tempers" and newness of life through divine power. Though "finished" in heaven, it is begun and continued on earth, and relates concretely to the way in which we conduct ourselves among our fellow men in this world.

5. Salvation relates to the whole life of man, which rightly seen is a stewardship. Since we are God's "bought with a price," "there is no employment of our time, no action or conversation, that is purely indifferent. All is good or bad, because all our time, as everything we have, is not our own." [61] Everything we do has religious significance. We have no right, for example, to spend money on "costly apparel," because such expenditures decrease our ability to minister to human need. When a tax was imposed on silver plate and Wesley received in May 1776 a form letter demanding a declaration of his silver, he replied: "I have two silver teaspoons at *London*, and

---

[60] "An Earnest Appeal to Men of Reason and Religion," 4. Works, VIII, 3-4.
[61] Sermon, "The Good Steward," IV, 2. Sugden, II, 478.

two at *Bristol.* This is all the plate I have at present; and I shall not buy any more while so many round me want bread." [62]

6. Salvation is realized within a community, and in this sense is itself social. "Solitary religion," declared Wesley, "is not to be found" in the gospel. " 'Holy solitaries' is a phrase no more consistent with the Gospel than holy adulterers. The Gospel of Christ knows no religion but social; no holiness, but social holiness." [63] The converts of the Wesleyan revival were introduced into a fellowship in which social, economic, and racial differences were transcended in a shared experience of redeeming love. Class meetings, bands, and societies became laboratories in which the priesthood of all believers was tested and proved, channels for works of charity, and centers from which Spirit-filled men went forth to live their faith in a larger society.

It remains true that Wesley never carried out fully the social implications of his theology. "Social holiness" meant for him not the transformation of social structures to accord with the divine will, but holiness experienced by persons who found mutual strengthening in Christian fellowship, and who practiced their faith in all their relations with their fellow men. The notion of social salvation in the sense of institutional reform would have been alien to his mind. As Waldo Beach has put it, "Wesley had no notion of seeking to redeem society through legislation." [64] In politics he remained a conservative Tory. For the most part, he did not challenge the economic and social institutions of his day, but with all his energy he sought the regeneration and transformation of the human beings affected by them. In practice, therefore, Wesley's ethic was chiefly individual, as was the scriptural holiness which he sought to "spread through the land." His social views were largely derived from ethical principles related to individuals.

Yet this primary concern did not prevent him from dealing critically on many occasions with the social evils of his time. He castigated unfair business practices (inflated charges for goods or services, exorbitant interest, ruthless competition),[65] attacked the manufacture and

---

[62] Journal, VI, 126 n.

[63] *The Poetical Works of John and Charles Wesley,* ed. G. Osborne (London: Wesleyan-Methodist Conference Office, 1868), I, xxii.

[64] *Christian Ethics*—Sources of the Living Tradition, edited by Waldo Beach and H. Richard Niebuhr. Copyright 1955, The Ronald Press Company, p. 361.

[65] Sermon, "The Use of Money," I, 1-6; II, 1, 6-7; III, 1, 4-5. Sugden, II, 314-20, 322-25. Here appears Wesley's oft-quoted counsel to Christians, "Gain all you can," "Save all you can," "Give all you can."

use of alcoholic beverages,[66] pointed out the iniquity and folly of war,[67] and in his last letter applauded William Wilberforce in his battle against "that execrable villainy," slavery. "Go on," he wrote, "in the name of God and in the power of His might, till even American slavery (the vilest that ever saw the sun) shall vanish away before it." [68]

Moreover, he himself engaged unceasingly in a wide variety of enterprises which sought to relieve suffering or improve the daily lot of all sorts and conditions of men. The words of Waldo Beach are an accurate summary of these activities:

He visited English prisons many times, preaching to their inmates and commenting bitterly in his letters on the misery of prison conditions. He set up a simple loan society among his Methodists to help keep his poor followers from the clutches of the pawnbrokers and out of debtors' prisons. He fought hard liquor as much for economic as for moral reasons. He edited a *Christian Library*, fifty volumes of extracts from Christian literature, for popular use. He established a free medical dispensary and wrote a book of simple home remedies for sickness, called *Primitive Physic*, which ran to twenty-three editions. He established a home for widows and a school for poor children.[69]

Sometimes Wesley's ethical concern for people was rather negative in nature, aiming to release them chiefly from the sins of the flesh. For example, as evidences of the reality of men's experience of "the power of God unto salvation" he lists the following: "The habitual drunkard that was is now temperate in all things; the whoremonger now flees fornication; he that stole, steals no more, but works with his hands; he that cursed or swore, perhaps at every sentence, has now learned to serve the Lord with fear and rejoice in Him with reverence; those formerly enslaved to various habits of sin are now brought to uniform habits of holiness." [70]

It must be remembered, however, that in the barren, poverty-stricken life of eighteenth-century England, from which multitudes

---

[66] *Ibid.*
[67] "The Doctrine of Original Sin: I," II, 10. Works, IX, 221-22.
[68] *Letters*, VIII, 265.
[69] *Christian Ethics*—Sources of the Living Tradition, edited by Waldo Beach and H. Richard Niebuhr. Copyright 1955, The Ronald Press Company, p. 362.
[70] "To Dr. Gibson, Bishop of London," June 11, 1747. *Letters*, II, 290.

sought escape in sensuality and indulgence, this kind of message was precisely what was initially needed. Further, those who were convinced by Wesleyan preaching that the love of God was meant even for them gained a new self-respect which paved the way for a more positive social witness in succeeding years. The famous letter of the Duchess of Buckingham to Lady Huntingdon gives a clue to the change wrought among social outcasts by Wesley's gospel of salvation. The doctrines of the Methodist preachers, she wrote,

are most repulsive and strongly tinctured with inpertinence and disrespect toward their superiors in perpetually endeavouring to level all ranks and do away with all distinctions, as it is monstrous to be told that you have a heart as sinful as *the common wretches that crawl on the earth.*[71]

This proclamation that every man is called to be a child of God, personally experienced as true by multitudes previously without hope, was to exert an incalculable political and economic effect in nineteenth-century England and America. The "common wretches" were moved to oppose the powerful forces which had condemned them to lives of poverty and meaninglessness; to work industriously, to buy books instead of liquor, and to seek better educational and cultural opportunities for their children. Vastly changed was the self-image and outlook on life of those who learned to sing, with Charles Wesley:

> He owns me for His child,
>   I can no longer fear:
> With confidence I now draw nigh,
> And, "Father, Abba, Father," cry.

As Halford E. Luccock has written:

The new confidence as a result of religious experience was the "flower in the crannied walls." If you can see all there is in that, the sense of the human and divine resources for human life, you can understand the gathering struggle of the nineteenth century for human rights against injustice and exploitation. When that religious experience, that realized sonship to God, that enhanced personality, that conviction that all men are on an equality

[71] J. Wesley Bready, *England: Before and After Wesley* (New York and London: Harper and Brothers, 1938), pp. 211-12.

before God, is let loose in the lives of men, we can say with Mark Antony, "Mischief, thou art afoot. Take what course thou wilt." [72]

With the way thus prepared, men influenced by Wesley carried much farther than he the social implications of his religious message. The nineteenth century witnessed a powerful thrust toward legislative reform and institutional change. Specifically, historians and social scientists have noted strong influences from the evangelical revival in the antislavery movement led by Wilberforce, social and economic reforms like those provided in the Factory Acts, the Ten Hours Act, the Mines and Collieries Act, and the industrial extension acts; the temperance movement; the formation of the YMCA and the Salvation Army; the organization of societies for the prevention of cruelty to children and animals; and kindred developments. Marquis W. Childs and Douglass Cater conclude that "out of the light kindled by Wesley and the evangelical revival came the great drive for reform movements that has had a direct and continuing relationship to the life of the past 100 years." [73] With this judgment Kenneth E. Boulding concurs, asserting unequivocally: "It was not the economists who liberated the slaves or who passed the Factory Acts, but the rash and ignorant Christians." [74]

---

[72] Frank M. Liggett (ed.), *The Book of the Sesqui-Centennial of American Methodism* (Baltimore: Frank M. Liggett, 1935), p. 105.

[73] *Ethics in a Business Society* (New York: New American Library of World Literature, 1954; a Mentor Book), p. 61.

[74] *Religious Perspectives of College Teaching in Economics* (New Haven: Edward W. Hazen Foundation, n.d.), p. 18.

CHAPTER THREE

Wesleyan Emphases in Methodism Today

METHODIST THEOLOGY HAS INEVITABLY UNDERGONE GREAT changes since Wesley's day. An adequate account of the nature and causes of those changes would require not only an examination of the major thought-currents of the nineteenth and twentieth centuries, but a survey of the theologies of men like Richard Watson, John William Fletcher, Joseph Benson, Miner Raymond, Thomas O. Summers, William B. Pope, Borden P. Bowne, Henry C. Sheldon, Olin A. Curtis, Edwin Lewis, Albert C. Knudson, and Harris Franklin Rall, not to mention a considerable number of more recent thinkers. Such a survey lies outside the scope of the present inquiry. It is important, however, to ask to what degree the major emphases of John Wesley remain vital in Methodist circles today, and particularly to examine the social significance of those which are still affirmed.

A. Contemporary Acceptance of Historic Doctrinal Emphases

There are several clear indications that most of the Wesleyan doctrines continue to be held, at least in theory. A notable statement on the church issued by the British Methodist Conference in 1937 lists "three features of the original message" on which "particular stress has always been laid": the doctrine of the witness of the Spirit, or assurance; the need for believers to strive toward holiness or perfect love; and the practice of Christian fellowship.[1] The Methodist Church of New Zealand asserts that "Methodism has always placed her emphasis" on Christian experience and the life of the Christian com-

[1] *The Nature of the Christian Church according to the Teaching of the Methodists* (London: Methodist Publishing House, 1937), p. 35.

munity guided by the Holy Spirit, repentance, faith, and holiness.[2] The New Zealand Methodist membership manual discusses the following as "Doctrines Specially Emphasised by Methodism": universal sin and guilt, salvation for all, assurance and adoption, and sanctification and Christian perfection.[3]

A clue to the status of traditional Wesleyan teachings in contemporary American Methodism is found in the frequency with which the hymns of Charles Wesley appear in the *Methodist Hymnal,* as well as in the theology of the hymns included. Of a total of 564 hymns, fifty-four are by Charles Wesley. Whether this disproportionate number from the pen of one author springs from a denominational spirit, acceptance of Charles Wesley's ideas, devotion to the tunes to which his hymns are set, or something else, it is difficult to determine. Analysis of the fifty-four hymns discloses the presence of major Wesleyan doctrinal emphases as follows: sin and repentance, in three hymns; justification by faith (implying sin and repentance), in thirteen; the witness of the Spirit, in seven; salvation for all, in two; and sanctification or perfection, in eleven. No evidence is available to indicate how frequently these hymns are sung by Methodist congregations.

Speaking at the Sesqui-centennial of American Methodism in 1934, Albert C. Knudson listed as the major theological contributions of Methodism the primacy of religious experience, a clear-cut theism, a clear-cut doctrine of human freedom, and the transforming power of the Holy Spirit.[4] In 1947 appeared the volume entitled *Methodism,* an outgrowth of a conference of chairmen and registrars of Annual Conference Boards of Ministerial Training, sponsored by the Commission on Courses of Study for Methodist Ministers. Four of the "Distinctive Emphases" dealt with in successive chapters in Part II are doctrinal: "Salvation for All," by Robert E. Cushman; "God Can Be Experienced," by Nels F. S. Ferré; "Freedom from Rigid Creed," by Umphrey Lee; and "The Search for Perfection," by Harris

[2] *Towards the One Church* (Christchurch, New Zealand: National Council of Churches of New Zealand, 1954), p. 15.

[3] *Our Fathers' Faith and Ours: a Manual of Membership of the Church of New Zealand* (Auckland: Board of Publications of the Methodist Church of New Zealand, n.d.), pp. 88-92.

[4] "The Theological Contributions of Methodism: Their Further Extension," *The Book of the Sesqui-Centennial of American Methodism,* ed. Frank M. Liggett, pp. 123-32.

Franklin Rall.[5] Missing is any separate consideration of repentance or justification by faith; however, this probably does not mean that these doctrines are viewed as unimportant, but that they are not judged to be "distinctively" Methodist.

A major section of the Episcopal Address of 1952 stated in twelve concise paragraphs "What Methodists Believe." Three of these affirm belief in salvation from sin (stressing forgiveness by grace through faith, and the new birth), Christian experience, and Christian perfection.

Such evidence clearly indicates continuing stress on the major emphases of John Wesley except the universal availability of salvation. The absence of references to this doctrine in contemporary statements does not mean, however, that Methodists no longer believe it, but rather that it is no longer an issue, or else is so taken for granted that it no longer needs emphasis. The doctrine of election is receiving penetrating reinterpretation among many theologians today, but Calvinistic predestination is not a live option for most Methodists. However, official and semiofficial utterances assume the abiding importance of sinful man's need for repentance, justification by faith, firsthand religious experience, and growth in holiness. These doctrines are not affirmed to the exclusion of others like the authority of the Bible, the universal Fatherhood of God, the worth of man as a child of God, or the church, and often they are not stressed as much as these. They are clearly not so central for Methodists today as they were for John Wesley and early Methodism. Nor are they always derived from Wesley; in many instances they are more directly traceable to other influences. But they are an important part of the witness of Methodist Christians. Whether they are socially significant or not is another question, to the examination of which we must now turn.

B. Contemporary Social Significance of Historic Emphases

1. SINFUL MAN'S NEED OF REPENTANCE

Recognition of the reality and power of sin was far from absent

[5] William K. Anderson, ed., *Methodism* (Nashville and New York: The Methodist Publishing House, 1947), pp. 103-147. More accurately, these emphases are characteristic rather than distinctive. Each of them has been stressed by other Christian communions.

among Methodists even when emphasis on the social gospel was at its peak.[6] A major ground of social and political action has been the desire to change conditions, rooted in selfishness, which have stunted the growth of persons, or to guard men against their tendency to seek special privileges at each other's expense. Robert Moats Miller recognizes this even as he takes the churches to task for too readily identifying "their crusades of prohibition, pacifism, Christian socialism, and all the rest" with the will of God. "Misguided as these crusades may have been, their very existence pointed up the gulf between things as they were and things as they ought to be. Wisely or unwisely, they represented attempts on the part of the churches to face up to terrible evils." [7]

Some Methodists participating in such movements have been definitely influenced by Wesley's teachings concerning sin. For example, Harry F. Ward in 1921 acutely applied to the social situation then obtaining the early Methodist stress on sin and divine judgment:

The one condition for admission to the first Methodist societies, "a desire to flee from the wrath to come and to be saved from their sins," has peculiar pertinence to the present situation in modern society. The sinfulness of some of its essential features is plain enough by this time. . . . The wrath that is being stored up against the day of wrath by the continuance of this sinfulness is evidenced by recent and present happenings in Europe. It may be that once again a historic religious grouping will form around the conviction of social sinfulness and the consequent search for social salvation. In this case those who to-day have the spirit of Methodism should be able to carry its technique over into the new sphere of social consciousness and expression and help those who are seeking to escape the wrath and be saved from the sins of the present social order to find what are the true fruits of this desire and what works are evidence of its continuance.[8]

In the main, Methodist social thought in America has probably drawn more heavily on the total Protestant and Christian heritage regarding the nature of man than it has on Wesley himself. It has been strongly influenced, for instance, by Washington Gladden and Walter Rauschenbusch. Yet this very circumstance suggests the pres-

---

[6] See below, Chapter IV, pp. 84 ff.

[7] Robert Moats Miller, *American Protestantism and Social Issues, 1919-1939* (Chapel Hill, N.C.: University of North Carolina Press, 1958), p. 345.

[8] "Which Way Will Methodism Go?" *Methodist Review*, 104 (1921), 695.

ence in many socially conscious Methodists of the early twentieth century of a realism concerning sin which was not unlike Wesley's. Much nineteenth-century Wesleyan thought seemed to them unduly individualistic and pietistic. But in Gladden and Rauschenbusch they found a stirring social message coupled with an insistence that individual regeneration is a necessary foundation for enduring social change. H. Richard Niebuhr observes that both thinkers

distinguished themselves from their liberal contemporaries by keeping relatively close to evangelical notions of the sovereignty of God, of the reign of Christ, and of the coming kingdom. In Rauschenbusch especially the revolutionary element remained pronounced; the reign of Christ required conversion and the coming kingdom was crisis, judgment as well as promise. . . . He continued to speak the language of the prophets and St. Paul.[9]

Methodist leaders like Bishop Herbert Welch, Bishop Francis J. McConnell, John R. Mott, and Worth M. Tippy, and later thinkers like Georgia Harkness, Harold A. Bosley, and Walter G. Muelder have not only stressed the social dimension in sin but also insisted on the need for social repentance. Various statements of Annual and General Conferences have concurred, especially in recent years, in relation to the devastation of World War II, American responsibility for the cataclysms at Hiroshima and Nagasaki, and the growing threat of nuclear destruction on a world scale.

The wide use by Methodists of certain hymns of social concern suggests that this awareness of man's need to repent of corporate evil extends to multitudes of ordinary church members. Frank Mason North's "Where cross the crowded ways of life" not only portrays vividly the human situation marked by "selfish strife," "wretchedness and need," "thresholds dark with fears," "lures of greed," "hearts of pain," and "restless throngs," but calls on Christ for the healing through which the

> Sons of man shall learn Thy love
> And follow where Thy feet have trod.

Harry Emerson Fosdick, confronting "the hosts of evil round us"

[9] H. Richard Niebuhr, *The Kingdom of God in America* (Chicago: Willett, Clark and Company, 1937), p. 194.

69

which scorn Christ and "assail His ways," prays for freedom from fears and doubts, to work and praise. He asks God to cure men's "warring madness," control their pride, and shame their "wanton, selfish gladness." Finally he prays:

> Let the search for Thy salvation
> Be our glory evermore.

A similar spirit of contrition breathes through the fourth stanza of John Haynes Holmes' stirring summons to service, "The voice of God is calling":

> From ease and plenty save us;
>   From pride of place absolve;
> Purge us of low desire;
>   Lift us to high resolve.

Almost the whole of Rudyard Kipling's hymn, "God of our fathers, known of old," is a confession of the emptiness of military dominion, the transitoriness of human pomp and power, and the sin of nationalistic boastfulness, coupled with a plea for forgiveness from "an humble and a contrite heart."

> For heathen heart that puts her trust
>   In reeking tube and iron shard;
> All valiant dust that builds on dust,
>   And guarding calls not Thee to guard;
> For frantic boast and foolish word,
> Thy mercy on Thy people, Lord!

Only one of these hymns was written by a Methodist.[10] Likewise, there is nothing peculiarly Methodist about their content. Their popularity among Methodists reflects the influence of the social gospel movement in American Protestantism in general, and perhaps represents in part a reaction against the intense individualism and the other-worldliness of some of Charles Wesley's hymns. But they are sung so generally by Methodist congregations that they may be safely assumed to express convictions widely held among Methodist people.

[10] Frank Mason North. The hymns are Numbers 465, 279, 454, and 497 in *The Methodist Hymnal*.

Even when due allowance is made for the lack of attention to content often so characteristic of hymn singing, these and similar hymns suggest that the awareness of man's need to repent of corporate as well as individual evil extends to multitudes of ordinary church members.

2. JUSTIFICATION BY FAITH

Officially, Methodists believe with classical Protestantism that we are saved not by living righteously, but by the forgiving grace of God which, accepted in faith, bears fruit in the life dedicated to God. In 1920 Harris Franklin Rall wrote, "Methodism still believes . . . in a life that is more than a belief in effort. . . . The final ground of assurance is in that mercy of God which men lay hold of by faith." [11] The Episcopal Address to the Southern Methodist General Conference of 1930 emphasized that salvation comes not through righteousness, or ritual, or intellectual assent to doctrine, but through faith alone. "The faith that saves is the personal trust of the repentant and believing sinner in the gracious and forgiving Savior." [12]

Similarly, in affirming belief in salvation from sin the Episcopal Address of 1952 declared:

This experience comes through faith in Jesus Christ as Saviour and Lord. The act involves penitence for past sins and the acceptance of His mercy and forgiveness. Salvation comes not by our own striving or any achievement of merit. It is the free gift of God's grace who "shows his love for us in that while we were yet sinners Christ died for us." Thus God takes away our sins, restores His image in our hearts, and grants to us a new birth, another chance, through the unmerited love of His Son and our Saviour, Jesus Christ.[13]

Whether this is actually the working belief of Methodists at the grass roots is not so clear. In fact, Leland H. Scott believes that the nineteenth century brought in "the main body of American Methodists" a gradual decline in emphasis on God's redemptive grace and a corresponding increase in what he calls a "moralistic temper." "Methodism's inherent concern for practical holiness gained ascendance as a prime determinant, increasingly dissociated from that

<hr />

[11] "Methodism Today," *The American Journal of Theology* 24 (1920), 487-88.
[12] *Journal*, 1930, p. 356.
[13] *General Conference Journal*, 1952, p. 157.

71

orientation in redemptive grace which had been integral to Wesley-anism." [14] Robert E. Cushman likewise maintains that Methodists in the mid-twentieth century largely hold the opinion of Wesley before his Aldersgate experience in 1738—that the Christian life is the work of man. They therefore seek perfection through imitating Christ, overlooking that "we must come to know Christ as reconciler and redeemer before we can follow him as Lord." [15] These judgments may be extreme, but they do call attention to a widespread attitude. Many Methodists, apparently forgetting their Protestant heritage, view deeds of righteousness more as the cause or condition of forgiveness than as its fruit and fulfillment. While rejecting ceremonial works as incapable of winning the divine favor, they seem to regard ethical acts as somehow able to earn salvation.

In principle, belief in forgiveness by grace through faith should increase social sensitivity. As the experience of God's forgiving love arouses the grateful response of an ethical life, it can hardly fail to exert a positive effect on the individual's group relations. A sense of dependence on the divine forgiveness should make us less self-righteous, more humble, and more charitable and forgiving toward others, such as alcoholics and convicted criminals. But there is no way of determining the extent to which this actually occurs. Moreover, most Methodist discussions of justification by faith have omitted consideration of its social dimension.

However, some contemporary writers find social meaning deeply imbedded in the doctrine. Thus Albert C. Outler points out that since "he who would be forgiven must himself forgive, . . . the way of reconciliation to God is never unilateral; it always reaches out toward neighbor and community." [16] In the judgment of Everett Tilson, the Pauline doctrine, "By grace we are saved through faith" (Eph. 2:8-9), raises serious questions in the area of race relations. Since God receives us into his fellowship solely on the condition of our grateful acceptance of his free gift, on what basis do we set up "additional prerequisites for the joint participation of other men with

---

[14] "Methodist Theology in America in the Nineteenth Century," *Religion in Life*, 25 (1955-56), 94-95.

[15] "Theological Landmarks in the Revival under Wesley," *Religion in Life*, 27 (1957-58), 118.

[16] *Psychotherapy and the Christian Message* (New York: Harper and Brothers, 1954), p. 236.

us in a branch of this fellowship?" In offering forgiveness God ignores qualifications like nationality, race, and sex; can we therefore soundly claim "membership in the fellowship of the forgiven if we respect such factors?" On the other hand, if in approving integration we assume an attitude of superiority because of our supposed freedom from race prejudice, "do we not thereby deny the doctrine of salvation by grace?" [17]

Such applications make plain that this historic Protestant emphasis has potentially profound significance both for the daily decisions of Christians on social questions and for the development of a Christian theology of society—a significance which deserves much more careful attention than it has received.

3. THE WITNESS OF THE SPIRIT

Probably no contemporary affirmation of the doctrine of assurance is more definitive than the declaration of the Episcopal Address of 1952, "We believe in Christian experience." The paragraph continues:

It is the privilege of every redeemed soul to know his sins are forgiven and to be assured, through the co-operating witness of the Holy Spirit with his spirit, that he is a child of God. Reason, like the Law, may be the schoolmaster leading us to Christ. Yet our deepest assurance is not the result of reason but of repentance and faith. Our faith is often and unashamedly suffused with intense feeling. Yet our assurance arises not out of emotion but out of the radiant certainty of an indwelling Christ, whose mercy has cleansed us, whose love has saved us, and whose presence within our hearts has given us power and victory. The experience of the whole man, evaluating Scripture, tradition, and reason, through the vital action of the Holy Spirit, becomes the ultimate authority in religious certainty.[18]

Beginning with the heart of Wesley's emphasis on the Spirit's witness, this statement goes on to develop a doctrine of religious authority rooted in the total activity of the Holy Spirit. The "fruits of the Spirit" are implied in the reference to "power and victory," but not explicitly discussed. William R. Cannon is somewhat more definite. Describing the doctrine of assurance as "Methodism's most distinctive doctrinal characteristic," he declares that it "gives personal

[17] *Segregation and the Bible* (Nashville: Abingdon Press, 1958), pp. 105-6, 112.
[18] General Conference *Journal*, 1952, p. 157.

expression to the working reality of the Holy Ghost," and provides experiential proof that Christ not only died for us but "lives in us and manifests his power daily in what we do and in what we are." [19]

The Episcopal Address to the General Conference of 1944 agreed with Cannon in viewing the doctrine of experience as central in Methodism. After listing the major emphases of "the evangelical theology," it continued:

The fact that Methodist theology revolves about personal experience is clear. The salvation in which Methodists believe means much more than the forgiveness of actual sins and entrance into a heaven of eternal bliss after death. It means a personal experience of God beginning with conversion and continuing every step of the way to perfect love.[20]

None of these statements, however, attempts to relate the Christian experience of the individual to his social responsibility. This connection was made in 1908 by Herbert Welch in a discussion of the traditional Methodist insistence on the primacy of experience and life. From the first, he wrote, Methodism

has disentangled religion from creed and ceremony. Its emphasis has been always on experience, the root of life, tested by the life that grows out of it. The Methodist theory of Christianity, then, lends itself most naturally to a socialized religion, related to every political and industrial question.[21]

There have also been occasional hints of a connection between the possibility of a direct experience of God by each believer and the worth of persons which is a major ground for democracy and human rights. In 1941 Bishop Paul B. Kern discussed the struggle between the regimented control of the totalitarian state and the disciplined freedom granted the individual in a true democracy. "In this battle," he asserted,

Methodism takes her place. She is by historic tradition the foe of conventionalized morality or of dead ecclesiastical dictatorship. Her doctrine

[19] "The Ecumenical Emphasis in Methodist Theology," Proceedings of the Ninth World Methodist Conference, ed. Elmer T. Clark and E. Benson Perkins (Nashville: The Methodist Publishing House, 1957), p. 191.
[20] Journal, 1944, p. 156.
[21] "The Church and Social Service," Methodist Review. 90 (1908), 710.

of the dignity and worth of the human heart, of the incontestable value inherent in common men and women, is a denial of every philosophy that is built on mass regimentation or servility to prideful puppets. The human spirit must be free to seek happiness, to pursue truth, to quest for God.[22]

Other similar passages might be cited. Yet it must be admitted that Methodists have seldom explicitly developed the revolutionary social implications of the doctrine of personal religious experience which they prize so highly. An official membership manual affirms: "The strongest point of Methodist doctrine is that each man is responsible for his own relationship to God."[23] But no suggestion is given as to what this means even for religious freedom, not to mention other rights, freedoms, and responsibilities. Probably the emphasis on religious experience has exerted an indirect, unconscious influence on the social thinking of Methodists, but very seldom has the relationship been specifically explored.

4. SANCTIFICATION AND PERFECTION

Probably no doctrinal problem has occasioned so much internal controversy in American Methodism as the issue of holiness. At various times during the nineteenth century, in both the northern and southern branches of the church, groups arose which insisted on the centrality in Christian faith of entire sanctification and the "second blessing." Claiming loyalty to the views of John Wesley, such groups often manifested little of his spirit or his healthy concern for the totality of human life. Emphasizing holiness as "spotlessness from the world," and intent on winning their own salvation, they tended to withdraw from responsible participation in the life of society, and readily fell prey to feelings of self-righteousness and an extremely judgmental attitude toward the "worldly" Christians who did not share their views.

Methodism as a whole recoiled from such interpretations of sanctification, and repudiated the aberrations of the holiness movement. Several regional divisions resulted in the formation of new denominations. In other instances the extremists remained within the church as minorities with little influence. The problem remains a real one

[22] *Methodism Has a Message!* (Nashville: Abingdon Press, 1941), pp. 23-24.
[23] *Membership Manual of The Methodist Church for Teen-agers* (Nashville: The Methodist Publishing House, 1951), p. 51.

even today in some local communities, where Methodist churches sometimes find themselves in competition with vocal and aggressive holiness congregations.

This experience has inevitably left its mark on Methodist attitudes. As Harris Franklin Rall has pointed out, the belief in entire sanctification, literally conceived as "a conscious and final experience at a given time," is no longer generally held. Yet "there remains the emphasis upon the fact that religion means holiness of life, a holiness which is alike the gift of God and the task of man." [24] Thus Methodism, while recognizing the sinfulness of man, continues to stress the positive possibilities open to him through the activity of the Holy Spirit. In fact, the Episcopal Address of 1952, affirming Christian perfection as a Methodist belief, uses language not very different from that of Wesley himself:

God's grace is manifested not only in the forgiveness of our sins but is also creatively redemptive, the power that works in us to make us perfect in love. Nothing short of perfection, Christlikeness in thought, word, and deed, can measure God's loving purpose for us. It is our faith that the fundamental change wrought in the individual by regeneration is a dynamic process which by growth in grace moves toward "mature manhood, to the measure of the stature of the fullness of Christ." We may quench the Spirit and fall from grace but our divine destiny is perfect love and holiness in this life.[25]

According to William R. Cannon, Methodism asserts that God

lifts a man who accepts His grace above the power and sway of sin and gives him the force of character to be in actuality what in ideal he aspires to become. Saintliness, therefore, is introduced into the behaviour of common life and is the norm of conduct for every Christian. The single motive of the good man is love, inspired of God in keeping with the example of Jesus Christ.[26]

Albert C. Outler illustrates this hopeful view in his discussion of "the human possibility" as seen by depth psychology and the Chris-

[24] "Methodism Today," American Journal of Theology, 24 (1920), 488.
[25] General Conference Journal, 1952, p. 157.
[26] William R. Cannon, The Theology of John Wesley (Nashville: Abingdon Press, 1946).

tian gospel. Asking what the prospects are for human maturation and fulfillment in this world, he takes his stand with those who reply: "Christian salvation is a real change of heart and character and it launches a process of growth in grace which is aimed at the full maturation and stability of faith, hope, and love." This doctrine "takes sin with all seriousness," recognizes that even mature Christians experience "tension between self-assertion and the rule of God," and knows that the human life span is ordinarily not long enough for the growth of Christian love. But with high confidence in God's grace and man's capacity for faith, it affirms "that God *intends* to make *saints* of men. . . . Man was made to be blessed—he was made to grow in grace 'toward the fullness of the stature of the perfect man.' " [27]

Until the twentieth century Methodists have interpreted holiness almost entirely in individual terms. The British Congregationalist R. W. Dale (1829-1895) was sharp in his criticism of the evangelical revival of the eighteenth and nineteenth centuries, and of Methodism in particular, for their failure to carry out the social implications of the doctrine.

There was one doctrine of John Wesley's—the doctrine of perfect sanctification—which ought to have led to a great and original ethical development; but the doctrine has not grown; it seems to remain where John Wesley left it. There has been a want of the genius or the courage to attempt the solution of the immense practical questions which the doctrine suggests. The questions have not been raised, much less solved. To have raised them effectively would have been to originate an ethical revolution which would have a far deeper effect on the thought and life—first of England, and then of Christendom—than was produced by the Reformation of the sixteenth century.

Dale noted particularly that the revival shrank from politics, "regarded literature and art with a certain measure of distrust," and in business was "content with attaching Divine sanction to recognized virtues," while hardly touching the new ethical problems which were then emerging.[28]

[27] *Psychotherapy and the Christian Message*, pp. 183-84.
[28] Quoted by George Elliott, "Religion and Righteousness," *Methodist Review*, 94(1912), 57.

The General Conference of the Methodist Church of Canada in 1918 voiced a similar criticism, in adopting a remarkable report of its Committee on Evangelism and Social Service which included an approving reference to Dale's statement.

Had the Methodist doctrine of holiness, or perfect love, been followed in all its social and economic implications, Methodism would have been the home of that passion for human brotherhood, religious in its intensity, which has been shown by many groups of men and women outside the church. . . . The cruelties of the industrial system in the factories and mines of England, the heartlessness which permitted the growth of slums and kindred conditions in the cities, and the social and economic subjection of the poor, would have been the subjects of our persistent attack, and England would not have had to wait for Lord Shaftesbury and other reformers to do the work they did.[29]

In recent decades, however, various writers have interpreted sanctification socially as well as individually. As early as 1908 Katherine Stowe Abel showed that the term *sanctify* when applied by Jesus to himself means not merely *set apart* in a negative sense, but "set apart for the Father's work in service of sinful humanity." Sanctification is never completed until its social aspect leads the soul to the cross where Jesus gave himself for the world. To "walk in love" sacrificially for the sake of others is the essence of nearness to God.[30]

More concretely, C. W. Barnes saw in the discovery and discharge of man's social duties the test of the conversion which Christ sought:

This is the "new sanctification," the redemption of society, the cleansing of the social order from all sin—that is to say, selfishness, injustice, and wrong. The "new sanctification" is the making sacred of all life. All days are holy days. All men are in holy orders. At the anvil as well as in the pulpit toils the "man of God." Is the ministry a "sacred calling"? Yes. Is the anvil a "sacred desk"? Yes. Does the one make the other less sacred? No. To make *all* life sacred does not make any part of it less so. This, then, is the "new holiness," "the higher life," "the sacred righteousness" for which the modern world prays.[31]

[29] *Journal of Proceedings of the Tenth General Conference of the Methodist Church* (Toronto: William Briggs, 1918), p. 341.
[30] "Social Aspects of Sanctification," *Christian Advocate*, 83 (1908), 170.
[31] "The New Sanctification," *Methodist Review*, 94 (1912), 80.

In 1921 a similar extension of sanctification was called for by the editor of *The Methodist Review*, who nine years earlier had quoted approvingly the incisive criticism of Dale.[32] In an editorial note following an article by Harry F. Ward, George Elliott wrote:

The preacher should ground himself thoroughly in the religious and Scriptural basis for a new social order. Those who resent sermons on current industrial problems would have to keep silent as to an honest exposition of the prophet Amos, the Lord's Prayer, or the Sermon on the Mount. The Prophets and the Evangelists will help the preacher to become a true prophet and an evangelist. "Holiness to the Lord" must be written not only on the sacred vessels of the sanctuary but on all the tools of trade; not only on the bells of the priestly robe, but on car and shop bells as well. Entire Sanctification means the consecration of all life, the social order as well as the individual life. So shall the Kingdom come! [33]

The extension of sanctification to society was called for also by two statements emerging from Southern Methodist bodies. The Second General Missionary Conference held at Lake Junaluska, N. C., in 1913 affirmed that Methodism has a mission to society as well as to the individual. "Society is not made up of separate, isolated individuals. Society is a unit. . . . We are all bound up in one bundle." Further, it is folly for the doctor to attempt to save people from typhoid fever when sewers are polluting the water supply. "We must look to the water supply. We must apply the gospel of entire sanctification to society in its entirety." [34]

The Southern Methodist Episcopal Address of 1930, read by Bishop Edwin D. Mouzon, defined entire sanctification as "the complete unification of personality, the organization of the self about Jesus Christ as its center," then went on to declare that this embraces all of the individual's relations with his fellows. "The ultimate aim of evangelistic religion, therefore, is that all human relationships should be sanctified, that life in its totality should be brought under the power of Jesus Christ." [35]

[32] *Ibid.*, p. 36.
[33] *Methodist Review*, 104 (1921), 695.
[34] G. B. Witten (ed.), *The Junaluska Conference: A Report of the Second General Missionary Conference of the Methodist Episcopal Church, South* (Nashville: Board of Missions of the M. E. Church, South, 1913), pp. 115 ff.
[35] *General Conference Journal*, 1930, p. 357.

In similar fashion, Francis J. McConnell found social holiness implied in a full understanding of the "entire sanctification" of the individual. "The ideal of entire sanctification is that all parts of a man's nature are to be made subject to the law of the spirit of Christ—all a man's political and industrial and social relationships." [36]

James A. Beebe applied this conception to the international order. While World War I was still raging he dared to appeal for "patriotism's sanctification," by which he meant bringing political and international relations under the control of Christian morality.[37]

Harry F. Ward in 1921 related the doctrine of holiness to that of conversion, maintaining that these two historic teachings of Methodism should help her to provide leadership for a social order based on solidarity of interest and purpose rather than conflicting partial interests. Early Methodism, wrote Ward,

gave its first members both the joy of a great assurance and a discipline for the improvement of life. It then sent them onward toward perfection, training them into a practical force for the spread of scriptural holiness throughout the land. Apply either of these doctrines to the social order and where do they put the people called Methodists in the division between the Christians who want the church to leave economic affairs alone and those who seek to Christianize the economic order with all the rest of life? [38]

In a recent statement L. Harold DeWolf pleads for the union of the personal and the social in Christian ethics. Noting the tendency of liberal and neo-orthodox Christians to accommodate to the world in personal ethics while challenging it on social issues, and of conservatives to accommodate on social issues while refusing conformity in personal ethical practice, he insists that either position is seriously wanting. Truly Christian discipleship dare not accept "either the social condition of a world divided by artificial barriers of race, class, and nation, and filled with suspicion, fear, and hate, or, on the other hand, the sensuality, vulgarity, dishonesty, and materialistic hedonism that prevail in personal morals." DeWolf pleads for a "Christian asceticism" which goes much deeper. "It is a heeding of Christ's command, 'You . . . must be perfect' (Matt. 5:48). It is the earnest,

---

[36] "Christianity and the Present Crisis," *Zions Herald*, 94 (1916), 235.
[37] "The Christianization of Patriotism," *Methodist Review*, 101 (1918), 240.
[38] "Which Way Will Methodism Go?" *Methodist Review*, 104 (1921), 694.

humble quest for the total sanctification of life in every sphere." [39]

Albert C. Outler espouses a somewhat similar conception when he declares that historic Christianity seeks both "the highest and fullest development of human selves" and "the fulfillment of God's design in human life and history."

The Christian evangel, when rightly proclaimed, emphasizes that men should, in actual relations with God and their fellows, experience genuine spontaneity of love and trust; they must come to know the meaning of justice, mercy, and community (Micah 6:8). The Christian ethic is an ethic of responsibility which puts concern for persons foremost because of the abundant revelation of God's concern for all and each of His children. It aims at the transformation of culture through the mind and will and heart of Christ.[40]

Statements like these make plain that many Methodists, especially in the early decades of the century when the social gospel was most influential, have extended Wesley's teaching by interpreting holiness in social terms. Nevertheless, the evidence does not indicate that this interpretation has been general, or that it is now representative. Several considerations would seem to rule out such a conclusion.

1. Only a few of the utterances cited represent corporate judgments.

2. Only rarely since the 'twenties has sanctification or perfection been viewed specifically as a basis for social concern.

3. The paragraph on Christian perfection in the Episcopal Address of 1952 is wholly individualistic.

Recent years have brought considerable emphasis on the need for an effective Christian witness in all phases of men's common life. Typically, however, this has been based on doctrines like the kingdom of God, the church as the extension of Christ's redemptive ministry, the priesthood of all believers, the ministry of the laity, or Christian vocation. Wesleyan notions of scriptural holiness and perfect love may lie somewhere in the background exerting an unconscious influence. But sanctification has for many today a bad odor, suggesting a socially irresponsible, purely personal, sanctimonious piety or a

---

[39] *The Case for Theology in Liberal Perspective* (Philadelphia: Westminster Press, 1959), p. 148.

[40] *Psychotherapy and the Christian Message*, p. 177. This statement appears in the context of Outler's discussion of "the human possibility" of saintliness already cited (above, pp. 76-77).

holier-than-thou quest for individual salvation, while the search for perfection, even by individuals, is widely rejected as the expression of a moralism invalidated by a realistic understanding of human sinfulness. .The rehabilitation of the idea of holiness and the exploration of its social meaning might give Methodism today a heightened sense of the relevance of the gospel to the life of society and increase the effectiveness of its social witness.

C. Summary

We have examined the twentieth-century social significance of all of the major Wesleyan emphases except the universal availability of salvation. The omission of this Arminian doctrine implies in no sense the judgment that it is socially irrelevant, but simply the recognition that it is not explicitly cited as a ground of social concern. Actually it is so deeply imbedded in the Methodist theological outlook that it has probably predisposed thoughtful and sensitive Methodists to seek the good of all sorts and conditions of men. Specific evidence is lacking, but one can hazard the guess that those who assume God's redemptive concern for all men, and who have acted on this assumption in evangelism and missionary endeavor, are likely to support other activities designed to advance the welfare of all.

As far as the other doctrines are concerned, our survey has yielded the following conclusions: Methodist social concern has been rather strongly influenced by a recognition of human sin, its destructive effects in society, and man's patent need for repentance. The doctrine of justification by faith has had relatively little discernible direct effect on Methodist social attitudes though some recent writers find in it important social implications. The stress on personal experience has in some instances heightened a sense of social responsibility, but has seldom been specifically related to the social scene. Finally, the doctrine of sanctification has creatively stimulated the social thinking of able Methodist leaders, who have called for its serious application to society as well as to individuals, but this interpretation has not won general acceptance.

There is thus no direct line leading from these theological emphases to social action. Some elements have aroused social concern and stimulated action. Others have not had this effect. Variety of influence also appears among different thinkers and in different periods. On the whole, however, the net effect of the historic Methodist doctrines as now interpreted has probably been the encouragement of serious social thinking, responsible social action, and a hopeful view of the possibility of social improvement. At the Sesqui-Centennial of American Methodism in 1934 Albert C. Knudson declared:

The fact is that Methodist teaching has a special adaptability to the social needs of modern times. It has never limited the divine grace to any particular individuals, but has extended it to all, and in principle has always believed in the possible moral transformation of human society itself through the agency of the Divine Spirit. According to Methodist teaching society is not necessarily immoral. It is not permanently condemned to its present evil and sinful state. The current idea that it is so condemned is simply a hang-over from early Calvinism. It has no place in Methodist theology.[41]

Knudson's view is based primarily on faith in "the transforming power of the Holy Spirit," which he discusses as one of four modern Methodist emphases. A rather similar conclusion is reached by a recent statement of the Methodist Church of New Zealand, on the basis of a combination of emphases: Christian experience, the life of the Christian community guided by the Holy Spirit, faith, and holiness. Methodism, say the New Zealand Methodists, "has developed a distinctive life and ethos," which "may be seen in the approach to social and ethical questions. . . . When Methodism is true to herself, this ethos is characterized by joyous religious experience within the church, and by a strong social righteousness within the community." [42] These words could probably be applied with equal accuracy to American Methodism, though only with the same proviso—when it is true to itself.

---

[41] "The Theological Contributions of Methodism: Their Further Extension," *The Book of the Sesqui-Centennial of American Methodism*, ed. Frank M. Liggett, p. 130.
[42] *Towards the One Church*, pp. 15-16.

CHAPTER FOUR

Basic Christian Beliefs in
Methodist Social Thought

OUR EFFORT TO PORTRAY THE RELATION BETWEEN METH-
odist theology and social thought and action may be likened to the
photographing of a landscape with two different lenses. Until now we
have used a telephoto lens, which has given us a close-up view of the
characteristic doctrinal emphases of John Wesley and their status
today, while leaving out of the picture other important aspects of the
theology of Methodists.

Now we change to a wide-angle lens, permitting a view of the
whole range of Christian doctrine as it affects Methodist social attitudes. When using the telescopic lens we focused attention on a
particular section of the landscape which we had selected in advance
for special study. Now we shall try to examine the whole broad vista
before us and report what we see. Inevitably part of what we see will
lie in the territory already photographed. Now, however, we shall view
it in relation to the total panorama. We shall be chiefly concerned with
what Methodists think, not as representatives of the Wesleyan tradition, but as Protestant Christians. Our concern will be to discover
the implications for social thought and action which twentieth-century
Methodists find in the basic structure of their Christian belief.

Accurate photography requires more than a good camera with the
right lens. Before the pictures are taken, the shutter speed must be
adjusted to the movement of the subject, the size of the aperture must
be regulated according to the amount of light reflected, and the lens
must be focused according to the distance between the subject and
the photographer, with provision for adequate "depth of field"—the
zone in front of and behind the subject in which sharp reproduction

84

is possible. Particular theological convictions are usually expressions of larger structures or movements of thought, and can be understood only when the direction and nature of these movements are taken into account. Christian beliefs are also affected by lights and shadows, so that the same words may mean different things to different people in different contexts. Likewise, ideas emerge understandably only when the focus permits them to be seen in relation to both their immediate foreground and their historical background. Therefore, to portray accurately the theological foundations of Methodist social attitudes we must first sketch the major twentieth-century theological developments in which Methodists have shared. To this survey we now turn our attention.

A. Theological Movements Involving Methodists

1. PIETISTIC CONSERVATISM

At the dawn of the twentieth century most Protestants in America were conservative in theology. For several decades the impact of liberal ways of thinking had been making itself felt. Evolutionary science and the historical and critical study of the biblical writings, among other influences, had led many to re-examine and reformulate their religious beliefs. But this very process called forth a sharp reaction among Christians who saw in the new movements a deadly threat to the authority of the Bible and other central convictions of their faith.

In 1895 the Niagara Bible Conference listed six essentials which it believed must be defended at all costs: the inerrancy of the scriptures, the deity of Christ, the virgin birth, the substitutionary blood atonement, the bodily resurrection, and the visible, physical second coming of Christ. In 1910-12 appeared a series of twelve booklets, *The Fundamentals*, containing essays by various authors affirming the necessity of these doctrines, the historical accuracy of the miracle narratives of the Bible, and related ideas. Many persons who accepted these beliefs as fundamental and necessary came to regard as unchristian all who disagreed, and refused to maintain Christian fellowship with them. Those who adopted this exclusivistic position composed the 'fundamentalist" movement, which was vigorous and aggressive until the mid-twenties, declining considerably thereafter.

However, fundamentalism has continued to flourish in many local churches of large denominations which are congregational in polity,

and in a variety of smaller sects. Today many Christians with a fundamentalist heritage are disassociating themselves from some features
of the earlier movement, and prefer to describe their theology as neo-
evangelical. Their leaders are content to affirm the inerrancy of the
Scriptures "in the original manuscripts," are highly critical of the
typical fundamentalist lack of social concern, and are entering rather
freely into communication, written and oral, with Christians who do
not share their doctrinal position.

Fundamentalism, in the precise historical sense of the term, has
never made great headway among Methodists. With their traditional
subordination of doctrinal formulations to Christian experience and
life, they have seldom been ready to refuse fellowship with other
Christians on doctrinal grounds, and the connectional polity of the
denomination has made it impossible for local congregations to isolate
themselves. Individuals and groups have, of course, left the church,
but efforts to set up fundamentalist doctrines as normative for either
clergy or laity have always failed.

Nevertheless, multitudes of Methodists have held some or all of the
fundamentalist beliefs, while affirming also other historic Christian
doctrines like the Trinity, human sinfulness, conversion and the new
birth, and eternal life. Often, though by no means always, this theologically conservative outlook has been accompanied by an extremely
conservative social orientation.

In the first few decades of the present century this combination
frequently found expression in a largely pietistic view of the Christian life and the role of the Christian and the church in society. The
task of the church was conceived as that of winning converts to Jesus
Christ and helping those who were born again to live a spiritual life
unspotted from the world. Stress was laid on the individual's attainment of moral rectitude and personal purity, and negatively on avoidance of those sins which were found to interfere with individual holiness. Considerable attention was thus devoted to the evils of drinking,
sex immorality, gambling, and amusements like card-playing, dancing,
and theater-going. Seldom did this ethic lead to action aiming to
change social institutions. It brought forth occasional efforts to curb
gambling or enforce Sunday closing laws, but the only large-scale
exception to the individualistic pattern was support of legislation to
prevent the manufacture and sale of alcoholic beverages.

Methodists holding this point of view greeted the social gospel, aiming as it did to change social conditions, with suspicion and opposition. To them it represented partly a failure to come to grips with the reality of sin and the need for personal conversion, and partly an effort to compensate in external activity for shallowness of belief and absence of true spirituality. The functioning "social policy" of pietistic conservatism was thus to accept institutions much as it found them, while performing within them the task which it regarded as centrally important—the regeneration of individual men and women. Such reborn Christians, it was often assumed, would inevitably lift the level of community morality and bring about some social improvement, but this must always be secondary and incidental to the discharge of their responsibility for bringing persons to a saving knowledge of God.

2. LIBERAL THEOLOGY AND THE SOCIAL GOSPEL

Contrasting sharply with fundamentalism was the liberal theology which originated in the latter part of the nineteenth century and reached the peak of its influence in the third decade of the twentieth. The application to the biblical writings of the same canons of historical investigation as were used in the study of other ancient manuscripts yielded a wealth of information concerning the authorship, dates, and religious, social, and political backgrounds of the biblical books. This recognition of the human factors involved in the writing of the Scriptures became for many Christians an avenue to new understanding of the problems which they had encountered in biblical study. Against this background the theory of biological evolution was seen, not as a disproof of the basic meaning of the creation narratives in Genesis, but as illuminating the method followed by God in his creation of the world and man. The world of universal law assumed by the physical sciences suggested a God who wrought his purposes not by miraculous interventions from without, but by regular, orderly processes within nature. Influences like these led to important changes in both the method and the content of Christian theology.

Basically, liberalism is not a position or a body of belief, but an attitude and a method. It is marked by a spirit of free, reasoned inquiry and an open-minded search for truth. Among moderate Christian liberals this method has usually involved (1) an attempt to re-

87

discover the human experience out of which a particular doctrine arose, and (2) an effort to restate the problem and its solution in the thought-forms of today. Obviously such a procedure can readily lead to different results when used by different people, so that there can be no one liberal theological position. However, liberal theology of the type most characteristic of Methodists did lead to doctrinal emphases which won wide agreement, and which may be briefly summarized here.

These emphases include the following: (1) reliance on past and present religious experience, broadly interpreted, rather than on any infallible book, church, or creed, as the chief source of religious knowledge; (2) a historical approach to the Bible which sees it as the record of God's progressive revelation of himself to inspired men; (3) respect for science and scientific method and concern for a co-operative relationship between science and religion; (4) belief in the immanence of God in nature and human life, which are therefore seen as revelatory of the divine; (5) insistence on the real humanity of Jesus and on the importance of his historical life and teachings as our highest disclosure of the character and purpose of God; (6) a high estimate of human nature, centering in belief in the sacredness and worth of each person as a child of God; (7) insistence on the relevance of the Christian religion to the whole of man's life here and now, with correspondingly less stress on eternity; and (8) a view of the kingdom of God which conceives it primarily as the increasing realization of the divine purposes in human history.

Theological emphases like these led naturally to a social interpretation of the Christian gospel. A God who is actively at work in his world must be concerned when social conditions thwart the attainment of his goals for human life. If persons have an infinite value in the sight of God, all barriers to their fullest development as his children must be removed. If the kingdom of God so central in Jesus' teaching is to be eventually realized within history, men are responsible for doing everything possible to hasten the triumph of justice and love in human society. Motivated by such ideas, Protestant leaders formulated proclamations like the Social Creed adopted by the Methodist Episcopal General Conference of 1908, and called on Christians to join their efforts with God's in building his kingdom.

Fundamentalist attacks on liberalism proved largely unavailing, and during the early part of the twentieth century it gained strength steadily to become the dominant American theology. About the end of the third decade, however, criticisms like those of Reinhold Niebuhr in America and Karl Barth in Europe began to take effect. Attack centered on the liberals' reliance on human experience and reason, instead of an objective divine revelation, as ways to religious truth; their over-emphasis on the divine immanence and the kinship of man with God; their failure to fathom the depth of man's sinful estrangement from God; their muting of the note of divine judgment; their primary trust in human effort rather than divine grace; their optimistic view of history; and their this-worldly conception of the kingdom of God. Exponents of a late form of the social gospel were criticized for assuming, in forgetfulness of man's inward disorder, that a Christian society could be attained through institutional reform and changes in man's social environment.

Criticisms like these, reinforced by the shattering effect of a worldwide economic depression, the rise of Hitler, and World War II, exerted a powerful influence, and liberalism waned. Many of its representatives, like Reinhold Niebuhr, changed to a more "realistic" position; others held to their basic liberal outlook while modifying it in important respects. Meanwhile a younger generation of Christian thinkers has attained influence, a majority of whom represent different orientations.

Yet liberal theology is far from dead. Many of its representatives have listened receptively to the charges of the critics and sought to profit by them, while rejecting some criticisms as unfounded or unjustifiably extreme. The result is what may be termed a neo-liberal or liberal evangelical theology.

While differing from each other in details, theologians of this persuasion are in essential agreement on emphases like the following: They continue to stress the importance of intellectual freedom in theological inquiry. They regard scientific and philosophical inquiry as relevant to the search for religious knowledge. They conceive doctrine as the exposition of the truths implied in the total religious experience of the Christian community, past and present, while viewing that experience in turn as the human response to the revelatory activity of God. Regarding the biblical writings as the record of God's unique self-disclosure and redemptive activity culminating in Jesus

89

Christ, they are deeply interested in the theology of the Bible. They assert both the immanence and the transcendence of God. They affirm, on the one hand, the sinfulness of man and the primacy of the divine grace in salvation; and, on the other, the need of man's repentant, faithful, obedient response and the positive possibilities of human life empowered by God. They base their hope for the coming of the kingdom primarily on the divine initiative and power, but insist on the necessity of the free co-operation of committed men. They expect the kingdom to come partly within history, but in its fullness only beyond history. They lay great stress on ethical living and social concern as necessary expressions of the Christian's relation to God, but relate them more closely than did their predecessors to the total structure of Christian belief.

3. NEO-REFORMATION AND REALISTIC THEOLOGY [1]

The criticisms of liberalism already noted were the negative side of a many-sided movement of great power and influence. At the end of World War I, Karl Barth, Emil Brunner, and their European followers turned anew to the Bible, seeking there a definitive Word to man not subject to the ambiguities and distortions which they found in man's subjective experience and reason. The result was the birth of the "crisis" (judgment) or "dialectical" theology, which drew heavily on the doctrinal emphases of Paul, Augustine, and the Protestant Reformation, and which was also influenced by the thought of the nineteenth-century Danish existentialist Søren Kierkegaard (1813-1855), who previously had been largely overlooked outside his own country.

In the mid-twenties Reinhold Niebuhr, then a liberal Reformed

---

[1] No one term adequately characterizes the movement here described. "Neo-orthodoxy" is partly accurate, since the thinkers involved do reaffirm certain classical Christian doctrines, but in a new, post-liberal setting and often with new interpretations. However, they are thoroughly liberal in their use of historical criticism in biblical study, and their treatment of some doctrines as "myths"—symbolic, pictorial statements of religious truths incapable of adequate expression in ordinary rational terms—departs widely from orthodoxy. "Neo-Reformation" oversimplifies the complexity of the movement and overlooks some of the factors which in some thinkers are dominant. But in the main it is probably the best single term, open to fewer objections than any other, and is therefore used here. "Realistic" is added because it is probably more acceptable to those thinkers who rely heavily on psychological and sociological analysis, and do not think of themselves primarily as returning to any historical point of view. However, neither term should be used as a stereotype, or allowed to obscure the wide variety found among the thinkers whose similarities it is meant to suggest.

pastor in Detroit, began to probe within human nature for an understanding in depth of human social disorders which he increasingly felt to be lacking in liberal thought. He too was strongly influenced by Biblical and Augustinian sources, the Reformation thinkers, and the thought of Kierkegaard. With this background he developed a "realistic" theology centering in an emphasis on the sinful pride which inevitably leads man to put himself in the place of God, which infects even his noblest motives and acts, and which makes especially difficult the moral ordering of human social relations.

Influences stemming from these and related sources have wrought far-reaching changes in twentieth-century American theology. These developments cannot be accurately portrayed as a compact and unified whole, since sharp differences are often evident between Barth and Niebuhr and their followers, and since there are may variations in emphasis from thinker to thinker. However, a considerable number of thinkers manifest broad agreement in the following respects. They are marked by strong stress on human sinfulness, the shallowness of human pretensions, and man's inability in his own strength to achieve worthy ends; assertion of the incapacity of human reason to attain true knowledge of God, and skepticism concerning or opposition to the philosophical investigation of religion; insistence on the otherness and the sovereignty of God; reliance on the authority of revelation accepted on trust, and on the events centering in Jesus Christ as the decisive (or sole) locus of the divine self-disclosure; a deep sense of man's need of divine grace, and corresponding stress on salvation by grace through faith; concern for submitting human ideas and aspirations to the definitive Word of God in the Bible, hence devotion to Biblical theology, combined with acceptance of the historical-critical approach to the Biblical writings; a tendency to guide ethical decisions by the absolute demands of God as personally encountered in Christ, rather than by universal principles applied to particular situations; serious doubt concerning the possibility of long-range or over-all improvement in earthly society; insistence on the centrality of divine action in the coming of the kingdom of God; the expectation of the fulfillment of the kingdom beyond rather than within history; and a serious concern with eschatology and hope in God's ultimate victory.

91

The leadership of the movement in America has been characterized by a strong social concern. In this respect two features stand out:

1. It shares the insistence of liberalism on the social relevance of the Christian faith, carries forward the deepest intent of the social gospel, and asserts emphatically the social responsibility of the Christian.

2. Impressed as it is by the self-centeredness of human nature and the power of sin in the depersonalized structures of society, it envisages the attainment in history of only very relative and limited goals, with the tares growing side by side with the wheat until the end. Its representatives speak not of building the kingdom of God on earth, but of achieving proximate justice, exhibiting the Lordship of Christ in a sinful world, and practicing love toward one's neighbor as an expression of Christian obedience. What Christians can accomplish in society is limited, but they are responsible under God for acting to curb injustice and for seeking the best means of achieving relative ends, leaving the outcome in God's hands.

Neo-Reformation thought has been criticized for its denial that any truth about God or human destiny can be learned from sources (e.g., philosophical investigation) independent of the Christian revelation or apart from Christian commitment; the dualism between God and the world involved in its rejection of divine immanence; its failure to perceive, in opposing revelation to experience interpreted by reason, that divine revelation itself must be experienced and related to other experience; its failure to recognize, in its extreme stress on human sinfulness, the potentiality for positive good in man empowered by divine grace; and its failure to offer adequate constructive guidance for man's ethical decisions in society.

However, this point of view is today dominant in the theological leadership of American Protestantism. So far it has not penetrated deeply into the thinking of the laity; possibly it is too sophisticated for ordinary Christians at the grass roots. But it is strongly represented on the faculties of the major theological seminaries, including Methodist schools, and is exerting profound influence on successive generations of men and women in training for the Christian ministry. In Christian social ethics the views of Brunner and Niebuhr are particularly influential.

4. OTHER MOVEMENTS

In addition to the major types of thought already discussed, several other tendencies have had varying degrees of influence among American Methodists, and should therefore be mentioned here. For example, standing in some respects at the opposite pole from Neo-Reformation theology are the theistic naturalists. Though radically liberal in their methodology, they reacted against moderate Protestant liberalism because it was not thorough in its acceptance of scientific method. Such thinkers regard nature as ultimate and think of God as that process within nature which sustains and advances the realization of values in human life. Some theistic naturalists, like Henry Nelson Wieman, have reinterpreted certain basic Christian doctrines, such as sin, forgiveness, salvation, and the resurrection of Christ, in naturalistic terms. This point of view has commanded respect and some acceptance among Methodist thinkers, but is not numerically strong in Methodism. Its social orientation is in general similar to that of the liberals, and grounded in some of the same doctrines as in liberalism, though the doctrines themselves are very differently interpreted.

Christian existentialism also is represented among Methodist thinkers. It often appears in connection with a Neo-Reformation point of view, but also finds espousal among theologians who do not hold this position. It is of course strongly influenced by Kierkegaard, and usually in some respects by the thought of Paul Tillich. Christian existentialists ordinarily stress, among other things, man's predicament as a finite being whose very existence involves estrangement, inner conflict, and anxiety, and whose concern for his own destiny prevents objective intellectual judgment on ultimate issues; man's need to commit himself and act in faith without sufficient rational knowledge of alternative claims; and Christian faith as the answer to the meaninglessness which would mark human existence on any other basis. Existentialists are keenly interested in the arts and in literature, especially biography, poetry, and the novel, and often cultivate close relationships with persons who through these media wrestle with the crucial problems of personal existence. Existentialists vary in the extent and direction of their social concern.

Finally, it should probably be pointed out that some Methodist leaders think of themselves primarily not as adherents of liberalism,

Neo-Reformation thought, or any other position among those mentioned, but simply as middle-of-the-road Protestants and Methodists. As we noticed in Chapter Three, some aspects of the Wesleyan tradition continue strong, and recent years have witnessed in some quarters a renewed interest in Wesleyan theology and liturgical practices. Ethically, those who stress their Methodist heritage customarily emphasize the life of practical service to God and man in personal and social relations, under the power and guidance of the Holy Spirit.

B. Major Christian Beliefs Related to Social Thought

In the perspective of the preceding account of the theological movements which have involved Methodists, we are now ready to examine directly the basic Christian beliefs of Methodists in relation to their social convictions. Where does one look for this kind of information regarding a large, non-creedal Protestant communion? In the case of The Methodist Church, obvious sources include the published volumes of its theologians and other leaders, the books used in its schools of theology and in the courses of study prescribed for its ministerial candidates who do not attend seminary, editorials and articles in church periodicals, the pronouncements of General and Annual Conferences, communications of the Council of Bishops, the sermons of its ministers, its church-school curricular materials, and publications of its general boards and agencies. This chapter and Chapter Five are based upon a fairly extensive examination of sources like these. It is evident that such documents vary a good deal in representativeness, and it is not easy to estimate fairly their relative validity. Usually, however, in this study preference has been given to the writings of theologians, General Conference statements, and Episcopal Addresses, as probably most likely to reflect accurately the thought of the church.[2]

No documentary study can reveal with sufficient definiteness the thinking of the rank-and-file membership of the church. It is there-

[2] In evaluating General and Annual Conference pronouncements, it must always be remembered that such statements are arrived at by majority vote on the basis of committee reports and floor debate. Often large minorities hold a different position from the one adopted, so that on controversial issues the relative size of the vote for and against is an important factor in any fair interpretation. Nevertheless, the General Conference remains the supreme legislative body of Methodism, and its actions must be taken seriously as representing officially the preponderant judgment of the church's elected leadership at a particular time.

fore desirable to provide some opportunity for the members to speak for themselves. The questionnaire method, in spite of its shortcomings, seems to be the best means of attaining this end. Accordingly, a questionnaire dealing with religious, ethical, and social beliefs and social action was distributed in 1959 to a stratified random sampling of Methodists living in all parts of the United States. An interpretation of the results of this study will be given in Chapter Six.

The documentary materials disclose repeated references to the bearing of particular Christian beliefs on social problems. Therefore the natural and logical method of reporting our findings is to report what Methodists say regarding the social implications of these beliefs. The doctrinal areas most frequently involved are the ethical authority of the Bible, the nature of God, the nature of man, Christ and salvation, the church, and the kingdom of God. In each area we shall first consider utterances from the earlier part of the century up to approximately 1935, and then those from the later period, observing chronological order within each period as far as it is possible or relevant. This procedure should enable us to note changes in theological emphasis, and to relate interpretations of specific socially relevant doctrines to the underlying positions which they reflect.

In many Methodist discussions of social questions the doctrinal presuppositions of the attitudes expressed are more implicit than explicit, hence difficult to discover. Further, some expressed doctrinal concepts are peripheral to discussions of social issues, seeming to provide not foundations of social beliefs but rather theological or biblical justification for positions advocated on other grounds. However, in such cases it is well-nigh impossible for the interpreter to ascertain, from the printed page only, when such doctrinal affirmations are rationalizations or external additions and when they are real foundations. Where clear evidence is missing, therefore, we shall take statements at their face value, and simply report what we find.

1. THE ETHICAL AUTHORITY OF THE BIBLE

The statement on "The Church and Social Problems" adopted in 1908 by the Methodist Episcopal General Conference, meeting in Baltimore, began with the declaration that the teachings of the New Testament contain "the ultimate solution of all the problems of our social order." This judgment of the original "Social Creed" accurately

95

expresses a presupposition widely characteristic of Methodists during the early part of the century—that authoritative ethical norms for men's social relations are to be found in the teachings of the Bible, and particularly in the New Testament. For the most part Methodist leaders were not biblical literalists, and during these decades they came rather widely to accept the historical-critical approach which recognized different levels of spiritual and ethical insight in various parts of the Scriptures. But they were convinced that the Bible contained the Word of God, and that in its writings, properly understood, the authentic will of God for man's life in society is disclosed.

Repeatedly the utterances of the great Hebrew prophets were cited as containing principles valid for our day as well as theirs. Amos' demand for justice, Isaiah's judgment against those who "add field to field" and "grind the face of the poor," and Jeremiah's call for personal and social righteousness were applied to the acquisitiveness and materialism of modern society. Isaiah's plea to Judah for obedience to God and trust in him rather than in human alliances and military power was seen as divine revelation and practical wisdom for modern nations as well as for eighth-century Judah. The universalism of Second Isaiah, proclaiming a God who is "Creator of the ends of the earth" and Lord of all human history, was presented as normative for the attitudes of twentieth-century American Christians toward other nations and races.

Even greater reliance was placed on the ethical teaching of the New Testament. "The apostolic virtues," wrote Bishop Herbert Welch in an early article, "are largely social." Paul's and Peter's lists of the Christian graces, "the fruit of the Spirit," include not only individualistic qualities like joy, peace, fortitude, and faithfulness, but also justice, love, self-control, and patience. "One has but to follow these social virtues into their various applications to discover the precepts of all social righteousness and all social service." [3] When Ernest Fremont Tittle presented the resolution adopted by the Methodist Episcopal General Conference of 1932, providing that future General Conferences should meet only in cities offering advance assurance that there would be no racial discrimination or segregation in hotel accommodations, he supported it with the words of Paul: "Here there cannot be Greek and Jew, circumcised and uncircumcised,

[3] "The Church and Social Service," Methodist Review, 90 (1908), 709.

barbarian, Scythian, slave, free man, but Christ is all, and in all." [4] Other passages in Acts, Paul's letters, and the other epistles were frequently quoted as revealing what God expects of Christians today.

However, the highest authority was assigned to the teachings of Jesus himself. The earliest form of the Social Creed declared that the evils of civilization will disappear "when the spirit of Christ shall pervade the hearts of individuals, and when his law of love to God and man shall dominate human society." The church stands for "the recognition of the Golden Rule and the mind of Christ as the supreme law of society and the sure remedy for all social ills." [5] In 1916 the General Conference of the Methodist Protestant Church declared the "great need of the hour" to be "the application of the principles, precepts, and doctrines of the Gospel of Christ." [6]

Twenty years later the same body, accepting its responsibility for social righteousness, called for the vigorous application of "the principles of Christ" to the problems of politics, amusements, sex and family, crime, and poverty.[7] A speaker in the Southern Methodist General Conference of 1930 found progress toward such application in the signing of the Kellogg-Briand Pact outlawing war. The pact, he asserted, was "shot through with the light that shone in Bethlehem. The inspiration is the man of Galilee." [8]

Utterances like these obviously reflect the faith not only that the teachings of Jesus and other biblical precepts express at least partially the purpose of God for society, but also that Christians can through reference to them discern the divine will for society today and can by fulfilling and applying them help advance the kingdom of God on earth.

Recent years have brought marked changes in the Protestant understanding of the Bible. Earlier conceptions made much of progressive revelation, finding a development from primitive Old Testament beginnings to the ethical monotheism of the prophets and the New Testament teaching of the universal love of God. Now the Bible is viewed increasingly as salvation-history (*Heilsgeschichte*)—the history

---

[4] *Journal*, 1932, pp. 259-60. Dr. Tittle offered a similar resolution at the General Conference of The Methodist Church in 1944. It too was adopted.

[5] *The Doctrines and Discipline of the Methodist Episcopal Church*, 1908, par. 59, pp. 479, 481.

[6] *Journal*, 1916, p. 105.

[7] *Ibid.*, 1936, p. 75.

[8] *Ibid.*, 1930, p. 305.

of the revelatory events in which God has acted to deliver men from bondage and to call them into a new relation to him in the covenant community. It is a redemptive drama in two acts, reaching its climax in Jesus Christ and pointing toward the final consummation of God's purpose when the curtain of history goes down. The essential biblical message is a kerygma or proclamation which declares the deeds of God, past, present, and future, and calls for man's response.

The spread of this conception among Methodists has inevitably wrought changes in their interpretation of the ethical teachings of the Bible. Many now find it impossible, for example, to think of Jesus as a teacher offering guidance for the gradual reconstruction of society. Jesus did not believe, declares Paul Ramsey, that the gospel of love would avail to resolve the evil in many life situations.[9] Nor did "Jesus' call to the strenuous way of limitless love" lay down "the method for making all the world the kingdom of God." On the contrary, Jesus proclaimed that the kingdom was already effective. Men could live free of fear and practice love and forgiveness just because God was about to bring the present age to an end and give them the kingdom.[10] But this expectation was not realized.

Some thinkers, impressed also by the first-century setting and the eschatological aspects of Jesus' ministry, believe it impossible to extract from his teachings universal principles for the guidance of modern Christians in situations very different from those he faced. Others maintain that to interpret his teaching primarily as ethical standards which men ought to obey is to substitute legalism for the essential gospel of one who was not a law-giver, but above all the Redeemer and the Mediator of the forgiving, reconciling love of God. For others, the expectation that men can succeed to any marked degree in patterning their lives after his is unrealistic, overlooking the hard facts of human sinfulness.

For the most part, however, though recent developments have decreased the tendency to look to the Bible for ethical prescriptions, they have not undermined its ethical authority. The Bible, writes Bernhard W. Anderson, is the " 'holy ground' on which God confronts

[9] "A Theology of Social Action," *Social Action*, Vol. XII, No. 8 (Oct. 15, 1946), pp. 4-5.
[10] *Basic Christian Ethics* (New York: Charles Scribner's Sons, 1950), p. 37.

man with his humbling and forgiving Word." Hence Christians return to it again and again for understanding of their vocation and destiny. Its proclamation of God's mighty acts is "accompanied by an appeal to men to serve Him with the full gratitude and devotion of the heart." It also contains the contemporary word which we need, for it is the medium through which God calls men today to faith and obedience.[11]

J. Robert Nelson exhibits a broadly similar point of view in affirming the authority of the Bible for the church. In every special problem of authority, in social action as well as in faith and worship, the church is responsible for seeking "that course of thought or practice which comes closest to being in full accord with the Word of God, known in Jesus Christ and the Scriptural testimony to Him." [12]

Though Paul Ramsey regards Jesus' "primitive eschatology" as mistaken, his Basic Christian Ethics is biblical throughout, with repeated use of the ethical teachings of Jesus. In fact, he maintains that in the ethic centering in the welfare of the neighbor "human thought gains an Archimedean point on which to stand and judge the world." All civilizations are "absolutely bound" to serve the neighbor's good

in obedient love. Christian ethics may claim to be relevant in criticism of every situation precisely because its standard derives from no particular situation and is not accommodated to man's continuing life in normal, historical relationships; and this in turn is true in point of origin precisely because of Jesus' apocalyptic view of the kingdom of God.[13]

In contrast to the views of writers like Ramsey, some Methodist statements of the past twenty-five years continue to express the spirit of the liberal social gospel. For example, the latest version of the Social Creed asserts in connection with a statement of its theological basis:

The Methodist Church must view the perplexing times and problems which we face today in the light of the teachings of Jesus. Jesus taught us

---

[11] "The Bible," A Handbook of Christian Theology (New York: Meridian Books, 1958), pp. 35, 39.
[12] The Realm of Redemption (Chicago: Wilcox and Follett Co., 1951), p. 118.
[13] Basic Christian Ethics, p. 44.

to love our neighbors and seek justice for them. To be silent in the face of need, injustice, and exploitation is to deny him.[14]

In the fall of 1958 the Council of Bishops observed the semicentennial of the Social Creed by addressing a "Message to The Methodist Church" which reaffirmed the principles of the creed and related them to today's issues. The bishops reasserted "unchanged" the creed's "recognition of the Golden Rule and the mind of Christ as the supreme law of society and the sure remedy for all social ills," and summoned all the ministers of the church again "to the fearless but judicious preaching of the teachings of Jesus in their significance for the moral interests of modern society." [15]

Meanwhile a number of Methodist theologians, while recognizing the pronounced eschatological element in Jesus and the New Testament, assert an essential continuity between the ethics of the new age to come and that by which Christians by God's grace are called to live now. On this basis they continue to look to the teachings of Jesus for definite guidance, though no detailed blueprints, for individual and social life today. Two examples may be cited.

Writing in 1940, Harris Franklin Rall insisted that "Christianity is not a supernatural, authoritative, and unchanging set of rules." The gospel offers neither a new law nor an example for meticulous imitation. "The earlier 'social gospel' was mistaken in its efforts to find directions in the Bible for a new economic order, and the liberalism which sought to solve modern intellectual difficulties in religion by reducing it to an ethical emphasis misconceived the New Testament." The ethics of the gospel is rooted in the character of God, who is redemptive good will; it calls men to trustful surrender to him and domination by his spirit.

What this means is disclosed concretely in the spirit of Jesus, as indicated in his life, teachings, and death. It centers in a love which is positive and creative good will for all men. "Its basic principle is social. It is solidaristic, not atomistic, for it roots in the God of good will in whom all men are one as children and brothers." This

---

[14] *The Doctrines and Discipline of The Methodist Church* (The Methodist Publishing House, 1956), par. 2020, p. 703. This passage has remained unchanged since the revision of the creed by the first General Conference of The Methodist Church in 1940. Hereafter the various editions of this publication will be designated simply as *Discipline*, with the date.

[15] Adopted in Cincinnati, Ohio, Nov. 13, 1958.

100

ethics offers no programs for social reconstruction; nevertheless, its principles and attitudes "have a decisive meaning for our day." It "passes definite judgment upon our social institutions and processes and holds up definite ideals, without attempting to indicate the exact means of their achievement." [16]

L. Harold DeWolf combines realism with confidence in the applicability to life now of the ethics of the New Testament:

The spirit represented by the Beatitudes, the whole Sermon on the Mount, the life of Jesus, and the many ethical teachings of Paul, is capable of being only ambiguously enacted in this present life, but even imperfectly realized it is in continuity with the spirit of the eternal kingdom of God. Hence the most practical prayer of petition we can utter here, in this corrupt and perplexing life, is, "Thy kingdom come, thy will be done, on earth as it is in heaven." [17]

Marked differences have appeared in Methodist interpretations of the nature and scope of the Bible's ethical authority. Nevertheless, there is broad agreement on the reality and primacy of that authority. Clarence Tucker Craig has expressed well the conclusion to which our study has led. After pointing out clearly the differing views of biblical authority in the ethical and social areas, he is still able to write: "If the Bible is used by a Spirit-filled inquirer, in the light of the best traditions of the Church, the moral experience of the race, and an accurate knowledge of the contemporary situation, it will prove an invaluable source of guidance in dealing with our social and political problems." [18] However restricted at times may be its applicability, and however remotely men approximate its goals, the Bible provides for Methodists their major guidance to the will of God for human relations.

2. GOD

On the whole, Methodists in the twentieth century have probably related their social thought to their belief in God more than to any other aspect of their Christian faith. The greatest meaning for Chris-

[16] *Christianity; an Inquiry into Its Nature and Truth* (New York: Charles Scribner's Sons, 1940), pp. 262-66.
[17] *The Case for Theology in Liberal Perspective*, p. 171.
[18] "A Methodist Contribution," *Biblical Authority for Today*, ed. Alan Richardson and Wolfgang Schweitzer (Philadelphia: Westminster Press, 1951), p. 44.

tian social relations appears in three central affirmations concerning God: his universal creatorship and fatherhood, his sovereign righteousness, and his reconciling love. Since representatives of differing theological points of view agree in stressing all three of these concepts, we shall follow a topical order in presenting their ideas.

a) Creatorship and Fatherhood

In the earlier decades of the century there were fairly frequent allusions, usually without much elaboration, to the fatherhood of God and the brotherhood of man implied in it. A typical expression of this is found in the "Korean Creed," written by Bishop Herbert Welch and a committee of Korean Methodists in 1930, and widely used by American Methodist congregations since its publication in the Methodist Hymnal in 1935. The seventh of the eight affirmations declares: "We believe in the Kingdom of God as the divine rule in human society, and in the brotherhood of man under the fatherhood of God." [19] Most statements of this kind asserted or assumed the responsibility of those who worship God as Father to treat their fellow men as brothers in one family.

Later utterances develop with greater care the implications of this aspect of Christian faith in God. In the statement of theological bases added to the Social Creed in 1952, the first belief affirmed is "that God is Father of all people and races, that Jesus Christ is his Son, that all men are brothers, and that man is of infinite worth as a child of God." [20] The current Membership Manual for youth and adults concurs: "Belief in the fatherhood of God leads to belief in the brotherhood of man. The implications of these two beliefs call for us to cast off exclusiveness and to accept all persons as brothers under God." [21]

Georgia Harkness applies this conception specifically to international relations. "It is a clear Christian conviction," she writes,

that God is the creator of all men and "hath made of one blood all nations of men for to dwell on all the face of the earth." A Christian conscience, when it is sensitive to the gospel, is thereby committed to an international outlook. This involves the obligation to regard and respect all men as

[19] This affirmation of faith also appears on pp. 139-40 of The Book of Worship for Church and Home (The Methodist Publishing House, 1944).
[20] Discipline, 1956, par. 2020, p. 703.
[21] Manual of The Methodist Church for Young People and Adults, 1951, p. 36.

sons of God, treating them with mercy, sympathy, courtesy, and understanding.[22]

As a matter of fact, this conviction has been a major foundation for Methodist efforts to replace narrow nationalism with international understanding and co-operation for the welfare of humanity as a whole. Specifically, it provided a dominant theological imperative behind the Crusade for a New World Order in 1943 and again in 1953, and it is implicit and often explicit in the ongoing work of the Board of World Peace.

Similar inferences have been drawn regarding race relations. The insistence of Jesus, declared the Episcopal Address to the General Conference of 1944,

was that our supreme loyalty is not to race, or fatherland, or earthly family, but to the family of God. That is the goal for which every sincere Christian works. While we wait for its attainment we are to bring the spirit of love into all the relations we sustain with each other; we are to be brotherly with every man and just with every race.[23]

In this context the bishops rejected the assumption of the inherent superiority or inferiority of any race and grounded racial variety and interdependence in the purpose of God. In the same spirit Bishop Paul B. Kern wrote a decade earlier: "To despise another man because his background is different from ours and his skin is a shade off color, is not only blind stupidity but practical atheism." [24]

All of the statements and actions cited so far seem to stand essentially in the liberal social gospel tradition. Writers representing a Neo-Reformation or "realistic" orientation reach basically the same conclusions. However, on the whole they are less inclined to speak in terms of the moral "ought" derived from the view of God as Father and Creator, and somewhat more likely to stress the inner alienation of men from God that obstructs their realization of true community with each other.

Everett Tilson illustrates this approach in discussing the questions which he feels are raised for people on both sides of the race issue

[22] The Modern Rival of Christian Faith, p. 105. Cf. pp. 191-92.
[23] Journal, 1944, p. 729.
[24] The Basic Beliefs of Jesus (Nashville: Cokesbury Press, 1935), p. 164.

by biblical faith in God as Creator. For advocates of segregation it poses questions like these: In attaching so much importance to differences in skin color, do you not deny that "the only difference of really decisive significance is that which separates, not one group of men from another, but every man from his Creator?" For all you are and have and hope for you are as dependent on your Maker "as the man who *inherited* parents of another race." What right have you then to regard the color of your skin as a basis for favored or separate treatment at the hands of men?

Similarly, integrationists need to ask themselves: Do you base your demand for integration merely on the humanistic assumption of the equality of man, or "on the equal dependence of all creatures on their Creator"? Do you think of your Creator as a useful ally in the struggle for integration, or "do you think of your support of integration as one aspect of your creaturely obligation to your Creator?" [25]

Waldo Beach represents a somewhat similar concern when he writes:

It is through those outward arrangements created by integration that best can be realized the inner ethic of reconciliation, the recovery of interpersonal community—not the meeting of Negro and white groups, self-conscious of their racial equality, but a family reunion of individuals who are all the children of one Father.[26]

Yet the difference between the two theological standpoints should not be exaggerated or stereotyped. Evangelical liberal Christians, too, are concerned to remove the inner blocks to harmonious interpersonal relations by helping people to find their true being in God. And Tilson asserts with the liberals that "both testaments deny the possibility of rightly worshiping God so long as we hate our fellow men, brethren with us in his family, whom he wills that we should love and help." [27]

The creatorship of God has been for Methodists the ground of another principle of social significance—that of stewardship. If God is the Maker and Sustainer of heaven and earth, then our material and human resources are not ours but his, to be used in accordance with

[25] *Segregation and the Bible* (Nashville: Abingdon Press, 1958), pp. 102-3.
[26] "A Theological Analysis of Race Relations," *Faith and Ethics*, ed. Paul Ramsey (New York: Harper and Brothers, 1957), p. 224.
[27] *Segregation and the Bible*, p. 130.

his ends. The Social Creed affirms the faith of the psalmist that "the earth is the Lord's and the fulness thereof," going on to assert that "our own capacities and all we possess are gifts of the Creator, and should be held and used in stewardship to him." [28] Likewise Albert Outler declares that the Christian acknowledges his gifts and powers as "divine endowments, to be received and exercised in faithful stewardship and service to 'the neighbor' and to all mankind." [29]

The General Conference of 1944, emphatically affirming stewardship as the Christian view of man's relation to the soil, called on Methodists "to recognize their responsibility to God for the conservation, development, and the right use of the total resources of the rural community." [30] Various Methodist writers have taken the same view of atomic energy, stressing man's responsibility to God to use it for constructive purposes.[31]

Man's ultimate accountability to his Creator is also the major foundation of "the responsible society," which is receiving great emphasis in the ecumenical movement. As Walter G. Muelder has shown, in this view "society is responsible to God, who is the ultimate source of all true value and its preserver." From such responsibility come ethical and social fruits like "practical urgency, the majesty of justice, religious freedom, and universal solidarity." [32] Men who are aware of their accountability to God also recognize their obligations to each other. Thus a truly responsible society is one in which each member freely acknowledges his responsibility to God and his neighbor, and in which those who exercise power see themselves as responsible to God and the people affected by their acts.

b.) *Sovereign Righteousness*

For Methodists God is not only Creator and loving Father; he is also the Sovereign who rules his world in righteousness and demands righteousness in his worshipers. Definitely present amid the comparative optimism of the teens and twenties was the insistence on the inviolability of God's moral laws which are written into the structure of society. The note of stern judgment against economic

[28] *Discipline*, 1956, par. 2020, p. 703.
[29] *Psychotherapy and the Christian Message*, p. 227.
[30] *Journal*, 1944, p. 724.
[31] See for example Georgia Harkness, *Understanding the Christian Faith*, p. 173.
[32] *Foundations of the Responsible Society* (Nashville: Abingdon Press, 1959), pp. 35, 21.

injustice was sounded by leaders of the social gospel movement like Harry F. Ward, who in 1921 could write of "the wrath that is being stored up" because of the sins of the social order.[33] As early as 1919 Ernest Fremont Tittle appraised the causes of World War I from the perspective of a prophetic faith which knows that the flouting of God's moral order brings inevitable disaster. "Humanity," he wrote, "has been seeking a false objective and has been compelled to retreat." Anyone would be "strangely blind" who traced the war only to Germany's mad bid for empire. German intrigue ignited smoldering passions, but the total European situation was such that

only a miracle such as never occurs could have prevented eventual war. When nations build their lives on the assumption that the ultimate forces of the universe are material forces, not spiritual, and put their trust in might, not right, war is inevitable. Diplomacy may delay it, but cannot finally prevent it.[34]

Since the 'thirties the implications of the divine sovereignty have received much more careful attention, and by thinkers of all theological standpoints. Conscious of an earlier stress on man and the frequent tendency of Christians to assume that the kingdom would come mainly through human effort, Harold Bosley declares, "We've had the wrong center. We've got to recover a consciousness of God, his sovereignty and the absoluteness of his claim upon us." [35] Harris Franklin Rall, writing on American Methodism (especially its view of the church), in preparation for the Lund Conference on Faith and Order (1952), reported that "in its preaching it has been insistent on the transcendent holiness of God, the sovereignty of God." [36]

The implications of this conception for human social relations have been frequently treated. The General Conference of 1944 asserted, in adopting a report on the conditions of peace, "God is the Ruler of the world; nations as well as individuals are subject to his law." [37] Stressing likewise the "exacting moral demands" of God, Georgia Harkness points out the part played by individual and national selfish-

---

[33] "Which Way Will Methodism Go?" *Methodist Review*, 104 (1921), 695.
[34] "Priest or Prophet?" *Methodist Review*, 102 (1919), 555-56.
[35] Interview with the MESTA research team, Boston, March 4, 1959.
[36] R. Newton Flew (ed.), *The Nature of the Church* (London: Student Christian Movement Press, 1952), p. 336.
[37] *Journal*, 1944, p. 726.

ness in the causation of World War II, and insists that persistence in policies similarly motivated lays the foundation for new war. "We cannot sow the wind and not reap the whirlwind. . . . God sets before us life and death; we must choose." [38]

In much the same way Paul B. Kern has related the divine judgment to the economic process:

God never intended that so much of this wealth should be held by so few of his children, and He who heard the cry of the poor and downtrodden in an ancient day will not spare any economic system that enriches a favored minority and consigns to poverty and unspeakable sorrows the vast majority of the peoples of the world.[39]

Robert S. Michaelson expresses the foregoing convictions in somewhat Niebuhrian terms when he writes of the self-idolatry of the nation which "flaunts its own righteousness and self-sufficiency before God and the world." Such a course leads to "corruption within, challenge from without, and eventual dissolution. Self-exaltation is an acid which eats away at the foundations of life. Attempts to live as one's own sovereign gradually sever the roots which lie buried in the only true ground of sovereignty and power." [40]

The divine sovereignty has also been seen as a major ground of Christian concern for human rights, freedoms, and responsibilities. Since man's ultimate responsibility is to God alone, he must be free to fulfill it.

The divine will is normative for all; therefore each must be granted the right to obey it in accordance with conscience in all areas of life, and none has the right to lay demands or restrictions on others which would prevent such obedience. Only so can man realize the central meaning of his existence.[41]

Further, since God's rule is righteous, those subject to him are responsible for treating one another justly and have the right to be so treated. The same fundamental freedoms should therefore be extended

[38] *Understanding the Christian Faith*, pp. 173-74.
[39] *Methodism Has a Message!*, p. 115.
[40] "The Kingdom of God in America and the Task of the Church," *Faith and Ethics*, ed. Paul Ramsey (New York: Harper and Brothers, 1957), p. 280.
[41] S. Paul Schilling, "The Christian Bases of Rights, Freedoms, and Responsibilities," *The Church and Social Responsibility*, ed. J. Richard Spann (Nashville: Abingdon Press, 1953), p. 19.

to all men. This conviction has often motivated Methodists in such activities as opposition to congressional investigating methods which undermine freedom of thought, advocacy of nondiscriminating immigration legislation, and support of efforts in the United Nations to secure fundamental human rights.

Finally, the doctrine of the divine sovereignty is applied by Waldo Beach to the whole realm of church-state relations. He finds in it rather than in separation the Protestant starting point of a sound theory. Immediate and far-reaching implications are involved in the affirmation of the kingship of God over all realms of life.

Far from excluding religion from political life, it means that ideally the public order would be infused with and guided by Christian norms, that the state be regarded as one of the divine "orders" created, judged, and redeemed by God. . . . The "religion of Protestants" is certainly not only a private matter of faith . . . it is also an outward expression of faith in works, with unavoidable political implications.[42]

c) Redemptive Love

God is active in history not only as Lord and Judge, but also as Redeemer. Even his judgment which upsets the self-centered schemes of men is not an end in itself, but a means of restoring humanity to its true vocation. Partly by frustrating our own short-sighted purposes he seeks to guide us toward his own perfect goals. The social significance of God's redemptive activity received relatively little attention from Methodists at the beginning of the century, but in recent years has been thoughtfully developed.

The God revealed in Jesus Christ, declares Tittle, is

the living God, who is working for the redemption of individuals and of society. . . . It is He who begets in men a growing discontent with themselves and with social conditions which breed injustice, violence, and cruelty. It is He who prompts men to seek a just and enduring peace and who mightily aids them in every true and righteous undertaking.[43]

This faith in God as Redeemer is one of the theological assump-

[42] "Issues Between Catholics and Protestants," *Religion in Life*, 23 (1954), 190.
[43] "Implications of the Christian Faith for a Just and Enduring Peace," *When Hostilities Cease* (Chicago: Methodist Commission on World Peace, 1941), p. 103.

tions with which A. Dudley Ward supports the church's social witness in general and her concern for better race relations in particular.[44] Waldo Beach roots racial redemption primarily in the reconciling love of God to which men respond by practicing reconciliation toward each other.

We are redeemed racially, as in all other areas of life, by the grace of God, by an obedient and glad response to his forgiving and recovering work in human life. We are not the initiators, but first the recipients, then the reflectors of love. "We love, because he first loved us." We forgive as we are forgiven.

In so responding the Christian is clear-sighted enough to discern the distance between the kingdom of God and integration or other human arrangements. Hence he does not place his trust in any such provisions as final, but step by step commits himself to love for his neighbor in radical obedience to the God who in Jesus Christ has acted to redeem both.[45]

3. Man

Hardly less prominent than the Christian view of God in Methodist expressions of social concern is Christian teaching concerning man. Again and again various aspects of the nature or status of human personality are cited as foundations for action in behalf of social goals. Two in particular require consideration here—the worth and the sinfulness of man.

a) *The Worth of Persons*

Prominent in the development of the social gospel was the conviction that persons should always take precedence over institutions or material things. In 1927, for example, the Michigan Annual Conference of the Methodist Episcopal Church declared: "The church stands for the making of men; industry, with few exceptions, stands for the making of profits. The Christian motive and the profit motive are irreconcilable." [46] The demand for social legislation sprang from the realization that long hours of labor, low wages, and the

---

[44] "The Christian in His Social Relations," *Christian Action*, May 18 and 25, 1958.
[45] "A Theological Analysis of Race Relations," *Faith and Ethics*, ed. Paul Ramsey, p. 222.
[46] *Information Service*, Federal Council of Churches, Oct. 22, 1927, p. 3.

absence of safety measures stifled human personality and prevented its rightful development. Such action usually assumed, on the basis of the teachings of Jesus, the sacredness of persons as children of God, but was usually not related to a carefully wrought Christian doctrine of man.[47]

As the years passed, however, this relationship received increasing attention, and both official statements and the writings of individuals have frequently and specifically cited the unique worth of man as a major foundation for social concern. Typical of the former is the statement in the current Social Creed: "All persons have supreme value in the sight of God, and ought to be so regarded by us. We test all institutions and practices by their effect upon persons." Whenever personality is oppressed, we therefore seek its emancipation, enrichment, and redemption.[48] Representative of many individual utterances is the declaration of Harris Franklin Rall that Christianity has with reference to society a fourfold task: "to assert the sacredness of human personality; to set free the spirit of man from the divisive forces of selfishness, hatred, and fear; to reshape the institutions of our social life so that they will minister to humanity and not be the exploitative instruments of the few; to show how the life of the individual is fulfilled in the life of the group, and the life of the group in that of the larger whole." [49]

For the most part, such statements ascribe infinite worth and dignity to all men, on the basis of their creation by God. All are made in his spiritual image for fellowship with himself, and all are his sons. Moreover, all men are the objects of his saving love disclosed in Christ. "God so loved the world" (John 3:16).[50] Jesus' concern embraced not only Jews, but also Samaritans, an Ethiopian eunuch, a Roman centurion's servant, and a Syro-Phoenician woman. He made

[47] In some instances a doctrine of man was clearly stated, asserting the supreme worth of man as a child of God, but not related to social concern. For one example see Borden Parker Bowne, Personalism (Boston: Houghton Mifflin Co., 1908).

[48] Discipline, 1956, par. 2020, p. 703. See also the statement in the Episcopal Address of 1944, endorsed by the General Conference (Journal, 1944, pp. 728-29), and the affirmation, "We Believe in Man," in the Episcopal Address of 1952 (Journal, 1952, pp. 156-57).

[49] Christianity, pp. 23-4, 32. See also Paul B. Kern, The Basic Beliefs of Jesus, p. 23; and Georgia Harkness, The Modern Rival of Christian Faith, p. 44.

[50] All Scripture quotations in this book are from The Revised Standard Version of the Bible (copyrighted 1946 and 1952 by the Division of Christian Education, National Council of Churches; and used by permission).

110

plain that Naaman the Syrian and a widow of Sidon properly received the ministrations of the prophets of God. No distinctions of race, nationality, class, or sex make any difference in God's attitude toward men. All are persons, inestimably worthful because they are the object of his creative and redemptive concern.

It has sometimes been pointed out, however, that in another sense sonship to God is limited to those who have accepted his offer of redemption. Bishop James H. Straughn, for example, calls for a clearer interpretation of "the dignity of man."

Almost in the same breath in the record of Christ's divine birth is "Thou shalt call his name Jesus: for he shall save his people from their sins." There is nothing dignified about sin. The dignity here is what Jesus does for man. To apply the phrase to mankind in general, unredeemed, is a false estimate.[51]

Though the bishop overlooks the inestimable value imparted to man through both the creative and the redemptive activity of God, he reminds us of the deeper reaches of sonship experienced only by those who yield to God their trustful, repentant response. "All who are led by the Spirit of God are sons of God" (Rom. 8:14; see I John 3:1, 2). From this point of view, as Albert C. Knudson has shown, we are not born, but reborn, children of God.[52] Even on the purely human level, the full father-son relation involves much more than biological kinship. It includes mutual trust, the sharing of life's highest meanings, and rich daily companionship. Something akin to this—yet vastly different too, since the God who reconciles us to himself so far transcends man—is what is meant by sonship to God in the second sense. Those who in loving trust commit their lives to Christ and his way receive "power to become children of God," who were "born, not of blood nor of the will of the flesh nor of the will of man, but of God" (John 1:12-13).

A large majority of the Methodist writers who assert that man is infinitely worthful as a son of God, and should be treated accordingly, use the term in the first of these two meanings. They do not there-

[51] *Inside Methodist Union* (Nashville: The Methodist Publishing House, 1958), pp. 165-66.
[52] *The Doctrine of Redemption* (New York: Abingdon Press, 1933), p. 87.

fore deny the second meaning, and most of them no doubt would affirm it, but they do not make much use of it in discussing the nature of man as a ground of social concern.[53] The de-emphasis may sometimes be deliberate, from a fear of lessening the sense of social mission, since in some instances stress on the second meaning has been accompanied by a rejection of the first and a dismissal of all social obligation toward persons considered unregenerate.

Such writers are clear, however, in insisting that the supreme value ascribed to persons is not inherent in human nature as such, but rooted in man's relation to God. The General Board of Education, for example, has been quite explicit on this point. In 1952, in a statement of the theology underlying the curriculum, it asserted that Christian belief in human dignity is based on faith "that man is made in the image of God to love and serve God." [54] The latest revision of this statement in 1958 declared: "The worth of man is not something that man can claim for himself but is derived from God's purpose for him. The dignity of man, in the Christian understanding, is rooted in the destiny to which God has called him." [55]

In the judgment of a series of General Conferences, Episcopal Addresses, and many individual thinkers, the Christian affirmation of the sacredness of personality has far-reaching implications for the life of men in society. It condemns as wrong any system of production which places individual gain above community welfare, and demands that economic activity seek above all the satisfaction of human needs. It calls for struggle on a world scale against hunger, poverty, disease, and illiteracy. It requires strenuous effort for the abolition of war and support of political agencies to give effect to the will to peace. It points to total abstinence from alcoholic beverages and opposition to the organized liquor traffic. It rules out discriminations based on race, color, or creed. It demands the extension of fundamental human rights and freedoms to all men. It provides a firm foundation for democratic forms of government and demands that Christians take

[53] However, note the stress laid on the redemptive activity of God in Christ, below, pp. 119 ff.

[54] *Educational Principles in the Curriculum*, p. 12.

[55] "Foundations of Christian Teaching in Methodist Churches" (unpublished, 1958), IV, pp. 4-5.

seriously their political responsibilities. It offers an important basis for democratic procedures in education, secular and religious. These are illustrative of the wide range of the applications made.[56]

Such appeals for action imply also that men empowered by God have grounds for expecting real social improvement. Probably this expectation has nowhere been stated more emphatically than by G. Bromley Oxnam in his most recent book (1958). He declares that when man utilizes the resources of religion and science and his God-given reason, he can "abolish war and establish peace, fashion economic justice, and set up racial brotherhood. It is an affront to God . . . when we make light of the capacities with which he has endowed us." Oxnam recognizes the power of self-interest, and of the evil represented by the concentration camps, gas chambers, and crematoria of Nazi Germany. But he refuses to think pessimistically of man as "a fallen creature," "disposed to evil."

This is not man as I see him. I see man as God's own handiwork . . . a being of infinite capacities. I am constantly aware of the love that is ever present in the homes of the world. . . . I know what men and women can be. I see man as fit for the incarnation of God; and in Jesus I see what he can become. I believe in man.[57]

However, not all Methodists display this degree of optimism, or share the generally liberal view implied in most of the positions thus far mentioned. For example, though Everett Tilson agrees that in the Biblical view man is a creature of God made in the divine image and related to God as son to Father, he is too much impressed by man's inclination to crown himself the master of his own destiny to expect great social advance. Men are equals in that they are all "equally dependent on God for the gift of life and a sphere in which to order it." They are invited by the biblical writers "to the imitation of God's attitude toward their neighbors, not from the belief that they will be able to build Utopia if they accept this invitation,

[56] General Conference Journal, 1940, pp. 659, 676; 1944, pp. 195, 731; Ernest Fremont Tittle, "Man as Christianity Sees Him," First Church Pulpit, Evanston, Illinois, IX, 15 (Feb. 29, 1948), p. 9; Georgia Harkness, The Modern Rival of Christian Faith, pp. 44, 90-99, 158; "The Church and Democracy," Religion in Life, 6 (1937), 3; "Foundations of Christian Teaching in Methodist Churches," I, p. 3.

[57] A Testament of Faith, pp. 168-69; see pp. 26, 157, 160, 164-65.

but in the conviction that they will plunge both themselves and their neighbors into hell if they do not." [58]

Paul Ramsey maintains that in Christian ethics motivation for valuing human personality is derived neither from man's created nature nor indirectly from man's capacity for responsive service to God, but "centrally from within that service itself." The value and the rights of personality are, as it were, read "backward from Christ into man." When a person in serving God "forgets his own claims and becomes in some measure a Christ to his neighbor," he attributes infinite value to the neighbor's personality. To be in the image of God is thus to do the work of love in valuing the neighbor for whom Christ died. Part of this work of love is participation in the reconciling task of creating community.[59] This view also provides a firm foundation for human rights. Since the central meaning of existence is found in man's acknowledgment of God in his life and the service of his neighbor in works of love, he must be free to fulfill this meaning.

The differences which have appeared in the thinking of Methodists concerning man are too acute to be glossed over. Yet they ought not to be allowed to obscure two crucial elements of agreement. In the first place, all the spokesmen whom we have surveyed agree that man's worth depends on his relation to God as revealed in Christ. Secondly, they concur in affirming that this relation calls on men to treat all other persons in accord with the value which all alike derive from God.

The position of Albert Outler conserves both of these agreements, while in some measure also bridging the differences. "The Christian perspective on selfhood," he writes, "is radically theocentric: man from God, man before God, man against God, man redeemed by God, man in communion with God, in and through the God-man." He points out that an authentic Christian doctrine of man must be rooted in faith in God as Creator and Redeemer. It sees man as image and beloved child of God, made for free fellowship with his Creator; it sees also man's finitude, sin, and error, and recognizes that his possibilities are radically dependent on God. Viewing man in this way, Christians "must seek for the ordering of life through God's righteous rule and redemptive grace, manifest in Jesus Christ." [60]

[58] *Segregation and the Bible,* p. 137.
[59] *Basic Christian Ethics,* 354-57, 365.
[60] *Psychotherapy and the Christian Message,* pp. 68-69, 53-54.

Such an ordering of life Outler believes possible since Christian faith sees in man not only original *sin* but also original *righteousness*. The image of God is sadly disfigured, but not destroyed, and amid the disorder is a "viable germ of justice" which God uses in remaking human nature after his original design.[61] Related to society, this suggests that realistic Christian love which does not expect to build Utopia has a more positive alternative than the avoidance of hell.

b. *Human Sinfulness*

It is impossible to look at man from a Christian perspective without considering his propensity to sin. Relatively speaking, this aspect was not so strongly emphasized at the height of the social gospel movement as it has been in later years. Probably this de-emphasis was in part a reaction against the pietistic preoccupation with individual sin and with conversion unaccompanied by social concern. Nevertheless, the responsible leaders of the social gospel manifested a much clearer awareness of the power of human sinfulness than is usually recognized today. Seldom did they overlook the rootage in selfishness and greed of the conditions which they sought to change, and seldom did they forget the religious dimension of these ethical wrongs. They believed neither that evil social circumstances were their own explanation nor that external changes alone would suffice to remedy them. As early as 1893 Frank Mason North pointed out that the problem of poverty "lies very close to the problem of sin. Sin is a primary cause of poverty, poverty a constant occasion for sin." [62]

In 1919 Edwin Lewis, discussing the relation between theology and the social gospel, suggested the possibility of an alliance based on the increasing tendency of theology to view sin as selfishness. If theology is to make "faithful use of its material," he wrote, it must revise the individualistic conception of sin. Sin he defines with Ritschl as "active contradiction to God," but he insists that the term must include whatever is in any way antipersonal, hindering the true self-realization of persons and therefore hindering the kingdom of God. He quoted with approval a passage from William DeWitt Hyde specifically designating typical evils of society as "phases of the one deadly and destructive principle, sin." [63] Lewis' definition of sin at this stage later proved

[61] *Ibid.*, pp. 259-60.
[62] "City Missions and Poverty," *Zions Herald*, 71 (1893), 33.
[63] "The Social Theology," *Methodist Review*, 102 (1919), 233-34. See Hyde, *Outlines of Social Theology* (New York and London: Macmillan and Co., 1895), p. 225.

unsatisfactory to Lewis himself. Nevertheless, it is clear that he took the stark reality of sin with all seriousness, and that opposition to its ravages was for him a basis for Christian action in society.

These are by no means isolated instances. Though the appeal for social action was probably based more frequently on men's responsibility for treating their fellows as persons, this usually carried with it the assumption that the failure to do so was a sin against God and man, as well as the conviction that opportunities for the expressing of such sinfulness must be circumscribed as much as possible. It remains true, however, that then as now many socially concerned Christians devoted more effort to the achievement of better social conditions than to the securing of inner change in persons. It is also true that less attention was given then than in more recent years to the effort to understand the meaning, scope, and power of human sinfulness.

Amid diversity of expression and variation in emphasis, Methodist theologians of the past quarter-century manifest a large measure of agreement in their interpretations of sin. In the main they continue to represent, as did John Wesley, a broadly Arminian tradition. This standpoint mediates between a one-sided, Pelagian stress on human goodness and freedom and an equally one-sided, Calvinistic, deterministic conception of divine sovereignty. Man's nature is neither so good that he can avoid sin by his own unassisted will nor so corrupt that he has lost all freedom. He has real freedom of choice, and so can accept or reject the divine grace, but this freedom is itself not an inherent capacity, but a free gift of God.

However, Methodist thinkers today, influenced by recent psychological, Biblical, and theological insights, are much more impressed than were their immediate predecessors by the extent and strength of the limitations on man's freedom. The major differences which appear hinge largely on the prominence given to free choice and consciousness of wrongdoing in the conception of sin.

Stressing the element of human responsibility, Albert C. Knudson agreed with F. R. Tennant in defining sin as "moral imperfection, for which the agent is, in God's sight, accountable." [64] Harris Franklin Rall concurs: "Sin is responsible wrongdoing viewed in its relation

[64] Basic Issues in Christian Thought (New York and Nashville: Abingdon-Cokesbury Press, 1950), p. 119.

to God." [65] L. Harold DeWolf, while insisting on the volitional nature of sin, distinguishes carefully between *formal* sin, "the wilful act of choosing contrary to self-acknowledged obligations," and *material* sin, "choosing contrary to the actual will of God, whether that will is known or not." [66] For Georgia Harkness, however, it is not only freely chosen attitudes and acts contrary to God's righteous will, but also "a sinful state of pride and rebellion against God from which not even the most saintly soul is wholly clear." [67] Going a step farther, Edward T. Ramsdell rooted men's specific sins in the radical sin of self-exaltation, in which man places himself instead of God at the center of his life; because of this he is alienated from God.[68] Similarly, Paul Ramsey regards sin as pride or anxiety "working through selfishness" (the opposite of "faith working through love"); it is "anxious self-centeredness or self-centered anxiety." [69] For Albert Outler, too, it is estrangement from God centering in unfaith or mistrust, man's determination to act by and for his unmastered self.[70] In the thought of Edwin Lewis sin is rebellion and self-assertion against God; it is supported by the activity of the adversary which in both nature and man operates to obstruct the divine purpose.[71]

Obviously there is a wide divergence between the strongly volitional-ethical view of Knudson and the views which locate sin in pride or mistrust. In the main, however, the similarities evidenced by these thinkers greatly outweigh their differences. None of them accept the doctrine of original sin in its traditional form. But L. Harold DeWolf, in spite of his stress on choice, lists seven truths symbolized by the Augustinian concept of original sin.[72] At the same time, those who make most of sin as a radical estrangement which penetrates the depths of man's existence insist that it is man's own doing. Thus Outler asserts that each man has "his own responsibility and share," [73] and

[65] *Religion as Salvation* (New York and Nashville: Abingdon-Cokesbury Press, 1953), p. 57.
[66] *A Theology of the Living Church* (New York: Harper and Brothers, 1953), p. 182.
[67] *Understanding the Christian Faith*, p. 102.
[68] *The Christian Perspective* (New York and Nashville: Abingdon-Cokesbury Press, 1950), pp. 130, 142-50.
[69] *Basic Christian Ethics*, pp. 290-91.
[70] *Psychotherapy and the Christian Message*, pp. 132-33.
[71] *The Creator and the Adversary* (Nashville: Abingdon-Cokesbury Press, 1948), p. 231.
[72] *A Theology of the Living Church*, pp. 199-200.
[73] *Psychotherapy and the Christian Message*, pp. 132-33.

Ramsey insists that sin originates from nothing besides man's own will; "every man is his own Adam, sin originates with him." [74]

It is safe to say, therefore, that the most influential contemporary Methodist theologians basically agree that sin involves a rupture of man's fellowship with God, and that this break cuts the root of human sociality as well. Moreover, they agree in recognizing the social havoc wrought by human sinfulness, the resulting need for action to restrict its evil effects, and the grave hindrances it places in the path of social improvement.

Various writers point out the necessity of collective action to protect men against their own tendency to take advantage of one another. Paul Ramsey asserts that "right policy for political society cannot be made without some basic reference to Christian realism concerning the necessity of restraining and remedying sin." [75] Since men frequently seek special privilege at the expense of others, the rights of all must be guarded through laws which apply equally to all alike. Democracy is possible, declares Everett Tilson, because man is created in the image of God. By the same token it is also necessary, "because man, even though God's creature, never completely escapes the temptation to usurp the place of God." [76] Albert C. Knudson, although more optimistic than Tilson, nevertheless insists that justice can be achieved only when appeals to voluntary action are supported by legislation, the strong arm of the state, and other forms of social compulsion.[77]

As another political corollary of the doctrine of sin, Waldo Beach shows the need for public policy to provide checks against the pride which infects the institutional life of the church itself, dividing the body of Christ into competing sects. The state must provide a "dyke against sin," protecting the whole church against "the imperialism of the parts." [78] Thus the need of social restraints on man's sinfulness is illustrated not only in areas like labor-management relations, civil rights, education, the family, and international affairs, but

[74] Basic Christian Ethics, pp. 306-7, 287-88.
[75] Ibid., p. 337.
[76] Segregation and the Bible, p. 122.
[77] The Principles of Christian Ethics (New York and Nashville: Abingdon-Cokesbury Press, 1943), p. 269.
[78] "Issues Between Catholics and Protestants," pp. 190-91.

also in the life of the very agency which is called to proclaim amid all of these the gospel of salvation.

4. CHRIST AND SALVATION

a.) God's Redemptive Act and Social Concern

According to Christian faith sin not only calls for action to limit its harmful effects on persons in an interdependent society; it also calls forth divine action to redeem the sinner and his sinful world. Like other Christians, Methodists believe that the climactic act of God for human redemption has taken place in Jesus Christ. Jesus is not merely an exceptionally good man, a superlative ethical and religious teacher, the greatest of the prophets, or a spiritual genius, but "the eternal divine Word made flesh and dwelling among men." [79] In him God acted as he has not before or since to heal the broken relation between him and his rebellious, idolatrous children. In his life, teachings, death, and resurrection we see God himself taking on himself the burden of men's sin in order to reconcile them to himself.

Within the framework of this central insistence on the Incarnation, Methodists have varied in their detailed interpretations of the person of Christ. Some have stressed his divinity, affirming with the Nicene Creed that he is "Light of Light, Very God of very God; Begotten, not made; Being of one substance with the Father." Others have emphasized his humanity, seeing in him one whose human center of consciousness was centered also in God, so that in him we see not only perfect man, but the very life and love of God himself. Most have sought to conserve both divinity and humanity within the unity of his personal life.

Similarly, Methodists have included followers of all the major theories of the Atonement. Some have insisted on some form of the penal theory represented by Calvin, according to which Christ in his sufferings and death bore the punishment demanded of sinful man by the justice of God, allowing the love of God to forgive sin. Some have been influenced by the theory (Irenaeus, Luther, Aulén) which stresses the deliverance of men from the power of sin and the fear of death through the decisive victory of God in Christ over the forces of evil. Others hold to some form of the moral or personal

[79] Episcopal Address, 1952. General Conference Journal, 1952, p. 155.

theory typified by Abelard, which centers the meaning of Christ's redemptive activity in his supreme revelation in life and death of the self-sacrificing love of God, which awakens men to repentance, love, and obedience. Many seek to conserve the features of permanent worth in each of these views. But beneath all differences in specific interpretations lies the confidence that in Jesus Christ God has acted decisively to restore the communion between him and mankind which sin has broken.

In this central conviction are important elements of social significance which were largely overlooked by Methodists in the early part of the century but are now clearly asserted. Men are objects of the redemptive love of God—sinners for whom Christ died. As such they have an immeasurable worth which they themselves should respect in themselves and in each other, and in terms of which they should act.

God has acted at infinite cost to redeem man. "We were bought with a price." [80] This central truth of the gospel becomes in the Methodist Social Creed the final theological basis for social action: "Since Jesus died for the redemption of human life, we believe we should live to help save man from sin and from every influence which would harm or destroy him." The sensitive, thankful recipient of God's saving grace will seek the maximum fullness of life for all whose need has called forth the self-giving love revealed in Christ.

The redemptive action of Christ includes also his resurrection, in which "we see God's eternal triumph over tragedy, and are empowered to press forward in faith and hope." In his victory we have the assurance that God's purposes for men will not be defeated but fulfilled. "The grace of God in Christ is available for redemption in all areas of life as we seek in penitence and obedience to do his holy will." [81]

b) *Social Salvation*

"Redemption in all areas of life." In varying ways twentieth-century Methodists have embraced a social as well as an individual conception of the salvation made possible in Christ. We have already seen evidence of this in the earlier decades in connection with pleas for "social sanctification." [82] In 1909 William M. Balch, a frequent

[80] I Cor. 6:20; 7:23.
[81] *Discipline*, 1956, par. 2020, p. 703.
[82] See above, pp. 75-81.

contributor to the *Methodist Review,* declared that salvation requires "the removal of those social conditions which render impossible or partial the exercise of saving influences upon individuals." [83] Likewise Edwin Lewis in 1919 saw the "larger outlook" as integral to the New Testament message. "From the time that John proclaimed the approach of the Kingdom until that other John saw all things made new the note is incessantly sounded that Salvation is to be socially realized." [84]

However, combined with the social interpretation was the insistence that social teaching and action must be rooted in inner transformation. "Mere ethical teaching," wrote the editor of *Zions Herald* in 1920,

will of itself accomplish little. Men are not going to cease to be selfish just because they are told not to be so. Character may be made by conscience, but conscience itself must be educated and re-enforced and inspired by the grace of God revealed in Christ. When men are drawn close to Christ they will be drawn closer one to another.[85]

In 1908 Bishop Herbert Welch, one of the framers of the original Social Creed, emphatically affirmed the wholeness of salvation and the falsity of separating individual and social change:

What God hath joined together let no man put asunder. Our need is not evangelism or social service, but evangelism and social service, now and forever, one and inseparable! This is not revolution, but the old, the natural, the inherent meaning of the religion of Jesus Christ. And this meaning the church must recognize and adopt if it is to serve the present age.[86]

That The Methodist Church today has adopted this understanding of the Christian faith is evidenced in a wide variety of official and individual statements representing different theological backgrounds which display virtual unanimity in this area. The Episcopal Address to the General Conference of 1944 noted that the conference which in 1784 founded the Methodist Episcopal Church declared that God's purpose in raising up the Methodists was "to reform the continent

[83] "Social Salvation," *Methodist Review,* 91 (1909), 749.
[84] "The Social Theology," *Methodist Review,* 102 (1919), 238.
[85] "Socialization Through Christianity," *Zions Herald,* 98 (1920), 750.
[86] "The Church and Social Service," *Methodist Review,* 90 (1908), 714.

and spread scriptural holiness over these lands." In approving this statement of purpose the bishops gave it a social as well as an individual interpretation.[87] Significantly, The Methodist Church's statement of the aim of missions, which forms the theological basis for the work of all three divisions of the Board of Missions, begins by asserting, "The supreme aim of missions is to make the Lord Jesus Christ known to all peoples and all lands as their divine Saviour," and closes with the words, "and to bring to bear on all human life the spirit and principles of Christ." [88]

Methodism, writes Waldo Beach, "is as intensely social as it is intensely inward. Salvation does not mean a private preparation for heaven; it means a life of moral purity and social concern." [89] Clarence Tucker Craig provides one of many illustrations of the truth of this judgment when he declares that the church

seeks to bring its Gospel to every phase of individual and social need. It seeks to spread the Gospel to the end of the world by testimony of faith and deeds of love. It seeks to minister to all the ills of humanity at the same time that it strives for the coming of a social order expressing more fully our Christian ideals.[90]

As noted previously,[91] some recent writers have pointed out profound social implications in the doctrine of salvation by grace through faith. For instance, he who has received forgiveness purely on the basis of the divine mercy cannot consistently set up other prerequisites, such as nationality, race, sex, or class, for the admission of other persons to full participation in the fellowship of the forgiven.

At times social action by Christians has been inadequately related to the full Christian meaning of salvation, being concerned, for example, with economic need alone, or conceived as accomplished mainly by men. But voices have always been raised to declare that all genuine salvation is basically the work of God, in which God-empowered

[87] Journal, 1944, pp. 161-62. See Minutes of Several Conversations (Philadelphia: Charles Cist, 1785), p. 3.
[88] Discipline, 1956, par. 1166, p. 295.
[89] Beach and Niebuhr (eds.), Christian Ethics, p. 362.
[90] R. Newton Flew (ed.), The Nature of the Church, pp. 251-52. See Georgia Harkness, The Modern Rival of Christian Faith, p. 143; and Paul Ramsey, A theology of Social Action, pp. 16-17.
[91] See above. pp. 65 ff.

men are called freely and responsibly to share. "It is wrong," writes Harris Franklin Rall,

to speak of a social "gospel" when all that is meant is social reform through human effort. We must learn to see God's saving work in all the life of man, social as well as individual. . . . God offers to men and nations his forgiveness and his help. That is salvation.[92]

5. The Church

During the early part of this century the doctrine of the church received only peripheral attention from American Methodists. Three main factors contributed to this circumstance: (1) Under the influence of the individualism of the era, the church was widely regarded as relatively extraneous to the Christian faith and the believer's relation to God. (2) The church was often seen as a purely human organization, an institution which threatened to divert to its own upbuilding energies which should be devoted to the kingdom of God. (3) The practical tasks of Christian service were felt to be much more important than the defining of doctrine. These influences can readily be discerned in the definitions of the church which did appear during the period. For Borden Parker Bowne, for example, it was simply "the organization for public religious worship, for religious instruction, and the administration of religious ordinances." [93] Harris Franklin Rall wrote in 1924: "The church is the fellowship of the followers of Jesus, and he is the bond of union." [94]

The *purpose* or *function* of the church was given more careful consideration, in which a live social concern was usually manifest. Thus in 1908 Bishop Herbert Welch declared: "To write 'Holiness unto the Lord' even upon the bells of the horses, to baptize all life into its rightful sacredness, to permeate all persons and all relationships with the spirit of Christ—this . . . is the purpose for which the church of Christ has been established and still exists." [95]

Frank A. Horne, a Methodist delegate to the Lausanne Conference on Faith and Order in 1927, was impressed by a report submitted by

[92] *Religion as Salvation*, p. 200.
[93] *The Essence of Religion* (Boston: Houghton Mifflin Company, 1910), p. 39.
[94] "Not Intellectual Credence but Personal Trust," in a Symposium, "The Faith Once Delivered to the Saints," *Methodist Review*, 107 (1924), 256.
[95] "The Church and Social Service," *Methodist Review*, 90 (1908), 711.

the section on "The Church's Message—the Gospel," of which Bishop Francis J. McConnell was chairman. According to this document:

The gospel is the sure source of power for social regeneration. It proclaims the only way by which humanity can escape from those class and race hatreds which devastate society, at present, into the enjoyment of national well-being and international friendship and peace. . . . Sympathizing with the anguish of our generation, with its longing for intellectual sincerity, social justice, and spiritual inspirations, the church in the eternal gospel meets the needs and fulfills the God-given aspirations of the modern world.[96]

In recent years a new interest has developed among Methodists, as among other Protestants, in the nature of the church. There is no lessening of concern for its task, but there is a much deeper desire to relate that task to a clearer understanding of the church's meaning, and a much more vivid awareness of the integral connection between being a Christian and being a member of the Christian community. As recently as 1950 the series of eight booklets on "Our Faith," published by The Methodist Church, omitted the church from the topics discussed. But in 1958 the Division of National Missions of the Methodist Board of Missions sought the aid of British and American Methodist theologians in connection with a consultation on the nature of the church and its ministry. In 1959 the National Methodist Town and Country Conference, meeting in Wichita, Kansas, devoted major attention to "the nature, purpose, and message" of the church.

Meanwhile Methodist theologians have been making significant contributions to a growing ecumenical understanding of the church. In addition to many articles and chapters in books by various authors, important volumes on the subject have been written by J. Robert Nelson, Albert C. Outler, and Claude Welch; and able essays preparatory to Faith and Order discussions have been written by Clarence Tucker Craig, Harris Franklin Rall, and others. This growing body of literature provides clear indications of what Methodists today think of both the church and its relevance to the life of society.

[96] "The Lausanne Conference: Impressions of a Methodist Layman," *Methodist Review*, 111 (1928), 47. H. N. Bate (ed.), *"Faith and Order," Proceedings of the World Conference, Lausanne, August 3-21, 1927* (New York: George H. Doran, 1927), pp. 462-63.

a) *The Nature of the Church*

Many Methodists follow Paul in conceiving the church primarily as "the body of Christ." "We, though many, are one body in Christ, and individually members one of another" (Romans 12:4-5; I Cor. 12: 12-30). Unlike Roman Catholics, however, Methodists use the term metaphorically. The church is not a superpersonal entity with a mystical life of its own, but a closely-knit community with Christ as its head. As Clarence Tucker Craig has pointed out, the analogy is singularly appropriate, since a body is a visible expression of both unity and diversity, an instrument for the expression of spirit, and an organism which develops through inner transformation.[97] The health of the church, like that of a physical body, depends on the faithful discharge by each member of his peculiar and indispensable function in the ongoing life of an interdependent whole. Even more, it depends on the willingness of each and of all together to act under the direction of Christ, the head (Col. 1:18; Eph. 5:23). The church lives only as it receives power, wisdom, and love from him.

Possibly still more characteristic of most Methodist thought is the conception of the church as "the people of God," the new community which fulfills and extends universally the revelatory and saving action begun by God in the covenant community of Israel. "You are a chosen race, a royal priesthood, a holy nation, God's own people" (I Peter 2:9). The church is the worshiping, trusting, loving, witnessing, teaching, serving fellowship of those who have been made new by the forgiving love of God in Jesus Christ. In the words of the Episcopal Address of 1952, it is "the community of which Jesus Christ is Lord and in which he works by his Holy Spirit." [98]

There is, of course, no conflict between these two New Testament conceptions. Both bring out clearly the church's essential nature, described by J. Robert Nelson as "the oneness between the living Lord and the community, as well as the unity of the members of the community one with another." [99] The synthesis is well suggested by Craig in his report for the American Theological Committee to the World Council Commission on Faith and Order preparatory to the Lund Conference of 1952. In answer to the question, "What is the church?"

[97] *The Universal Church in God's Design*, Amsterdam Assembly Series, Vol. I (New York: Harper and Brothers, 1949), p. 253.
[98] *General Conference Journal*, 1956, p. 157.
[99] "Church," *A Handbook of Christian Theology*, p. 56.

he replies in part: "It is the people who have given allegiance to God in response to his gracious call. It is a body witnessing to His rule by their trust and obedience." [100]

The dominance of these conceptions makes plain that for representative Methodist thought today the church is not merely a human association whose members are loosely joined together by similar interests, but a community created by God and united and empowered by his Spirit. It is a company of real men and women, affected by their frailties and limitations, and responsible for acting in the world, but nonetheless a body distinct from all other earthly groups in that it is a covenanted fellowship of those who have responded in faith to the redemptive action of God.[101]

Methodist thinkers today are joining with many other Christians in recognizing profound social significance in the Biblical understanding of the church. The church which was born at Pentecost and which is portrayed throughout the Book of Acts was a body which ignored distinctions of nationality, language, race, and class. By its very nature the church today is called to be a universal fellowship, binding together in deep mutuality all who answer the divine invitation. Within its own being it must be committed to the removal of unnatural barriers; and since it is commissioned to extend the divine offer to all men, the quality of its own Christ-centered life becomes in principle normative for the rest of humanity. This double implication is brought out effectively by Robert S. Michaelson, who insists that the church must itself incarnate the redemptive love it has received and also move in specific ways toward the redemption of society. God's gift

means a Church that is a society in which the barriers of race, culture, caste, and class are dissolved in and through the love of God in Jesus Christ. It also means the Church's striving to become a social pioneer, to take a place at the forefront in the struggle for social justice by engaging in well

---

[100] R. Newton Flew (ed.), *The Nature of the Church*, p. 253.

[101] Walter G. Muelder, "The Necessity of the Church," *Proceedings of the Ninth World Methodist Conference*, ed. Elmer T. Clark and E. Benson Perkins (Nashville: Methodist Publishing House, 1957), p. 144; Claude Welch, *The Reality of the Church* (New York: Charles Scribner's Sons, 1958), p. 48; J. Robert Nelson, *The Realm of Redemption*, p. 175; Harris Franklin Rall, *The Nature of the Church*, ed. R. Newton Flew, p. 332.

thought-out and concerted programs and by sponsoring bold experimentation.[102]

Much the same conclusion is reached by L. Harold DeWolf on the basis of the nature of love as understood and practiced by the New Testament church. That love is not an atomistic love in which an "I" confronts a "Thou," but a *koinonia* (fellowship) love in which all the "I's" and "Thou's" become a "We," united by the Holy Spirit and sharing "the unsearchable riches of Christ" (Eph. 3:8). To be in the church is thus to share a profound fellowship in which each individual, losing himself in the whole, finds fulfillment in new richness of meaning. "This *koinonia* love, this community in depth with God and with other human beings," is not content with passing on the treasure to others externally. It inspires instead the desire for the sharing of the treasure in intimate community. Such *koinonia* leaves no place for "ideals of *apartheid* or of 'separate but equal' rights." Assistance given or sent to other people, however generous, falls short of true Christian love, which seeks the breakdown of all artificial barriers, "that all may be one," as Christ and the Father are one (I Cor. 12-13; John 17; I John).[103]

b) *The Purpose of the Church*

The church does not exist for itself, but has a mission to fulfill in the world. The meaning of that mission is in fact implicit in the nature of the church as already discussed. The body of Christ is to grow as its members use their diversified gifts to bring other persons into a saving relation to its head, and the people of God are to "declare the wonderful deeds of him who called [them] out of darkness into his marvelous light" (I Peter 2:9).

The church exists, in short, to carry forward the ministry of reconciliation begun by Christ himself. "Both historically and metaphysically," writes Craig, "the church's function may be regarded as one of carrying on and extending the work of the earthly life of Jesus."[104] Similarly Nelson declares, "God created the Church to be the con-

[102] "The Kingdom of God in America and the Task of the Church," *Faith and Ethics*, ed. Paul Ramsey, p. 290. See Everett Tilson, *Segregation and the Bible*, p. 159.

[103] *The Case for Theology in Liberal Perspective*, pp. 142-43. See Claude Welch, *The Reality of the Church*, pp. 72-73.

[104] Report of the American Theological Committee, *The Nature of the Church*, ed. R. Newton Flew, pp. 251-52.

tinuing vehicle in the world by which His plan and purpose of salvation, testified to in the work of Jesus Christ, may be carried forward." [105] For Rall it is the channel through which "the living message of Christ is mediated to successive generations of men." In this sense he is willing to speak of the church as "a continuing incarnation," not in the Roman Catholic sense of a mystical identification of Christ and the church, but only "in so far as it realizes and expresses the Spirit that was in Christ." [106] Thus Rall's emphasis is actually much the same as that of Outler when he asserts that "in general Methodist teaching the church is not an extension of the Incarnation, but rather of *the apostolic witness*. The most important 'definition' of the church is by her *evangelistic mission*." [107] Statements like this evidence rather general agreement that the church, extending the work which Christ began, is summoned to proclaim and manifest among men the redemptive love and power of God.

Methodists have pointed out social implications in the church's purpose more frequently and explicitly than they have in connection with its nature. For Claude Welch the very mission of the church to the world requires it to identify itself with the world, testifying to Christ as Lord not only of the church, but "of the world and of every man." [108] Bishop G. Bromley Oxnam also—though from a very different theological background—sees social action as implicit in the church's goal: "When the Church sees its goals as the increase of the love of God and the love of brother, it is pledged to the expression of that love in the enthronement of God's will in the social order." [109]

How is the church to make the connection between these general objectives and the concrete problems confronting society? Bishop James C. Baker affirmed the church's responsibility for providing not blueprints, but guiding norms, for social relations: "We must work away at the task of bringing to the questions which the church may have no competence to settle, the Christian principles without which there can be no settlement." In terms of these principles, it must then "enlist all its members—and any others who will share in the task—

---

[105] *The Realm of Redemption*, p. 178.
[106] *Christianity*, p. 210; Flew (ed.), *The Nature of the Church*, p. 331.
[107] In an unpublished address at the Graduate School of Ecumenical Studies at Bossey, Céligny, Switzerland, in 1956.
[108] *The Reality of the Church*, p. 206.
[109] *A Testament of Faith*, p. 110.

in bringing to the Judgment Seat of Christ all our social, economic, and political life." [110]

If judgment is placed in a redemptive context, such a conception of the church's role seems implicit in most of the recent declarations of the Social Creed, and in most of the ethical and social pronouncements of the General, Jurisdictional, and Annual Conferences of The Methodist Church. Methodists have in the main taken it quite seriously. In fact, there is some evidence to indicate that Methodist ministers at least are somewhat more inclined than others to stress the church's obligation to influence society by proclaiming and interpreting the Christian way.

In a poll conducted for *Christianity Today* by the Opinion Research Corporation in 1958, 508 Protestant clergymen were asked to indicate which of ten possible tasks of the church they felt to be most important and which of lesser importance. To several tasks, such as world evangelization, preaching, and teaching the Bible, and advocating individual trust in and acceptance of Christ, Methodists assigned about the same degree of importance—in each instance very high—as did their brothers in other communions. The administration of the sacraments was seen as very important by 76 per cent of the total group polled but by only 62 per cent of the Methodists, while 23 per cent of the former and 35 per cent of the latter regarded this function as fairly important. This relative evaluation was reversed, however, when the social tasks were considered. Of the total group, 49 per cent checked "the interpretation of the moral side of social and economic issues" as very important and 43 per cent checked this as fairly important. Of the sixty-five Methodists included, 58 per cent viewed this as very important and 34 per cent as only fairly important. Similarly, 92 per cent of the Methodists listed "influence on community life" as very important, as compared to 76 per cent of the total group, while 23 per cent of the total group regarded this as only fairly important. To "expose evils of alcohol, gambling, etc." was regarded as very important by 57 per cent of the Methodists but only 44 per cent of the total number.[111] If data like these are representative, Methodist pastors believe that part of the task of the church is that of

[110] "The Church in the United States Maps a Plan," *Religion in Life*, 10 (1941), 394.

[111] Data used by permission of *Christianity Today* and the Opinion Research Corporation.

relating the ethical standards and resources of the gospel to the solution of the problems of society.

c) *The Ministry of the Laity*

Two conclusions are implicit in Methodist thought concerning the nature and purpose of the church. First, it is not enough for the church to proclaim ethical standards for society and rely on secular agencies to apply them. Secondly, the fulfillment of the church's role is primarily the responsibility of laymen. True community can be extended and redemptive influences brought to bear in all of life only as those who compose the redemptive fellowship make their Christian witness in their day-by-day relationships in society. Accordingly, new emphasis has recently been placed on the role of the laity, who are the church in the world.

Historically, Methodism has had a high conception of the importance of its lay members. The growth and vitality of the Wesleyan revival in England would have been impossible apart from the impassioned labors of its lay preachers and the dynamic witness in daily life of the rank-and-file members of the Methodist societies. The Methodist Protestant Church grew largely out of the demand for a recognition of the "mutual rights" of laity and clergy, involving chiefly full opportunity for laymen and local preachers to share in church government, although the dwindling importance of the local preacher in American Methodism has brought a decreased sense of lay responsibility for the totality of the church's task.

In the past the rights and responsibilities of laymen have ordinarily been conceived mainly in terms of the internal affairs of the organized church. In the thought of many this conception is now giving way to a much broader view which sees the laity as exercising a true ministry in the total life of society. John R. Mott hinted at this in a letter to Bishop Straughn when he asserted that lay responsibility must be stressed far more than in the past if the church is to play its proper part in "meeting one of the greatest needs of our day, namely, that of Christianizing the impact of our country on the non-Christian world and, to that end, the conquering of the untaken forts in our rear." [112]

The implications of this emerging view, strongly stressed in ecumenical circles today, are well expressed by Walter G. Muelder when

[112] James H. Straughn, *Inside Methodist Union*, p. 178.

he writes: "The church not only *has*, but *is* a ministry in the world. . . . All Christians are commissioned by faith in Christ to minister." [113] This is not, of course, a new idea. In the New Testament church each member had his ministry, and Luther's stress on the priesthood of all believers recaptured something of this early understanding. From time to time since the Reformation Protestants have seen it clearly, as when in 1902 W. E. McLennan observed: "The Lord never meant that there should be only one minister in a parish. He meant that there should be as many ministers as there are Christian men and women." [114] But today the ministry of the laity is being affirmed and interpreted with new clarity and power, and its social significance is increasingly recognized.

As Muelder declares, if the church is the whole people of God with a ministry to the world, it is called upon

to guide the fortunes of society, clarifying its goals and purifying its motives, . . . to be a righteous ferment in social institutions, . . . and to share Christ's reconciling power in the midst of social conflict. . . . A decision for Christ in the church means a dedication to him in the decision-making processes of everyday life.[115]

6. THE KINGDOM OF GOD

The concept of the kingdom of God, described by H. Richard Niebuhr as "the dominant idea in American Christianity," [116] supplied the major theological foundation for the social gospel movement in the early decades of the century. It continues today to provide a major focus for Christian social thought. Among Methodists it has exerted a powerful influence. Of the many questions which arise concerning the kingdom three have been especially prominent in discussions relating it to earthly society: (1) What is the nature of the kingdom? (2) What are the respective roles of God and man in its

[113] "The Future of the Ministry," *Zions Herald*, March 1959, p. 3.
[114] "The Place and Work of the Laity in the Church," *Methodist Review*, 84 (1902), 938.
[115] "The Future of the Ministry," p. 3. See L. Harold DeWolf, *The Case for Theology in Liberal Perspective*, p. 185; Georgia Harkness, *Understanding the Christian Faith*, p. 171.
[116] *The Kingdom of God in America* (Chicago: Willett, Clark and Co., 1937), p. xi.

coming? (3) Is it to be realized within or beyond history? We shall consider each of these in order.

a) *The Nature of the Kingdom*

During a long period of years prior to the twentieth century the kingdom had been largely spiritualized, being conceived as a condition of inward blessedness or as the heavenly city to come. Against this idea Walter Rauschenbusch sharply reacted, and many Christians followed him in insisting that the kingdom in the New Testament had to do with the day-by-day relations of flesh-and-blood human beings here and now. Thus there emerged a strong tendency to construe the kingdom mainly as the ideal earthly society in which God's will is done. The words of the editor of the *Methodist Review* in 1912 are fairly typical of the period. Jesus' aim, he wrote,

is the realization of the Kingdom of God in which the children of earth shall conform to the holy will of the Father as do the hosts of heaven. . . . The Gospel is the announcement of the Kingdom of God; a new social order in which mankind are brothers because sons of one Father.[117]

As a matter of fact, an interpretation of the kingdom very similar to this may still be found among Methodists. In 1949 Lucile Desjardins wrote that in the new Closely Graded Lessons for Intermediates the central concern was the "building of the world-wide kingdom of God on this earth." This includes the furtherance of "wholesome democratic group life." "The kingdom of God is the rule of God among men in which each person, regardless of race, or class, or economic status, has equal rights in relation to others." [118] Likewise in 1959 the Baltimore Conference asserted, in adopting the report of its Board of Social and Economic Relations, that God seeks "the establishment of the Kingdom of God on earth, which, whatever else it may mean, can be conceived as nothing less than the creation of a social order transfused with the Christian ethic and spirit." [119]

However, most recent interpretations do not go so far toward identifying the kingdom with a righteous human society. For example, in

[117] George Elliott, "Religion and Righteousness," *Methodist Review*, 94 (1912), 52-53.

[118] *Counselor's Guide to the Use of Closely Graded Lessons for Intermediates*, 1949, pp. 75, 10.

[119] *Minutes of the Baltimore Annual Conference*, 1959, p. 193.

1941 Ernest Fremont Tittle departed significantly from the earlier social gospel conception by adding a transhistorical dimension, while also pointing out that God rules even when men break themselves on his laws. "At all times," he wrote, "God reigns: we have the option of doing his righteous and loving will, or meeting disaster. The eternal kingdom of God is beyond the confusions of history. It may never be made fully manifest on earth." [120]

The Episcopal Address of 1952 also contained a recognition of the judgment implicit in the divine rule: "Beyond all human laws, customs, and opinions, there is one divine Law which remains absolute and unchanging. Men may break themselves and their civilizations upon that Law but the Law itself stands forever." [121] Nevertheless, the bishops' basic definition of the kingdom conceives God's reign in terms of the fulfillment of his will: "It is the reign of God in every department of society, the divine scale of values for every individual, group, and nation. As Christian perfection is the goal in the individual life, so is the kingdom of God in human society." [122]

"Neo-liberal" thought in Methodism agrees that the reality of the kingdom is demonstrated even in our disobedience, and that even as judgment its complete fulfillment lies beyond history. However, it continues to interpret the reign of God to mean centrally the actualization among men of the righteous, loving purposes of God, the coming into being of a divine-human community in which his love is shared and his will is done. Thinkers representing a "realistic" standpoint ordinarily maintain that men can only prepare for the future coming of the kingdom. However, they believe that Jesus' portrayal of the righteousness of God, in what he said and did and was, provides "the measure and meaning of human obligation" and "the standard for measuring the reign of God among men." [123] Christians are called to get ready for the kingdom by seeking to order their lives now by reference to its norms. Thus for both types of thought the kingdom is relevant to the earthly life of men in society.

b) A Gift or a Task?

The social significance of belief in the kingdom of God appears

[120] "Implications of the Christian Faith for a Just and Enduring Peace," When Hostilities Cease, p. 104. See also Everett Tilson, Segregation and the Bible, p. 117.
[121] General Conference Journal, 1952, p. 158.
[122] Ibid.
[123] Paul Ramsey, Basic Christian Ethics, p. 45.

vividly in connection with the manner of its coming. Marked differences in the views of Methodists on this question also emerge. When the social gospel was at the height of its influence it was widely assumed that the kingdom would come gradually as men increasingly patterned their social relations after the teachings of Jesus. "People and preachers together," wrote Francis J. McConnell in 1922, "are engaged in a regal task . . . actually bringing in the Kingdom of God on earth." [124] Such statements almost always took for granted the underlying activity of God, but, partly in reaction to an earlier tendency to wait passively for the kingdom, they summoned Christians to an active acceptance of their responsibility as those who were invited to citizenship in the kingdom.

The result was often a one-sided stress on human agency which has appeared occasionally even in more recent years. The following passages from church-school materials for intermediates, published in 1949, are illustrative: The Methodist Youth Fellowship is "the organization through which young people of the church work out their plans to help build God's kingdom on earth." A boy vows, "I will begin where I am now to change things so that the Kingdom of God will come in." "The church in the twentieth century is building the Kingdom of God in a troubled world." [125]

In recent decades, however, many warnings have been sounded against earlier assumptions that the removal of injustices or changes in political, economic, or social systems would make the kingdom real. Such exaggerated trust in external programs is also seen as indicative of a primary reliance on human effort instead of divine action, whereas the coming of the kingdom is mainly a gift of God. Already in 1932 John Paterson insisted: "The Kingdom of God does not come from beneath; it is from above. It is not a new environment men need; it is a new heart." [126]

This more realistic attitude finds expression in two main ways. Methodists with a liberal or neo-liberal perspective speak of the kingdom as basically the work of the spirit of God calling forth men's active response. According to the Episcopal Address of 1952,

[124] *The Preacher and the People* (New York: Abingdon Press, 1922), p. 147.
[125] *Intermediate Closely Graded Lessons*, 1949, Course IX, Part 3 B, Pupil's Book, pp. 105, 109; Course VIII, 3 B, Pupil's Book, p. 97; Leader's Guide, p. 56.
[126] "Some Ethical Insights of Prophecy," *Religion in Life*, 1 (1932), 54.

its creation is a co-operative task involving both God and man. . . . Its achievement is through the spiritual energy imparted by His spirit in human hearts, but its final consummation comes slowly through the joint efforts of God and man, working side by side, in the struggle to create a new and divine order and to make His will be done on earth as it is in heaven.[127]

Harris Franklin Rall declares that The Methodist Church, "while recognizing that all is of God . . . has affirmed God's grace in working through man and man's opportunity and obligation as working together with God, rejecting both activism and quietism." [128] Rall himself regards the kingdom as basically the gift of God which must be met by man's obedient trust; it is thus "both gift and task, Gabe und Aufgabe." [129]

Sharing essentially this view, DeWolf suggests that the figure of cultivating a vineyard is more appropriate to the actual situation than that of building the kingdom.[130] Georgia Harkness agrees, but prefers the analogy of Jesus' parable of the sower. Men are to sow the seed and fertilize the soil, but God brings the kingdom. Yet this involves human responsibility in the reshaping of physical and social structures.[131]

Quite different from this conception is the view which Paul Ramsey calls a "negative social gospel." "The measures adopted by Christian social action are not first of all for the implementation of Christian love. They rather serve the purpose of negative restraint, of eliminating glaring evil." But positively it is only God who brings the kingdom nearer. "Nothing man does can actually bring the kingdom, even though he must assume the task of restraining and holding within bounds the kingdoms of evil."

Ramsey, too, employs the analogy of the gardener, but in his view Christian social action "cultivates the garden to keep down the tares" rather than to help grow vegetables. It "must hinder all hindrances to the good life," thus preparing men to receive the kingdom when the Lord accomplishes it. Without such action "the kingdoms of this

---

[127] General Conference Journal, 1952, p. 158.
[128] R. Newton Flew (ed.), The Nature of the Church, p. 336.
[129] Christianity, p. 37.
[130] Trends and Frontiers of Religious Thought (Nashville: National Methodist Student Movement, 1955), p. 89.
[131] The Modern Rival of Christian Faith, p. 174.

world, and men in them, cannot be made ready to have God's will done in their midst." [132]

Tilson expresses a similar point of view. He affirms, for example, the Christian's responsibility for political action, but adds: "This does not mean that we may some day legislate the Kingdom of God into existence, but it does mean that we have no excuse for sitting on the sidelines while others legislate it out of existence." [133]

Views as diverse as the two we have expounded can hardly be reconciled. In their net effect on social action, however, they are closer together than might appear. Both assert emphatically the responsibility of Christians to act in society in accord with the ethics of the kingdom. Even though one may aim to kill weeds and the other to grow better tomatoes, if both actually cultivate the garden the result will be fewer weeds and better tomatoes. They can therefore hoe side by side. Yet the situation is not quite so simple. At many points the social policies sought by the two theories may diverge widely; in consequence one may want to grow potatoes and the other pole beans. Programs which seek mainly to restrain evil and those which aim primarily to advance the good will often converge, but at other times they are likely to differ sharply. Then it becomes all the more important that those who represent them continue to work with full mutual respect in the same garden.

c) *The Realization of the Kingdom*

Early in the century Methodists shared with most other Protestants a high degree of optimism regarding the earthly actualization of the kingdom. In 1920 Edwin D. Mouzon summoned the church to the "great battle that is to destroy all the strongholds of iniquity, that is to make America Christian through and through, and to bring in that glad day when

Upon earth's grateful sod
Shall rest thy city of our God.[134]

---

[132] "A Theology of Social Action," *Social Action*, Vol. XII, No. 8, Oct. 15, 1946, pp. 10-12. In Ramsey's view social action is in part the thoughtful modern Christian's substitute for an eschatology which he can no longer share. Not expecting the imminent end of history, he seeks to prepare for God's final gift of the kingdom whenever it comes.

[133] *Should Christians Drink?*, pp. 108-9.

[134] "Translating Christ into Our National Life," *Christian Advocate*, 95 (1920), 483.

As late as 1932 a "Washington observer" could say, according to the editor of *The Christian Advocate:* "Whenever I see a Methodist, I say to myself, 'There goes a man who really believes that some day the world is going to begin to "live happily ever afterward." ' " [135]

Even today a tempered hopefulness has its champions. G. Bromley Oxnam, for example, takes issue with theologians who expect the kingdom to be established only when God acts at the end of history to inaugurate a new order. He writes: "This, to me, is highly speculative. . . . I have never been able to see why God's purpose cannot be realized in history. . . . Jesus is for me the hope of the world, this world, and the next world. I believe in the Kingdom of God on earth realizable in time." [136]

In a similar vein, the Council of Bishops in 1958 took to task the "theologians who center attention upon 'the end of history,' 'the depravity of man,' and 'the second coming,' " and declare the kingdom "to be unrealizable in history." They went on to affirm: "The Christian faith holds that love conquers, that hearts can be strangely warmed, that both new men and a new society are possible here and now. It is thus that Jesus comes. It is thus the Holy Spirit works." [137]

But a strong tide is running against such optimistic expectations. Waldo Beach, a Methodist, joins with H. Richard Niebuhr, representing the Reformed tradition, in pointing out the failure of man's nineteenth-century hopes for "a warless, happy, and secure world. The sequence of the tragic events of the time seems to make the confidence in the realization of a Kingdom of God on earth a fond and foolish illusion." [138] Others point out that the Christian is a citizen of two worlds; since "this space-time world will always be imperfect and finite," no complete accomplishment of the divine purpose may be expected here. Yet we are called to live in the space-time world "always in the light of the eternal gospel." [139]

Thus the substitution of an eternal for an earthly perspective may become a solid basis for an ultimate optimism. Robert S. Michaelson, for example, after interpreting the kingdom in terms of God's sovereignty and providence, his grace disclosed in Christ, and his judgment,

---

[135] *Christian Advocate*, 107 (1932), 280.
[136] *A Testament of Faith*, pp. 59, 131.
[137] "A Message to The Methodist Church," adopted at Miami Beach, April 10, 1958.
[138] Beach and Niebuhr (eds.), *Christian Ethics*, p. 476.
[139] *Foundations of Christian Teaching in Methodist Churches*, II, pp. 1, 6.

presents it also as "a promise which constitutes our sole lasting hope." In this hope Christians may look forward with conviction to "the healing of the nations and the realization of the glorious liberty of the children of God." [140] Significantly, such faith in the final coming of the divine kingdom is proving for many today not an excuse for indifference to the problems of society, but a resource for concerned social action.

The connection appears clearly in the thought of L. Harold De-Wolf, who combines the recognition that the complete realization of the kingdom lies beyond earthly history with the conviction that God's rule then will be of a piece with what we know of his rule now. In DeWolf's view, the fact that the consummation of God's reign is described in the New Testament as a return of Christ evidences confidence that it will be in harmony with what God has revealed of himself in Jesus of Nazareth. It will therefore fulfill the deepest meaning of love.

The important substantial center of Christian eschatology is that, despite all the alternations and uncertainties of this present life, God will have the last word and his last word will but fulfill his word of love spoken in Jesus Christ. It is precisely by that word of love that we Christians are bound now to guide our personal and social action, and in it we find the very meaning of "life and history." [141]

C. Conclusions

Certain broad conclusions may now be drawn from our survey of the social implications which Methodists find in the basic structure of their Christian belief.

1. Since the early decades of the twentieth century there has been a trend toward greater concern with doctrinal questions and a more conscious, explicit effort to relate social thought and action to basic religious beliefs. For example, the social significance of the nature of the church and the bearing of God's redemptive act in Christ on the worth of persons were largely overlooked in the earlier years, but now have an important place.

2. Marked changes have occurred in the content of beliefs which

[140] Robert S. Michaelson, "The Kingdom of God in America and the Task of the Church," *Faith and Ethics*, ed. Paul Ramsey, p. 285.
[141] *The Case for Theology in Liberal Perspective*, pp. 180-81.

have been related to social attitudes since the beginning of the century. For example, there is now greater stress on the sovereignty and grace of God, the limitations and sinfulness of man, the difficulties in the way of social improvement, and the transhistorical reference of the kingdom of God.

3. Methodist social thought is now influenced predominantly by neo-liberal or evangelical liberal and by realistic or neo-Reformation theology. However, the older liberalism is still represented.

4. On the whole, official and semiofficial statements have been less affected by recent trends than have individual theologians. Many of the clergy whose positions of leadership enable them to influence church-wide declarations by their votes received their theological training when liberalism was dominant, and most lay delegates to official bodies are relatively unfamiliar with realistic and neo-Reformation theology.

5. Representatives of varying theological standpoints often conceive and express differently the reasons for Christian social responsibility, but agree overwhelmingly in asserting on theological grounds the reality of that responsibility. They also evidence considerable agreement in the social goals advocated.

6. The social thinking of Methodists has been more closely related to the basic beliefs they hold as Protestant Christians than to the doctrinal emphases particularly associated with the Wesleyan tradition.

Leaving aside now the earlier decades of the century, what do Methodists think today in the six doctrinal areas examined, as indicated by their utterances in the past twenty-five years? The major emphases which we have discovered can be summarized in a series of brief propositions.

1. Authoritative guidance for human social relations is to be found in the Bible. Its central message proclaims the deeds of God and calls men to respond in faith and love. Though it contains no blueprints, it discloses, particularly in the life, teachings, and death of Jesus, and in the religious and ethical teachings which he inspired, attitudes and principles which provide our major clues to God's will for society.

2. The central foundation of Christian social responsibility is faith in God and his mighty acts. Since God is the Creator and Father of

139

all men, his worshipers are responsible for treating their fellow men as brothers in one family. As righteous Sovereign and Lord of history, he demands righteousness in those who serve him; unjust social institutions and practices fall under his stern judgment, and cannot endure. As Redeemer who acts in reconciling love to restore humanity to its true vocation, he summons men to respond in attitudes and actions of reconciliation toward each other.

3. The Christian view of man calls forth serious concern for the welfare of men in society. All men are children of God, created in the divine image for fellowship with God, and all are the objects of his saving love disclosed in Jesus Christ; hence each person has an infinite worth which others are bound to respect. Because of the sacredness of personality under God, Christians should oppose all social practices which obstruct and support those which advance the fullest growth of persons. Man's fellowship with God and human community as well have been broken by sin; Christians must therefore act both to restrain and to redeem the sinner and to control the social consequences of sin and the conditions which encourage its spread.

4. God has acted in Jesus Christ at infinite cost to redeem sinful humanity. This imparts to men an immeasurable worth which they must respect, prompts grateful recipients of the divine grace to act redemptively toward each other, and provides a firm foundation for hope that God's purposes will ultimately be consummated. The salvation which God offers combines personal regeneration and social transformation. Dependent basically on divine action, its fulfillment awaits the faithful, obedient response of dedicated Christians through whom God works.

5. The church is the body of Christ and the covenant people of God, commissioned to carry forward Christ's ministry of reconciliation by manifesting to men God's redemptive love and power. It must therefore transcend within itself the barriers of nationality, culture, class, and race, and seek to bring the whole of human life into maximum harmony with the divine intention. This imparts primary significance to the ministry of the laity in their day-to-day relationships in society.

6. The kingdom of God means primarily the actualization in all human relations of God's righteous, loving will, but also his reign in judgment even when his will is violated. It is basically the work of

God; for some Methodists man's role is that of co-operating with God in realizing divine ends; for others, that of restraining evil and thus preparing for God's ultimate gift of the kingdom. Both views call on Christians to seek in society the largest possible measure of justice and love. Only partially realizable within man's finite existence, the kingdom will come in its fullness beyond history; faith in its final consummation is a resource for social action now in accord with its norms.

D. Methodism and Ecumenical Theology

Since we have been considering mainly in this chapter the beliefs which Methodists hold as Protestant Christians, it would be highly desirable to see them in relation to the convictions which inspire the social outlook of the ecumenical movement, of which Methodism forms a part.

Space does not permit such a comparison here. However, there is considerable evidence that the doctrinal considerations advanced by Methodists in support of social attitudes and policies broadly parallel those urged by the Federal and National Councils of Churches during the same periods, and to a lesser degree those emanating from the World Council of Churches since 1948. Neo-liberal influences are probably less strong in the National Council and still less so in the World Council, with neo-Reformation theology correspondingly stronger than in The Methodist Church. Yet it is a basic ecumenical conviction that the struggle for justice, freedom, and peace is God's will, hence integral to the life and witness of the church, and this conviction is supported by many of the same theological grounds as those noted above.

Three examples may be cited. In 1954 the National Board of the National Council of Churches declared:

God as we know him through Christ is the God of history, of nations and peoples, as well as of individual souls. It is his will that his Kingdom be realized among men and that his lordship be acknowledged over . . . every department of life, including economic institutions and practices. . . . All men are created in the image of God; and, though they are in history sinful and rebellious as the slaves of their own self-will, God seeks to redeem them from their self-centeredness.[142]

---

[142] "Christian Principles and Assumptions for Economic Life," September 1954.

One of the reports of the Evanston Assembly of the World Council of Churches affirmed:

Christian social responsibility is grounded in the mighty acts of God, who is revealed in Jesus Christ our Lord. . . . In the call to responsible social action, the promise and the commandment of the righteous and loving God require us to recognize that in every human being Christ Himself comes to claim our service. Responding to God's love in Christ and being aware of his final judgment Christians will act responsibly. . . . From Christ men receive the direction for their service, the obligation to share heartily in the world's work and daily tasks, and the responsibility to seek a better social and political life.[143]

Both nationally and internationally, the ecumenical movement has focused much attention on the church—its nature, unity, mission, and role in society. Since the Oxford Conference of 1937 intense labors have been devoted to a deeper understanding of the church as a redemptive community serving the redemption of the other communities of men. Much of the new emphasis on the ministry of the laity is an outgrowth of this endeavor. Our examination of Methodist thought on the church shows that Methodism has both contributed to and been stimulated by this new understanding of the church's nature and social significance.

The social pronouncements of the National Council of Churches and the voluminous literature of the World Council contain many other comparable indications of a broad similarity.

[143] *The Evanston Report*, ed. W. A. Visser 't Hooft (New York: Harper and Brothers, 1955), p. 112.

CHAPTER FIVE

The Beliefs of Methodists in 1959

THE PRECEDING CHAPTERS HAVE EXAMINED THE IMPLICATIONS for social concern of the religious beliefs of twentieth-century Methodists, as those implications are discovered in the published utterances of individuals and groups. The method has thus been that of library or documentary research. This type of inquiry is indispensable to such a study as this, and it has yielded important results. For two reasons, however, the research committee decided to supplement it with a more direct approach. First, no amount of information culled from the books and articles of particular thinkers or from the pronouncements of conferences of leaders can mirror accurately the thinking of the rank and file of Methodist people. Secondly, statements covering six decades cannot possibly disclose accurately the thinking of Methodists in 1959. In the attempt to overcome these difficulties at least partially, a questionnaire was devised dealing with religious, social, and ethical beliefs, and with social action. The results of its use, as they bear on the theme of this volume, will be reported in the present chapter.

The two forms of research have proceeded in large measure independently. The form and content of the questionnaire were finally determined from six to eight months before the writing of Chapters One to four, while the findings of the survey were not finally tabulated and available for interpretation until after the first draft of these chapters was completed. These circumstances may occasion some lack of integration of the results of the two types of research. On the other hand, they may make it possible to compare the findings of each method with those of the other. The net result will be a more factual account of how Methodists think and act than would otherwise be possible. No attempt has been made to revise the foregoing chapters to accord with the findings of the questionnaire. On the other hand, the discussion of the questionnaire will inevitably be related at many points to conclusions previously reached, and any desirable modifications will be indicated.[1]

The content of the study of Methodist beliefs is derived from responses received from 357 cooperating churches, 267 of which returned questionnaires from a stratified random sample of their membership. A combined membership of these churches constitutes 150,340 Methodists. A carefully chosen random sample of every tenth member chosen alphabetically was asked to respond to the questionnaire. The questionnaires then were returned to the pastor in a sealed envelope and forwarded to the School of Theology for processing. The number of questionnaires which were usable and which were processed totaled 5,020. Since the churches selected were statistically representative of the 22,435 Methodist churches, the data at most may be said to be representative of Methodism as a whole or at least representative of the 150,340 members of the co-operating congregations.

As we examine the results of the questionnaire, we shall be concerned not only with the evidence it affords regarding the theological convictions of Methodists today, but particularly with any light it may shed on the relation between these convictions and the ethical and social beliefs and activities of those who hold them. In order to facilitate comparisons, we shall follow the same order as that adopted in the preceding chapters. Attention will be directed first to the views of the respondents on the relation between doctrine and life; second, to their orientation with respect to the chief historic Methodist emphases; third, to their positions on the basic beliefs of ecumenical Christianity; and finally, to other evidence in the questionnaire concerning the bearing of their religious beliefs on their social views and acts.

One characteristic of the structure of the questionnaire must be kept constantly in mind if the findings are to be soundly appraised. Questions 1-20 and 26-44 offer a choice among four or five statements

---

[1] The full text of the questionnaire, with the results tabulated by jurisdictions, will be found in Appendix B to this volume. Also included are an account of the methodology, structure, and form of the questionnaire and an interpretation of the representativeness of its findings. Readers wishing more details than can be given in this chapter are therefore urged to consult Appendix B.

ranged on a continuum. In the nature of the case, adjoining statements normally shade into each other, like colors in the rainbow. In many instances, therefore, possible alternatives overlap; they are not mutually exclusive, nor are they meant to be. In answering these questions the respondent was asked to check under each heading the one statement which seemed to him to correspond most closely to his own belief, expressing better than any other what he regarded as centrally important. Thus the selection of a particular statement may be quite consistent with a recognition of important elements of truth in one or more of the other positions not checked.

A. Theology and Life

Question 13 concerns the extent to which belief is thought to influence conduct. Here a surprising 43.3 per cent adopt the extreme position that "what one believes is all-important, because it determines conduct," while 37.2 per cent affirm that "our actions are affected by our basic beliefs more than by anything else." Thus more than four out of five assert decisively the relevance of theology to ethical action. Only 7.2 per cent regard right conduct as "much more important than correct beliefs," and only 8 per cent are willing to take the position often expressed a generation ago, that "it doesn't matter what one believes—it's how he lives that counts." The jurisdictional scores reveal virtual unanimity, with the Northeastern Jurisdiction manifesting a slightly lower estimate of theological relevance than the others (38.7 per cent and 36 per cent favoring the first two positions cited, and 8.2 per cent and 11.9 per cent the last two). It is also interesting to note that the ministers largely agree with the total group. They score slightly higher on the first two positions (47.5 per cent and 41 per cent respectively) which assert the relevance of belief to conduct, but less than one per cent are willing to say that beliefs do not matter.

These returns seem to indicate, in theory at least, a trend toward greater theological concern in present-day Methodism. Or have the respondents replied as they thought they were expected to reply in a questionnaire originating in a School of Theology? The indications of question 13 are partly confirmed by the answers to questions 21-25, which suggest that well over a majority, and in some instances about three-fourths, derive from their religious beliefs principles which help

145

to guide their conduct and social policy on such questions as drinking, segregation, marriage, and divorce.[2]

Yet answers to some of the specific ethical and social questions suggest that in daily decisions religious beliefs are much less influential and various nontheological factors more weighty than the replies to question 13 indicate. It is difficult to find any clear relation between the religious beliefs affirmed and the attitudes expressed toward participation in war (question 27). Likewise, the two questions on race (28 and 29) reveal clear regional differences among those who manifest considerable theological agreement. Problems like these will be more fully discussed later in this chapter.[3] At the moment they are mentioned simply to show the need for caution in interpreting question 13. The fact remains that Methodists say that they regard religious beliefs as exerting powerful influence on conduct.

B. Major Methodist Emphases

In Chapters Two and Three we examined five major doctrinal emphases which are traceable to John Wesley and early Methodism. We discovered that four of these—sin and repentance, justification by faith, Christian experience, and holiness of life—continue to play their part in Methodist theology today, in some respects lending encouragement to social concern and in others socially neutral. It is now our task to explore the evidence regarding these four emphases and their social significance. The fifth historic Wesleyan doctrine, the universal availability of salvation, is not dealt with in the questionnaire.

1. SIN AND REPENTANCE

The notion of sin plays a very small part in the views of man disclosed in the survey. Only 3.9 per cent think of man primarily as "a creature of God who in sinful pride has rejected his Creator and deified himself," and only 4 per cent conceive him chiefly as "a being who has blurred the divine image in which God has created him." In sharp contrast, 78.2 per cent think of man primarily as "a rational being capable of knowing God and entering into fellowship with him," while 10.5 per cent avow the extreme humanistic position which

[2] For a more detailed discussion of these questions, see below, pp. 150-51.
[3] See below, pp. 155 ff.

146

sees man as "a product of nature whose innate powers for achieving goodness, truth, and beauty are almost unlimited."

However, the replies regarding sin itself imply a much less favorable view of man. A total of 38.6 per cent view it either as an inherited corruption (17.1 per cent) or as "a condition of self-centeredness and pride which distorts the wills of men and affects their best choices" (21.5 per cent). Almost 51 per cent, instead of rooting it in man's nature, define it chiefly as voluntary disobedience to the will of God, partly due to our involvement in society. But only 5 per cent dismiss sin as "anti-social conduct caused by ignorance or bad environment." [4]

These replies to questions 3 and 4 may indicate a real inconsistency. On the other hand, it must be remembered that under each topic the respondent was asked to check the statement which seemed to correspond *most closely* to his own belief. Many of the 78.2 per cent who agree that man is "a rational being capable of knowing God and entering into fellowship with Him" may believe this statement to express better than the others what they regard as *centrally important*, while still recognizing fully the seriousness of human sin. Some of these might feel no incongruity between this view of man and a conception which regards sin as a condition of self-centeredness affecting all of man's attitudes and actions. In this case there would be no serious discrepancy.

The answers to some of the other questions shed further light on Methodist views of sin. A total of 93.5 per cent define salvation (question 5) in ways which imply a clear recognition of the sin from which man needs to be saved. Here 2.1 per cent think of salvation as "going to heaven and escaping hell"; 41.4 per cent, as "peace and joy with God through His forgiveness of our sins"; and 50 per cent, as "power to live a new life in fellowship with God and man." For only 2.3 per cent does it mean only "the integration and highest fulfillment of the self in harmonious social relations." The replies to question 8 on how men are saved, question 11 on religious experience, and question 18 on the way to a more Christian society also indicate a serious attitude toward sin.

Thus the evidence of the questionnaire supports the judgment of Chapter Four that contemporary Methodists recognize the reality

[4] See above, pp. 115-18.

of man's sin and his need of repentance. What bearing this recognition may have on Methodist social attitudes is not apparent. However, that it is not a deterrent, and may be a stimulus, to social action is indicated by the fact that most of those responding believe in the possibility of social change and espouse policies directed toward improvement in specific areas. By substantial majorities they believe in support for the United Nations, conscientious participation in political life, the rehabilitation of criminals, and in general in progress toward the fulfillment of God's purposes in society. Data now to be examined suggest that this hopefulness is grounded partially in faith in the redeemability of man through the power and love of God.

2. Justification by Faith

The questionnaire indicates that a majority of Methodists still affirm what John Wesley called the "door of religion"—justification by grace through faith. Asked in question 8 how men are saved, 54.3 per cent agree with the reply, "by divine grace when they respond in repentance and trustful obedience." A few (3.9 per cent) take the more Calvinistic position and declare that salvation comes "entirely by divine grace," but the largest number recognize as did Wesley the need for man freely to accept the grace of God which redeems him.

A minority hold views which deviate from the historic Methodist and Protestant position. The intellectualistic answer that we are saved "by believing that Jesus Christ is the Son of God" is given by 10.6 per cent, and 1.5 per cent place their reliance on human effort alone, asserting that men are saved "by their upright character."

Approximately a fourth (24.6 per cent) find salvation taking place through "belief in Jesus Christ and upright living." Some of these may be advocating in effect the Roman Catholic concept of salvation by "faith and works." It seems likely, however, that "upright living" connotes for most respondents not obedience to the divine law conceived as earning salvation, but rather the deeds of faith and love which the New Testament portrays as approved and expected by God in those who receive his saving mercy.

As to the bearing of these views respecting the way of salvation on social attitudes and practices, the questionnaire offers little evidence. We can only reaffirm the judgment expressed in Chapter Four, that Methodist attitudes toward justification by faith have mostly an individual significance, neither strengthening nor weakening social concern.

3. CHRISTIAN EXPERIENCE

The replies to question 11 constitute a strong reaffirmation of the historic Methodist position on Christian experience. A total of 46.1 per cent subscribe to a thoroughly Wesleyan statement of the doctrine of the witness of the Spirit: "By the inner witness of the Spirit, every Christian can have a sure trust that through the sacrificial love of Christ his sins are forgiven and he is reconciled to God." The less specific affirmation that "Christians may personally experience the presence and power of God in their lives" is preferred by 41.5 per cent. Thus 87.6 per cent declare that a firsthand awareness of God of greater or less intensity is the normative expectation of the Christian life. Almost identically small minorities adopt the polar positions on this question, 3.9 per cent agreeing that "we cannot be sure whether our sins are forgiven; God alone knows," and 4 per cent favoring the broad interpretation that "we experience religion whenever we co-operate with our fellows in high ethical endeavors."

In view of this result, it is no occasion for surprise that as many as 34.6 per cent view the church (question 7) as "the community of those who have been renewed through Jesus Christ and empowered by the Holy Spirit." What is surprising is that almost as many (30.4 per cent) are willing to define the church simply as "a society of those who have joined together in their quest for the religious life." Since only 12.4 per cent do not affirm one of the central positions on Christian experience, the religious questers must include 18 per cent of the personal experiencers! Such an overlapping might consistently occur, since it may be assumed that some who quest will gain the experience they look for. "They that seek shall find." Yet if these 18 per cent have actually found spiritual reality, would they not be more likely to align themselves with those for whom the church is a spiritually renewed and Spirit-empowered community? Thus real doubt arises with respect to the large number who stress personal Christian experience. It seems altogether likely that some of them are not voicing their own considered judgment, but simply expressing approval of what they think Methodists are supposed to believe.

Nevertheless, even a liberal allowance for error would still leave

149

large percentages supporting the historic Methodist emphasis, thereby confirming the documentary evidence in Chapter Four. With regard to the social significance of the doctrine of assurance the questionnaire sheds no new light. In view of the near-universality of the 87.6 per cent and the absence from the questions on social beliefs of data related to this problem, we have no basis for concluding that belief in Christian experience either increases or decreases social concern.

4. HOLINESS OF LIFE

The replies to question 12, "Growth in Grace," indicate that the Wesleyan doctrine of sanctification and perfection is exerting more influence today than the evidence in Chapter Three suggested. It is true that only 11.9 per cent declare with Wesley that "Christians should expect through the power of God to attain perfect love in this life." But 81.9 per cent—the largest number to support any one position in the entire questionnaire—agree that "with God's help both individuals and society may progress toward the fulfillment of His purposes." This view goes beyond the individual expectations of the preceding one to include society, hence it occupies the fourth or extreme place in the continuum. In one respect it is less advanced, since progress toward fulfillment represents a more modest expectation than the attainment of perfect love.

Interestingly, the four out of five who affirm the possibility of individual and social advance are almost exactly matched by the 80.4 per cent who in question 15 affirm the abiding validity of the ethical principles of Jesus—implying that his teachings can be followed—and the 78.2 per cent who think of man (question 3) mainly as a rational being capable of knowing and having fellowship with God. Strong evidence of a real trend here is found in the fact that these scores represent three of the four largest concentrations of support for single positions appearing in any of the questions.[5]

Harmonious with these indications are the views on the kingdom of God (question 10). A total of 79.2 per cent conceive of the kingdom as either the righteous rule of God or the fulfillment of his purposes, two-thirds of them stressing the efforts of men aided by God and one-third the divine initiative which elicits man's co-opera-

---

[5] In question 36 the U.N. commands the approval of 79.6 per cent.

tion. Moving in the same direction are the 50 per cent in question 5 who view salvation as "power to live a new life in fellowship with God and man," and the 34.6 per cent who stress the empowerment of the Holy Spirit in their concept of the church (question 7).

Without much more detailed analysis it is impossible to determine the bearing of this generally hopeful attitude on specific social questions. It may be reflected in the 63.1 per cent who either favor total abstinence from alcoholic beverages (54.2 per cent) or go beyond this to urge work for prohibition (8.9 per cent); in the 93 per cent who see politics as an area of Christian responsibility; in the 69.7 per cent who emphasize the rehabilitation of criminals; in the 70.4 per cent who allow school teachers to join any "cause" organization so long as such membership does not interfere with effective teaching; and in the 68.4 per cent who grant to ministers the right to take on controversial issues any position which they regard as Christian.

In this generally harmonious symphony several dissonant chords are sounded. Almost three out of ten respondents (27.9 per cent) approve the use of alcoholic beverages if it is temperate and "within reason"—certainly a higher percentage of advocates of "moderation" than would have appeared a generation ago. An additional 3.5 per cent take a still more permissive attitude, holding that a Christian may drink either "without reference to religious scruples" (1.1 per cent) or socially to avoid offending his host (2.4 per cent). The replies on Christian support of or participation in war disclose the presence in many Methodists of a strongly nationalistic sentiment.[6] "Personal satisfaction and meaning in work" is for 37 per cent the highest value to be considered in the choice of an occupation, and another 5.5 per cent are content to list either "security in job and residence" (4.8 per cent) or "income and social status" (.7 per cent).

Nevertheless, the over-all impression is that of a body of Christians who think that through the power of God human life should and can move toward divine goals. The questionnaire does not mention sanctification or holiness, but a majority of those who have recorded their responses apparently believe in the possibility, for individuals and groups, of changes which point in the direction of the transformation of life which these terms connote.

[6] See below, pp. 176 ff, 289.

C. Basic Christian Beliefs

1. GENERAL ORIENTATION

A revealing picture of the relation of Methodists to typical doctrines of ecumenical Christian faith appears when the responses to questions 1-10, representing broadly an orthodox-humanist continuum, are tabulated together. For this purpose we need not now refer to the content of the specific answers,[7] but only remember that position one represents the extreme conservative orientation on each topic and position four or five the opposite pole. In each case the modal category (that checked by the largest number) is underlined twice and the second-ranking reply is underlined once.

Table 8

Scores of 5,020 Methodists on a continuum ranging from orthodoxy on the left to religious humanism on the right.

Question	Position					Write-In Answers	No Response
	1	2	3	4	5		
1. Bible	8.4	32.0	49.7	7.0		2.2	.7
2. God	10.0	60.1	11.4	11.3	3.0	2.6	1.6
3. Man	3.9	4.0	78.2	10.5		2.0	1.4
4. Sin	17.1	21.5	50.8	5.0		2.8	2.8
5. Meaning of Salvation	2.1	41.4	50.0	2.3		2.7	1.5
6. Christ	13.3	37.1	36.5	7.3		3.8	2.0
7. Church	6.3	23.7	34.6	30.4		2.5	2.5
8. Way of Salvation	3.9	10.6	54.3	24.6	1.5	3.5	1.6
9. Missions	19.9	42.9	23.3	8.5		3.4	2.0
10. Kingdom of God	12.7	26.4	52.8	1.8		2.4	3.9

The net impression yielded by this table is that Methodists on

[7] See Appendix B to this volume, pp. 275 ff.

their theological pilgrimage are walking down the middle of the road, with some preference for the "liberal" side of the middle. The modal category is always one of the middle positions, and only in two instances is the second-ranking position found at either extreme. But while three of the highest ranking scores are on the orthodox side of the scale and one is squarely in the middle, six are on the less orthodox side. Incidentally, the very small number of write-in answers and omissions suggests that the possibilities offered summarize acceptably the basic beliefs of the vast majority of Methodists, although in some instances it may indicate simply lack of the ability or the interest required to write an answer.

We turn now to a more concentrated examination of particular questions, notably those dealing with beliefs previously discovered to have definite social implications.

2. SPECIFIC BELIEFS

a) The Authority of the Bible

Approximately half of the respondents (49.7 per cent) affirm that the Bible, as "the unique historical record of God's revelation to inspired men . . . contains the Word of God" (question one). Willing to go still farther than this in asserting Biblical authority are 32 per cent who say that the Bible is the inspired word of God, although not all parts are of equal spiritual value. Only 8.4 per cent uphold the infallibility of the scriptures implied in the statement, "Every word is true because it came directly from God," and fewer still (7 per cent) represent the humanist extreme of treating the Bible as "one of several records of man's religious search." Thus 90 per cent trace the Biblical writings directly to the revelatory activity of God, though with variations in the role assigned to human agency.

A similarly high estimate of the validity of the ethical teachings of Jesus appears in the responses to question 15. The idea that these teachings were a kind of interim ethic, suitable for first-century Christians who expected the early end of the world but with limited application to us, is decisively rejected. Similar treatment is accorded the notion that Jesus' teachings set up general goals for Christians but which cannot be achieved in this world. These two statements together are supported by only 1.8 per cent. On the contrary, 80.4 per cent find in the gospels "basic principles which are just as valid now as

153

when first uttered." This is the next to the largest percentage of support accorded any statement in the entire questionnaire. Another 14.6 per cent view Jesus' teachings as "the most practical basis for human conduct." This may represent, as it was intended to do, approval for purely pragmatic reasons, but it may also connote for some a recognition of the realism as well as the truth of Jesus' teachings. Further evidence of the same kind is found in question 14, where 31.4 per cent —the second largest percentage—cite as the main reason for living a good life their conviction that "all Christians should follow the example of Jesus."

Such answers provide overwhelming confirmation of the conclusions reached in Chapter Four. Both investigations reveal Methodists as people who look to the Bible, and especially the New Testament gospels, for authoritative guidance regarding God's will for human relations.

b) God

The questionnaire yields little direct information on the social implications of the respondents' views of God, but it affords interesting clues nonetheless. The replies to question 2 on the nature of God disclose 82.8 per cent affirming views which definitely relate him to the life of his world. A clear majority (60.1 per cent) regard God as the trinitarian Lord "whose righteous will rules his whole creation." A total of 22.7 per cent find God working in nature and history, either as supremely personal Spirit realizing his purposes (11.4 per cent) or as the creative, perfecting power which supports the realization of values (11.3 per cent). Some of those who view God as "the awesome being, wholly other than man and the world, whom we encounter only in Jesus Christ" (10 per cent) may not relate him to the social scene. Yet historically many persons with this conception have courageously defied in God's name earthly dictators who sought to usurp his place. In the main, the answers tend to indicate agreement with the assertion of the sovereign righteousness of God noted in Chapter Four.

Similar reinforcement is found at two other points. On question 14 the main reason given (36.6 per cent) as to why a Christian should live a good life is simply that "it is the will of God." On question 20, 27 per cent, the second highest number, believe in safeguarding human rights chiefly because "man is ultimately responsible to God alone, and must be free to fulfill his responsibility." A somewhat different approach is made by a larger number (42.3 per cent), who maintain such rights to be important because "people should have unlimited opportunity to develop their capacities as children of God." Significantly, however, both groups, totaling 69.3 per cent, specifically relate support for human rights to the divine purpose.

c) Man

On the whole, the questionnaire indicates that Methodists hold an extremely optimistic view of man, which is all the more surprising in view of the tension, conflict, and insecurity of our time. On question 3 only 3.9 per cent regard man as a creature who in sinful pride has rejected his Creator, and only 4 per cent stress his having distorted the divine image in which he was created. The vast majority align themselves at the other end of the scale. A total of 78.2 per cent think of man as "a rational being capable of knowing God and entering into fellowship with Him," while 10.5 per cent find innate in him as a product of nature almost unlimited powers for achieving high values.

This picture is confirmed by the replies to question 10 on "Growth in Grace," where 81.9 per cent—the largest score for any category in the entire questionnaire—assert that "with God's help both individuals and society may progress toward the fulfillment of His purposes," and 11.3 per cent affirm that individual Christians "should expect through the power of God to attain perfect love in this life." It should be noted, however, that both of these statements root human accomplishment in the divine activity. A hopeful view of man is also implied in the view, previously mentioned and shared by 80.4 per cent, that the ethical principles found in Jesus' teachings remain valid today; only a being of high capacities could be expected to live by such principles. A similar view appears on question 20, where, as noted above, 42.3 per cent support human rights because men as children of God should have unlimited opportunity to develop their capacities, and where 14.3 per cent go beyond this to declare, as the chief basis for such rights, that man is by nature "a being of inherent dignity and worth."

A somewhat different note is sounded in the replies to question 4, where the orthodox side of the scale shows much greater strength. Approval of the traditional doctrine of original sin is affirmed by 17.1 per cent, while an additional 21.5 per cent adopt the view that sin is "a condition of self-centeredness and pride which distorts the

155

wills of men and affects even their best choices." A bare majority (50.8 per cent) define sin as "voluntary attitudes and actions partially due to our involvement in society, which are contrary to God's will," and only 5 per cent view it as "anti-social conduct caused by ignorance or bad environment." In each instance the Central and Southeastern Jurisdictions are noticeably more conservative than the others, showing respectively 28.8 per cent and 24.6 per cent who believe in original sin, 25.7 per cent and 26.4 per cent who consider sin a condition of self-centeredness and pride, and only 33.4 per cent and 39 per cent who conceive it as voluntary disobedience to God.

It is impossible satisfactorily to reconcile the replies to question 4 with those to the other questions cited. Yet the major tendency even in this question is in the same direction as that of the others, and the net impression given by all of them together is that Methodists hold a very high estimate of human nature—higher, indeed, than that expressed in the documents previously examined.

To what degree are Methodist attitudes on social questions consistent with this rather rosy picture of man? Here the evidence is ambiguous. Replies to the questions on war and race (27 and 28) reveal little correlation. The respondents emphatically reject the notion of inherent racial inferiority (only 1.9 per cent accept this), and 75.1 per cent believe that "members of all races should have the same opportunities." Yet of these three-fourths, 22.8 per cent want segregation continued in order to preserve racial purity, and the other 52.3 per cent believe that "present patterns must be changed gradually." Only 18.9 per cent maintain without qualification that all racial discrimination and enforced segregation should be abolished. This percentage is difficult to harmonize with the total of 56.6 per cent who support human rights because man is a child of God (42.3 per cent) or a being of inherent worth (14.3 per cent). Apparently many of these affirm rights in the abstract which they are not willing to grant to specific racial minorities. There is little correlation between their social and their religious beliefs.

A similar incongruity appears with reference to the Christian attitude toward war. Here 47.2 per cent accept the obligation to support their country in war "when its continued existence is at stake, apart from considerations of justice." This readiness to subordinate righteousness to national self-preservation hardly shows great respect for human worth, whether that of the war supporters who disregard justice or that of the possible victims of their injustice. Significantly, only 3.2 per cent have been led by the realization that nuclear war threatens universal destruction and makes justice impossible to refuse support for such war. Only 2.5 per cent take the full pacifist position of refusing to support or participate in war in any circumstance.

On the other hand, in question 37, quite consistently with a high conception of man, 69.7 per cent list as the main purpose of a prison "the rehabilitation of offenders and their restoration to normal life in society," while only 1.2 per cent conceive this purpose to be "the punishment of the enemies of society." The considerations listed as chiefly desirable in the choice of an occupation (question 38) also reflect a positive view of man. Only 5.5 per cent think primarily in terms of income and social status (.7 per cent) or security in job and residence (4.8 per cent), while 37 per cent maintain that occupations should be chosen mainly in terms of "personal satisfaction and meaning in work," and 50.6 per cent regard as decisive "the use of personal capacities" either in service to mankind (14.6 per cent) or in stewardship to God (36 per cent).

A similar impression is created by the answers to two questions dealing with international relations. For example, 45.4 per cent believe that economic and technical aid (question 35) should be "allocated on the basis of the needs of humanity as a whole," while about the same number (44.7 per cent) think that such allocations should "consider the welfare of the people involved as well as American interests." Likewise, with reference to the United Nations (question 36) only 3.7 per cent advocate unlimited national sovereignty, while 79.6 per cent support the UN as "our best political hope for world peace," and 9.8 per cent of the rest want the UN to be superseded now or soon by full world government.

There is thus among Methodists a good deal of evidence of social and ethical attitudes in real harmony with their theological beliefs concerning man, while in two crucial areas marked inconsistency is apparent.

d) Christ and Salvation

The response to question 6 reveals views of the person of Jesus Christ which support the high place accorded in questions 14 and

15 to the teaching and example of Jesus. The two views which presuppose the strongest belief in the relevance of Jesus to man's ethical and social life, while ascribing to him exalted authority, are affirmed by a total of 73.6 per cent. Of these 37.1 per cent view Jesus as "both divine and human," while 36.5 per cent think of him as "a man uniquely endowed and called by God to reveal Him to man." At one extreme 13.3 per cent conceive Jesus Christ as being "God Himself, not subject to human limitations"; at the other, only 7.3 per cent regard him simply as "one of the world's great spiritual teachers." Aside from these estimates of relevance and authority, the question sheds no light on the social implications of Methodist Christology. There is no question on the Atonement or the work of Christ.

A number of the questions state or imply positions regarding salvation from which significant conclusions can be drawn. For one thing, it is plain that for Methodists salvation is not unrelated to life here and now. In question 5 only 2.1 per cent think of it mainly as "going to heaven and escaping hell," and question 19 makes clear that even a primarily futuristic conception would not make irrelevant man's social problems here and now. An overwhelming 86.1 per cent state that belief in life after death either enhances our sense of social responsibility (47.4 per cent) or is one of the strongest motivations for such responsibility (38.7 per cent).

Salvation for 41.4 per cent means "peace and joy with God through His forgiveness of our sins," while 50 per cent view it as "power to live a new life in fellowship with God and man" (question 5). The first of these positions presumably is chiefly individualistic in application; the second could be so interpreted, but seems to imply also a social reference. The two leading answers to question 8 relate ethical conduct to the way of salvation: 54.3 per cent expect "repentance and trustful obedience" as the human response to the grace of God, and 24.6 per cent think that men are saved by belief in Christ and upright living. But neither of these specifically raises the question of social concern.

Two other theological questions yield markedly individualistic results. Almost two-thirds of all respondents interpret the chief aim of missions (question 9) in individualistic terms: 19.9 per cent take the traditional view that missions aim "to save those who know not Christ, and who will be lost unless He is made known to them";

and 42.9 per cent see the missionary's goal as that of bringing "individuals to accept and live by the good news" of God's redemptive love revealed in Christ. But 31.8 per cent take a broader view: 23.3 per cent think missions should seek "to release in both individuals and society the redemptive power of God . . . so that all human life may be made whole"; and 8.5 per cent conceive the aim primarily in social terms—"to improve the well-being of people by giving them new and improved methods of agriculture, industry, education, and health."

Individualism appears also in question 18. According to 44.8 per cent, twice as many as the second-ranking group, a more Christian society will come mainly through "the conversion of individuals to Jesus Christ." Some of these may think of a Christian society as one composed of Christians, without reference to social change. Among those for whom "a more Christian society" means changes in social institutions, this answer may indicate a belief either that conversion as such confers the will and the wisdom needed to solve the most serious social problems, or simply that the spiritual transformation of individuals is the primary condition of social advance. The first alternative seems largely ruled out by the fact that on question 17 only 8 per cent agree that "social change is no responsibility of the church, since if individuals are soundly converted social problems will take care of themselves." If the second interpretation is correct, then many of the 44.8 per cent do not differ greatly from the 22.6 per cent who expect a Christian society to come chiefly through "the efforts of individual Christians for social betterment."

Supporting a partially social conception of salvation is the fact that a total of 86.1 per cent of the respondents to question 17 view social change as a partial or major task of the church. A like inference may be drawn from the circumstance, previously noted, that approximately seven respondents out of ten think that prisons should serve a redemptive function, seeking primarily the rehabilitation of offenders. A similar implication is perhaps to be found in the views recorded concerning politics. Only 1.5 per cent view politics as "of no concern to the Christian, whose citizenship is not of this world," and only a few more (2.3 per cent) treat political activity as a necessary evil, participation in which Christians should avoid as much as possible to guard against contamination. In sharp contrast, 93 per cent think that politics should either "call forth the serious and intelligent concern of the conscientious Christian" (63.6 per cent) or be regarded by Christians "as a special responsibility" (29.4 per cent). Such replies suggest that many of the large number who see in the conversion of individuals the main path to a Christian society are agreeing verbally with what they interpret as an approved religious statement, but that they really recognize the importance of responsible sharing by converted Christians in the common life.

The evidence of the questionnaire on the social implications of Methodist views of salvation is thus not decisive either way. Interwoven with several strongly individualistic elements are unmistakable signs of broad social concern. Possibly this is an accurate indication of real ambivalence among Methodists in this area.

e) *The Church*

Responses to question 7 on the nature of the Christian church disclose little concerning the respondents' views of the church's social significance, but they provide interesting and important background. Strangely, only 23.7 per cent of the total group and 19.2 per cent of the ministers agree with the classical Reformation position and the thirteenth Methodist Article of Religion that the church is "the faithful congregation in which the pure Word of God is preached and the sacraments rightly administered." But another 34.6 per cent are quite consistent with the actual emphasis of historic Methodism in viewing the church as "the community of those who have been renewed through Jesus Christ and empowered by the Holy Spirit"— the "gathered church" conception of radical Reformation Protestantism. A strong majority (61.1 per cent) of the ministers take this position. The stress on renewal and community suggests that this view may contain positive implications for social change, although some groups who have held it have been strongly pietistic and otherworldly. A religious community is always social, but not necessarily interested in "social action."

Most difficult to explain in these replies is the support registered for the polar positions. At one extreme 6.3 per cent, including some clergymen, hold the essentially Catholic conception of the church as "the custodian of the authority and grace committed by God to the apostles and their successors"—though some of these may interpret

160

the statement to mean simply that the church is the ongoing carrier of the gospel. At the other extreme 30.4 per cent—the second-rank group —adopt a basically humanist view, regarding the church as "a society of those who have joined together in their quest for the religious life." If this is an accurate and serious expression, there is sound warrant for the judgment of some concerned students, that for many Protestants the church is little more than a social fellowship or merely one of the many purely human organizations.

The opinions expressed on the laity (question 16) are most revealing. More than a tenth of the respondents are content to assign to laymen a quite marginal role, 5.6 per cent viewing them as "those who are ministered to by the clergy who are the true church," and 5.1 per cent regarding them as "people in part-time Christian service." For six out of ten respondents (59.9 per cent) laymen are "non-ordained Christians whose function is to help the clergy do the work of the church." Only 24.8 per cent think of them as "members of the people of God called to a total ministry of witness and service in the world." If the ministers' scores were removed from these totals, the score for the third position would rise to 61.2 per cent and that for the "priesthood of the laity" position would drop to 23.1 per cent. It is also worth noting that the Central and Southeastern Jurisdiction totals are lower than the national totals for the third position (57.6 per cent and 53.7 per cent respectively) and higher for the fourth (33.3 per cent and 32.6 per cent).

No doubt some of those who adopt the third position interpret "the work of the church" broadly enough to include its outreach into society, but the function of assisting the clergy suggests a dominant emphasis on the church's internal affairs. At any rate, the replies to this question make plain that the currently stressed idea of the ministry of the laity [8] as the church at work in society has made relatively little headway among Methodists, possibly because it is not well known or understood.

However, when confronted directly with the question of the church's responsibility for social change, the respondents are emphatic in affirming it. A fourth (25.1 per cent) regard such change as "of equal importance with individual transformation," 9.4 per cent hold it to be "even more important than individual conversion, since social

[8] See above, pp. 150, 159; and below, pp. 261-64.

conditions greatly affect individuals," and 11.5 per cent go so far as to list it as "the all-important task of the church"—a total of 46 per cent who in varying measures stress the church's social responsibility. Another 40.1 per cent see social change as a partial concern of the church, while regarding it as secondary to individual transformation. Only 8 per cent state that the church has no responsibility in this area.

Yet Methodists differ considerably as to the nature of this responsibility. As mentioned earlier, relatively few (18.1 per cent) expect a more Christian society to come mainly through advocacy of measures for social betterment, while 22.6 per cent count chiefly on the efforts of individual Christians, and 44.8 per cent on the conversion of individuals to Christ as the main hope for social improvement. The latter group would probably point out, however, that to stress the role of the individual need not mean to overlook the contribution of the church which produces the conversions and nourishes and guides the individuals whose Christian lives are so decisive.

An extreme reflection of the uncertainty and difference of opinion characterizing Methodist attitudes on the church's social role is found in the response to question 29 on "Race in the Organization of The Methodist Church." The percentages for the four possible answers all reach two digits, with no position commanding the support of more than a third of those replying. At one extreme are 14.5 per cent who believe that the church should follow racial lines at all levels; at the other stand 33.2 per cent who hold that racial segregation should be abolished at all levels. Between the extremes are two groups almost equally divided; 19 per cent would allow the future status of the all-Negro jurisdiction and segregated Annual Conferences and local churches to be determined under permissive legislation; 20.4 per cent favor the immediate abolition of the all-Negro jurisdiction and the gradual elimination by permissive legislation of segregated Annual Conferences and local churches. Further uncertainty and disagreement are indicated by write-in answers totaling 3.6 per cent and by the absence of any response from 9.3 per cent—the largest total in these two categories for any question on religious and social belief except that on public power projects.

In the area of interdenominational relations the picture is quite different. Methodists are emphatically ecumenical in outlook. Almost two-thirds (64.2 per cent) favor co-operation with other Christian bodies "in activities that can be done together better than separately." Another 7.5 per cent would add to such co-operation efforts for full union with other Methodist bodies, while 22.4 per cent favor seeking full union with "all Christian bodies willing to explore the possibility."

What, then, may we conclude regarding the relation between the thought of Methodists concerning the church and their social thought and action? The net impression left by the questionnaire may be summarized in three propositions: (1) The respondents believe that the church has a real responsibility for the life of society. (2) They are in considerable doubt and disagreement as to how that responsibility is to be exercised. (3) Their views on the social role of the church lack Biblical or theological foundations. No clearly conceived doctrine of the church seems to play any effective part. Instead, pragmatic considerations are uppermost.

f) *The Kingdom of God*

The questionnaire discloses that Methodists hold attitudes concerning the kingdom of God which are broadly in agreement with those found in the individual and official statements previously studied. The term appears only in question 10, which focuses attention mainly on the respective roles of God and man in the coming of the kingdom. The replies suggest that in overwhelming numbers Methodists believe that the kingdom depends on the co-operative action of God and man. Of the 79.2 per cent who concur in this judgment, 52.8 per cent see the kingdom as "the fulfillment of God's purposes which depends mainly on the efforts of men aided by God," while exactly half as many (26.4 per cent) view it as "the righteous rule of God which depends mainly on God's initiative, but requires man's co-operation." Only 12.7 per cent conceive the kingdom as "the supernatural reign of God to be established wholly by divine action," and only 1.8 per cent are willing to identify it with "the ideal social order to be built wholly by human wisdom and effort."

These statements contain conceptions of the nature of the kingdom, but since they are linked with primary judgments concerning the agency by which it comes, inferences about its meaning are risky. However, in view of the dominance of the two middle categories and the clarity of the insistence on man's part, it seems fairly safe to con-

163

clude that for these Methodists the kingdom includes the fulfillment of God's purposes in history and his reign in human society.

Implications concerning the nature of the kingdom appear also in the replies on the aims of missions, the coming of a Christian society, social change, and the teachings of Jesus. If the individualism noted in the first two of these also applies to Methodist thought concerning the kingdom, such thought will hardly generate deep social concern. On the other hand, the size of the percentage (86.1) of those who assign to the church real responsibility for social change strongly suggests that for many the kingdom is closely related to the total life of man here and now. A like inference may be drawn from the almost unanimous judgment (95 per cent) that human conduct should be guided by the teachings of Jesus, which centered in the kingdom of God.

D. Religious Belief and Social Action

In the closing section of Part I and in Part III the questionnaire attempts to discover clues to the relevance of the religious beliefs of Methodists to their actual decisions on social questions and their activities in several areas of social responsibility. Here a problem arises because of the fairly large percentage of persons who did not respond. On the theological questions the average percentage of omitted answers is only 2.5; in the ethical and social questions it rises slightly to 4.4. But on the questions related to social action an average of 17.6 per cent fail to reply. Possibly some found the formulation of these questions more complicated than that of the others and did not fully understand what was desired. Other omissions probably indicate lack of interest, lack of knowledge or previous thought sufficient to provide a sound basis for judgment, or uncertainty.

Questions 21-25 ask the respondent to indicate the nature of the guidance he derives from his religious beliefs in five problem areas. Percentages ranging from 27.0, with respect to economic and technical aid to other countries, to 42.6, on the drinking of intoxicants, assert that their religious beliefs give them direct guidance for their own conduct. Additional percentages from 33.6 to 37.8 indicate that while they derive no direct guidance, they do find moral principles to guide their own conduct and social policy as well.

The maximum extent of guidance relates to the drinking of intoxicants, where a total of 78.7 per cent align themselves in these two positive categories, while three out of four (75.4 per cent) acknowledge the two types of help in questions relating to marriage and divorce. Lower percentages avow receiving such aid regarding problems of economic and technical assistance (63.8 per cent) and participation in war (65.6 per cent). Questions of segregation occupy a median position (73.1 per cent) in this respect. This general pattern appears in the percentage of omissions, which is only 10.4 on intoxicants but reaches 15.6 and 14.8 respectively on war and economic and technical aid.

Methodists apparently feel more at home in applying their religious convictions to personal and domestic matters than to broad problems in international relations, which may actually affect their lives with equal intimacy. This judgment is confirmed by the replies to question 27, already discussed, which show a large number of persons definitely departing from the teaching of their church regarding support for war. Either the church's educational work has been less adequate in the international field, or else it has been outweighed by strong cultural factors or the common human tendency to focus attention on matters where direct involvement is thought greatest.

It should be added that percentages ranging from 6.1 to 11.2 acknowledge "indirect guidance" for conduct and social policy from their religious beliefs, and only a very few (from 4.3 per cent to 10.2 per cent) state that they receive no guidance, but make their decisions on a purely pragmatic basis. All in all, the responses reveal a large proportion of Methodists who at least say that their thelogy really influences their social action in varying degrees. This conclusion is reinforced by the evidence disclosed by question 13, already discussed.

The responses to questions 45-47 indicate that Methodists are serious in discharging their responsibility as voters. In national elections 83.5 per cent report that they vote regularly and 4.1 per cent fairly often. The total of those who say they never vote (2.9 per cent) and those who do not reply (8.3 per cent) is very close to the number of respondents below voting age, indicating that the exercise of the franchise by Methodists in national elections is nearly unanimous. Frequency of voting in state and local elections is slightly less. The strenuous efforts of political parties and all the agencies of mass communication to "get out the vote" suggest that this strong voting record may result more from social pressures than from religious teaching. Yet the record is so much higher than that of the general population that some influence from Christian conceptions of citizenship seems altogether likely. The questionnaire offers few clues to the criteria used in determining choices in voting.

Methodists express their social responsibility much less frequently by participating in nonchurch organizations concerned with social problems. On the national level 16.7 per cent of the respondents work through such organizations regularly, 17.2 per cent fairly often—a total of about one-third. But 39.8 per cent do so seldom or never, and 26.3 per cent make no reply. On the level of the local community, organized activity in social action is greater; here 33 per cent report regularly and 27.3 per cent fairly frequent participation. But 24.3 per cent say they seldom or never participate, and 15.4 per cent fail to reply—a total of almost 40 per cent who give no evidence of serious group effort to tackle social problems in their local communities.

Even less frequently do Methodists express their social concern by writing letters. Only 3.5 per cent report writing regularly to members of Congress. Although another 11.3 per cent write such letters fairly often, 29.4 per cent write seldom and 41 per cent never, with 14.8 per cent making no report. Still fewer—2.1 per cent regularly and 5.6 per cent fairly often—wrote to newspaper editors on social issues.

Objectively, these figures do not indicate a large amount of activity by Methodist people in social causes, and they provide no firm, unmistakable basis for claiming that religious beliefs increase social awareness or heighten responsibility. Nevertheless, the percentages of those who actively express social concern are probably higher than would appear in a poll of the general population. Though no figures are available, it is doubtful whether as many as 60.3 per cent of Americans work in their local communities through organizations which tackle social problems, and also whether as many as one-third of the general population belong to or support national organizations of this type. In view of the multiple demands of contemporary life, the record affords some ground for encouragement.

The replies to the questions (53-58) on sources of guidance and leadership in areas of social responsibility indicate little disposition to turn to church agencies for such guidance. Many Methodists do apparently look to their minister for such direction, and the questionnaire underlines the strategic importance of the pastor's role in this field. Some 33.5 per cent report that they look to him "much" for guidance and leadership, while 36.8 per cent turn to him "some"— a total of 70.3 per cent. In contrast, the following low percentages report looking "much" to the agencies listed: general boards and publications, 14.6; local church commissions on social action, 10.8; General Conference pronouncements, 10.1; National Council of Churches, 9.0; and non-Methodist national publications, 8.1.

A further sobering fact is that 14.4 per cent report turning even to their minister "little" (8.4 per cent) or "none" (6 per cent), and that 15.3 per cent do not reply. Thus practically three out of every ten members of Methodist churches give almost no indication that they ever expect guidance from their pastor as they face their social responsibilities. Of course this may indicate less a lack of ministerial influence than an absence of social concern by the persons involved. People who do not feel socially responsible do not look anywhere for counsel in discharging responsibility! But if this is the case, why do they not feel socially responsible? It must be remembered that these people represent our most active church members; at least three-fourths of the respondents are in church no fewer than half the Sundays in the year, and more than half of them are at worship three-fourths of the Sundays or better. Why this lack of connection between the presumed content of their worship and their lives in society? Furthermore, why are our other church agencies failing so largely to communicate with the rank and file of our church membership in areas where genuinely Christian guidance is so needed?

The picture presented by the questionnaire is thus a mixed one. The respondents appear as persons whose religious beliefs point toward active effort in behalf of social causes, and who think of themselves as guided in conduct and social policy by ethical principles rooted in religious belief, but whose avowed convictions do not find correspondingly vigorous expression in social action, and who do not regularly look for guidance in such action to the church which nurtured their beliefs. It seems likely that in many instances the actual norms of action are different from those professed.

E. Conclusions

Our analysis of the data yielded by the questionnaire leads to the following general conclusions: [9]

1. The respondents hold that religious beliefs strongly influence conduct, though often no consistent connection is discernible between the theological convictions and the ethical and social positions which they themselves affirm.

2. The authority of the Bible and the abiding validity of the ethical teachings of Jesus are emphatically asserted, while marked differences appear in specific applications.

3. Man empowered by God is seen as a being of high possibilities. In the main this hopeful view of man finds harmonious expression in the social policies advocated, but serious exceptions occur.

4. The reality of sin and man's need of repentance are clearly perceived. That this recognition is not a deterrent, and may be a stimulus, to social action is indicated by the fact that substantial majorities believe in the possibility of social improvement and espouse policies aimed toward achieving it.

5. A majority of respondents assert the Protestant doctrine of justification by grace through faith, but no clear social implications emerge.

6. A large majority support the historic Methodist emphasis on first-hand Christian experience; however, the data available do not warrant inferences regarding the effect of this belief on social concern.

7. Salvation is seen as definitely relevant to life here and now. Some apparently conceive it wholly in individualistic terms, while others broaden it to include social redemption and transformation.

8. God, it is maintained, is working in nature and history to realize his purposes, and his kingdom comes as men respond in obedience to his will. The life of society can and should move toward divine goals.

9. These Methodists believe that the church has real responsibility for social change, but they are doubtful and divided as to how this responsibility is to be exercised, and they do not relate it clearly to Biblical or theological foundations.

[9] It is expected that continuing analyses of the data will make available more detailed and concretely valuable results.

10. A large number of the respondents picture themselves as guided in moral and social questions by their religious beliefs, but on the whole there is little evidence that they actually find in those beliefs or the agencies which interpret them either strong motivation or major guidance for positive social action.

On the whole, the questionnaire discloses a lack among Methodists of any coherent pattern of belief and action. The lack itself is a proper subject of regret, but the disclosure is not. It goes without saying that this and other indications of the questionnaire should be subjected to stringent criticism. Other evidence may modify or even invalidate some of its findings. However, a major element of significance in this first-hand study of the beliefs of Methodists in 1959 may lie precisely in the fact that it focuses attention on the ambiguities, inconsistencies, and hiatuses which exist in the thinking and acting of Methodist people on religious and social questions. Such knowledge is a necessary first step in the direction of a more harmonious and mutually enriching relationship between their theology and their social thought and action.

CHAPTER SIX

Cultural Influences

IN THE PRECEDING CHAPTERS THE FOCUS HAS BEEN ON THE theological side of the relation between theology and social thought and action. We have examined primarily the religious beliefs regarded by Methodists as foundations of social concern or held by them as they think and act on social questions. However, the traffic on the street we are traveling moves in both directions. Religious beliefs not only affect social attitudes but are also affected by them. Our ideas concerning God, man, sin, and salvation, for example, do not grow in a vacuum, but amid a variety of other ideas, experiences, and practices which constantly influence them. Historically and environmentally, too, as Gordon Allport has observed, "religion is lock-stitched into the social and economic fabric." [1] The colors and patterns of this fabric affect not only the religious beliefs of individuals, but their ethical and social attitudes as well. Some consideration must therefore be given to the impact of these complex social and cultural factors on the religious and social thinking of Methodist people.

We shall begin by considering several typical examples of the influence of culture on theology itself. Then we shall turn to the impact of culture on social thought and action, examining three typical areas: (1) the influence of nationalism on the attitudes of Christians concerning war and peace; (2) the effect of economic factors on social thought; and (3) the bearing of racial influences on thought and action on social issues.

[1] Walter G. Muelder, *Religion and Economic Responsibility* (New York: Charles Scribner's Sons, 1953), p. 28.

A. Cultural Influences on Theology

One instance of the influence of cultural climate on theology it-self appears in the differing estimates of the significance of theology in British and American Methodism. Among Methodists in Great Britain there has been very little of the tendency, so apparent in the United States, to stress experience and conduct at the expense of doctrine. In view of the common Wesleyan heritage of the two Methodisms, it is hard to avoid the conclusion that the lower American estimate of the importance of theological inquiry is due in considerable measure to socio-cultural factors. Methodist circuit riders on the American frontier, busily engaged in a rough-hewn era in the task of saving souls, had little time for critical or constructive theological thinking, and readily defended their unfamiliarity with it by treating it as relatively unimportant. In later years the generally pragmatic, utilitarian, activistic temper of American life has tended to perpetuate and confirm this view of theology, sometimes carrying American Methodists beyond a Wesleyan subordination of doctrine to life to a superficial exaltation of heart over head and a corresponding lack of clarity and understanding in religious belief.

Another form of cultural influence on theology is evident in the impact of the scientific temper and the results of scientific investigation. The rise of liberal theology in the late nineteenth and early twentieth centuries is a graphic example of this kind of influence. The scientific postulate of the universal reign of law strongly supported the notion of the immanence of God in his world, and led many to reinterpret the traditional conception of miracle. The evolutionary hypothesis in biology profoundly affected Christian thinking concerning creation; strengthened biblical criticism and the concept of progressive revelation; stimulated the comparative study of religions, which were readily seen as successively higher stages of one process; and contributed greatly to the belief in progress and the kingdom of God as the increasing fulfillment of the divine purposes in history.

Influence of a very different kind is seen in the sharp reaction of theology to "scientism"—exaggerated notions of the nature and extent of scientific authority and the tendency to make the assumptions of the natural sciences determinative in religion and all of life. Such

171

attitudes earlier aroused theologians to criticism of mechanistic and deterministic world views which claimed the support of the physical sciences. More recently, they have helped to call forth a reassertion of the transcendence of God; emphasis on revelation as divine disclosure from above distinctively different from ordinary human ways of knowing; insistence on the uniqueness and absoluteness of the Word which God has spoken to man in Jesus Christ; and stress on the reality of discontinuity and disorder in human history.

The social sciences have also exerted strong influences on Christian thought. Sociology has affected both the methodology and the content of Christian social ethics, encouraging it to relate Christian norms to all of the fundamental problems of society, and providing valuable empirical data for its inquiry. Both behavioristic and Freudian psychology have challenged theology at crucial points, requiring it to undertake critical and constructive tasks which would not otherwise have confronted it. Depth psychology and psychotherapy are directly concerned with questions which have long been basic in theological inquiry, such as the nature of man, human finitude and freedom, sin and guilt, the resolution of conflict and insecurity, and man's quest for meaning and his need for healing or salvation. Frequent conflict between the two enterprises is giving way to an increasing measure of co-operation. In the process theological concepts have undergone both modification and enrichment. A whole new approach to "pastoral theology" has emerged, which in many seminaries now devotes central attention to pastoral psychology, counseling, and clinical training.

Philosophical inquiry has influenced the theology of Methodists and other American Christians in manifold ways, a few of which may be mentioned here. William James's pragmatism, though seldom fully embraced by Methodist leaders and often sharply resisted, served to reinforce a preference for the fruits of religion in life and to decrease concern for doctrinal clarity. The personal idealism of Bordon Parker Bowne, finding in personality the clue to a theistic interpretation of man, nature, and ultimate reality, has provided for many a philosophical confirmation of the Christian faith, and in turn deeply influenced their understanding of basic Christian doctrines. As John Deschner has said, "Much contemporary Methodist social concern—

172

one of the characteristic marks of the Methodist Church—has been reformulated and nurtured anew in this personalist tradition." [2]

While the naturalistic humanism of John Dewey has been rather uniformly rejected among Methodists, the development of his instrumentalism in educational theory has had a powerful effect on the philosophy of Christian education held by some leaders and followed to some extent by Methodists. Emphases on teaching as creative involvement of the learner rather than transmission of content alone, thinking as problem-solving, the experience-centered curriculum, and "learning by doing and by undergoing" have been widely welcomed in the circles of those responsible for Protestant education; and the conception of human nature implied in these emphases remains a subject of lively discussion among educators and theologians.

The theistic naturalism of thinkers like C. Lloyd Morgan, Alfred North Whitehead, and Henry Nelson Wieman has markedly influenced the theologies of many Methodist ministers and teachers who would not accept *in toto* the thought of any one of them. Today strong influence is being exerted by religious existentialist philosophy, with its insistence that man's personal involvement prevents detached judgment on ultimate questions, and its stress on the inevitability of presuppositions accepted on faith, man's radical freedom, and the necessity of decision and commitment in the absence of satisfactory rational knowledge of alternatives. Considerable numbers of Methodists, especially in the seminaries, find in existentialist ways of thinking an apt vehicle of expression for the central meanings of the Biblical revelation.

Social philosophies involve not only ethical judgments, but also theories and assumptions concerning the nature of ultimate reality. Competing views like Marxian communism, socialism, fascism, and *laissez faire* individualism have compelled Christian ethics to confront urgent social problems in relation to both the concrete realities of social conflict and the fundamental affirmations of Christian faith.

Finally, attention should be called to the part played by political, economic, and social factors in the theological changes which have occurred since approximately 1935, already noted in Chapter Four.

[2] "Methodism," *A Handbook of Christian Theology*, p. 231. Bowne was a Methodist theologian as well as a philosopher, so that he himself illustrates the influence of philosophy on theology, as well as that of theology on philosophy.

The world depression of the 1930's, the rise of Hitler, and the holocaust of World War II served to set the stage for the rejection or modification of the older liberalism. Other influences were still more weighty, such as one-sided elements in the earlier theology, needs deeply imbedded in the nature of man which were not being adequately met, the trail-blazing thinking of theologians like Karl Barth, Emil Brunner, and Reinhold Niebuhr, and the very nature of the Christian gospel itself. Also, the newer theology is actually in part a protest against earlier cultural influences on the content of Christian doctrine. Nevertheless, the social upheavals of our time have unquestionably helped to undermine the optimism of an earlier generation and prepare the way for the emphases which now hold sway.

B. Cultural Influences in Social Thought and Action

1. NATIONALISM AND THINKING ON WAR AND PEACE

With respect to support of and participation in war, the views of Methodists in the United States have been strongly influenced by the feelings and attitudes they hold as Americans. "In their attitude toward war," writes Robert Moats Miller,

the Protestant churches have reflected too faithfully their environment. Their critique of America's battles has been bounded by class and sectional lines and not by a transcendent loyalty to a super-historical church in the world but not of the world.[3]

In spite of some notable exceptions, this judgment is probably as accurate for Methodists as for other major Protestant groups.

Methodist utterances during World War I accepted in the main the prevailing attitudes toward Germany and her peculiar wickedness and responsibility. Christian idealism was marshalled to support the war which was to end war and save the world for democracy, and the victory of the Allies was hailed as a triumph for Christian civilization. One of the main events at the Southern Methodist General Conference of 1918 [4] was an address by Major Charles W. Gordon (Ralph Connor), a chaplain in the Canadian army. Major Gordon spoke of

[3] *American Protestantism and Social Issues, 1919-1939*, p. 8.
[4] The General Conferences of the Methodist Episcopal Church and the Methodist Protestant Church did not meet during the 19 months of America's direct participation in World War I.

his function as that of helping men to be better fighters, and giving them a sense that God had a stake in the war. He predicted that the war would be over "when two million Americans get over there" and land "the real American punch" on "the wicked, dark-hearted Germany."

And, brethren, that heart is darker than you know, and more wicked than you know, and more irreligious than you know; and all its wickedness is a part of its system. I do not discount any atrocity stories, for they are all true.

Victory, said the major, would mean that "righteousness will have been established in the world and the reign of brutalizing force will be forever broken." At this point the conference "burst spontaneously into cheers and prolonged applause." [5] In the same General Conference the Committee on Patriotic Resolutions approved the use of the buildings and organization of the church "for all war purposes consistent with Christian patriotism." [6] Sentiments similar to these were voiced in many church gatherings.

The years following World War I witnessed a marked spread, particularly among ministers and youth, of the spirit of Christian internationalism. With the signing of the Kellogg-Briand Pact in 1927 war was renounced as an instrument of national policy. In the late 'twenties and early 'thirties an unprecedented number of Christians, including many Methodists, took the pacifist position of refusing to support or participate in any war. During the 'thirties Methodist bodies generally supported legislation designed to maintain the neutrality of the United States by prohibiting shipments of arms to belligerents. In 1940 the Board of World Peace, various Annual Conference Commissions on World Peace, and multitudes of individual churchmen opposed the passage of the Selective Service Act.[7]

The Methodist General Conference of 1940, meeting eight months after the outbreak of World War II in Europe, continued vigorously to oppose nationalism in the name of Christian universalism. It

[5] *Journal*, 1918, p. 401.
[6] *Ibid.*, pp. 128-29.
[7] For Methodist attitudes and actions during this period see Walter G. Muelder, *Methodism and Society in the Twentieth Century*.

declared that "the church of Christ, which transcends races, nations, and classes, has an all-important contribution to make to the abolition of war and to the establishment of a just and lasting peace"; and that The Methodist Church, with representatives "in every part of the earth, must make its full contribution to this great end." The Conference therefore urged all Methodists to recognize that

absolute loyalty belongs to God. The Christian is bound to serve his own nation in all ways that are compatible with the Christian faith and the Christian way of life; but his supreme allegiance is due to God, whose love embraces all mankind. "It is the duty of the Churches to disentangle patriotism and religion and to teach fearlessly that state and nation belong to the sphere of relative, earthly values. God alone is absolute, and He alone has a claim to our unconditioned loyalty."

The Conference also endorsed the judgment of the Oxford Conference on Life and Work (1937) that "war involves compulsory enmity, diabolical outrage against human personality, and a wanton distortion of the truth," as well as being "a defiance of the righteousness of God as revealed in Jesus Christ." On this foundation it asserted:

The Methodist Church, although making no attempt to bind the consciences of its individual members, will not officially endorse, support, or participate in war. We insist that the agencies of the Church shall not be used in preparation for war, but in the promulgation of peace. We insist that the buildings of the Church dedicated to the worship of God shall be used for that holy purpose, and not by any agency for the promotion of war.

Aware of the growing threat of American involvement in the struggles then raging, the Conference held that "the United States should remain out of the present conflicts in Europe and the Far East," in order to preserve democracy in America and to be able to provide relief and rehabilitation in a war-shattered world.[8]

When the General Conference met again four years later the United States was in the thick of the war, and the life of every Methodist was affected. This time the Conference rejected a majority re-

[8] Discipline, 1940, par. 1716, pp. 773-74, 777-78, 775-76.

port of its Committee on the State of the Church, which took a position quite similar to that of 1940, in favor of a minority report[9] which committed the church to the support of the war effort:

In this country we are sending over a million young men from Methodist homes to participate in the conflict. God himself has a stake in the struggle, and he will uphold them as they fight forces destructive of the moral life of man. In Christ's name we ask for the blessing of God upon the men in the armed forces, and we pray for victory. We repudiate the theory that a state, even though imperfect, must not fight against intolerable wrongs.

While we respect the individual conscience of those who believe that they cannot condone the use of force, and staunchly will defend them on this issue, we cannot accept their position as the defining position of the Christian Church. We are well within the Christian position when we assert the necessity of the use of military forces to resist an aggression which would overthrow every right which is held sacred by civilized men.[10]

The deep misgivings and searchings of heart which accompanied this action were registered when, on the next afternoon, after long overnight deliberations of leaders representing both positions, the Conference adopted by unanimous vote another very different statement, which became a part of the Social Creed:

Christianity cannot be nationalistic; it must be universal in its outlook and appeal. War makes its appeal to force and hate, Christianity to reason and love. The influence of the Church must therefore always be on the side of every effort seeking to remove animosities and prejudices which are contrary to the spirit and teaching of Christ. . . . The methods of Jesus and the methods of war belong to different worlds. War is a crude and primitive force. It arouses passions which in the beginning may be unselfish and generous, but in the end war betrays those who trust in it. It offers no security that its decisions will be just and righteous. It leaves arrogance in the heart of the victor and resentment in the heart of the vanquished. When the teachings of Jesus are fully accepted, war as a means of settling international disputes will die, and dying will set the world free from a cruel tyrant.[11]

[9] Adopted in a "vote by orders," the laymen favoring it 203 to 119, the ministers 170 to 169.
[10] *Discipline*, 1944, par. 2016, pp. 574-75.
[11] *Discipline*, 1944, par. 2010, sec. 15, p. 557.

Both pronouncements remained as official expressions of the mind of the church—dramatic testimony to the clash of national and Christian loyalties in wartime. Much of the former statement dealt specifically with the situation existing when the country was at war; it was no longer applicable in 1948, and was not considered by the General Conference of that year. The unanimously adopted utterance, much more general in nature, was retained in the Social Creed of 1948,[12] and the essence of it was included also in the Social Creed as adopted in 1952 and 1956.

Similar evidence of the increasing power of nationalism in wartime appears at the Annual Conference level. In doctoral research at the University of Pittsburgh following World War II, James W. Gladden studied the changing positions of selected conferences during the years 1940 to 1943. His report is concise and self-explanatory. He writes that in 1940-41

all the conferences examined in the Northeastern, North Central, and Western Jurisdictions had committees [on world peace], were opposed to the church participating in war, forbade war use of the local church or the national agencies, urged the exemption of individual objectors, and wanted the United States as a nation to stay out of war. In the Southeastern Jurisdiction only five conferences had committees, four spoke out against the church being a part of war, four wanted individual exemption, and none asked the nation to stay out of the European conflict. . . . Whereas all sixteen conferences [the number studied] of the northern and western jurisdictions were opposed to church participation, only ten mentioned it in 1942. Six failed to state the conviction and also said nothing about the church agencies. Only three of the sixteen did not specifically mention supporting individual objectors. Only three spoke of an international organization, although study conferences which brought out such a need were supported by ten groups. In the south and southwest in 1942 only Virginia and North Carolina showed a measure of insistence upon the stand taken by the denomination in 1940. The Alabama Conference went all out in support of war. . . .

By 1943 only eight conferences refused church support of war. Only six out of thirty-two said, "We cannot bless war." Nineteen conferences before the war insisted on the right of the objectors; this had dwindled to ten by 1943. Only four actually endorsed the war effort but the language

[12] The statement of 1948 was a synthesizing one which was adopted with near-unanimity. Many delegates felt that it healed the breach of 1944.

of the speakers and the reports of the other committees suggest that there was a majority of feeling in other conferences that the church was "in the war." [13]

It should be pointed out, however, that the church was much less militaristic in the Second World War than in the First. In the main the war was not looked upon with enthusiasm as a great crusade for high ideals, but much more soberly and realistically, even agonizingly, as a manifestation of human sin which had to be fought through to the bitter end, but which at best could only remove Hitlerism and provide an opportunity for men to reconstruct the world on sounder foundations. Through its Commission on World Peace, the church gave counsel to its conscientious objectors and some financial support to those in Civilian Public Service Camps, who exceeded in number those of every other denomination except the historic "peace" churches.[14] While the war still raged, the church worked vigorously at the task of exploring the conditions of lasting peace. Methodists participated responsibly in the National Study Conferences on the Churches and a Just and Durable Peace sponsored by the Federal Council of Churches at Delaware, Ohio, in 1942 and at Cleveland in 1945, as well as in regional conferences like that at Hood College, Frederick, Maryland, in 1943. In 1944-45, under the leadership of the bishops, The Methodist Church embarked on a Crusade for a New World Order, designed to register Christian sentiment on international issues, particularly in favor of international collaboration instead of a postwar return to isolation. In such ways the basic universalism of the Christian faith was kept alive and given opportunity for expression.

Evidence of the continuing influence of nontheological factors in the thought of Methodists concerning war has already been noted in Chapter Five. In the MESTA questionnaire 47.2 per cent of those replying affirm their obligation as Christian citizens to support their

[13] "The Methodist Church and the Problem of War and Peace: An Analysis in Social Understanding." Reprint of an abstract of a doctoral dissertation, *University of Pittsburgh Bulletin*, Vol. 43, No. 2, Feb. 10, 1947.

[14] Of a total of 11,950 conscientious objectors enrolled in Civilian Public Service, the largest representations were as follows: Mennonites, 4,665; Church of the Brethren, 1,353; Friends, 951; Methodist, 673; Jehovah's Witnesses, 409. (*Directory of Civilian Public Service*. Washington, D. C.: National Service Board for Religious Objectors, 1947.)

country in war "when its continued existence is at stake, apart from considerations of justice." What explanation can be given for this willingness of so many to give higher priority to national self-preservation than to questions of right and wrong? Deeply imbedded nationalistic attitudes and traditional conceptions of patriotism no doubt have played important parts. Beyond these, considerable weight should probably be given to the current East-West conflict, portrayed as it so often is as a struggle for survival of one way of life or the other. Whatever the correct interpretation may be, it seems evident that in this instance, as before, factors rooted in the national culture have exerted a powerful influence.

2. THE EFFECT OF ECONOMIC FACTORS

The influence of economic circumstances on ethical and religious attitudes has been too clearly recognized and attested in recent years to need close scrutiny here. Nathaniel Micklem voices a judgment which most Methodist scholars would accept:

We shall not wisely dispute that there is a certain correspondence between social conditions and current theology, nor that Christian morality has been in fact accommodated to economic changes. A purely penal theory of the Atonement, for instance, cannot for long be maintained when even the secular courts regard punishment as being, at least in part, remedial. We may suspect, too, that the rise of Capitalism rather than increased ethical vision led to the abandonment of medieval strictures upon usury. To be sure, it is easier to argue that Calvinism produced Capitalism than vice versa, and Marx's almost exclusive emphasis upon the economic factor in the shaping of history is untenable, but the great influence of the economic situation upon Christian thought and conduct from age to age is matter for research, not for denial.[15]

Equally well recognized is the ease with which we find religiously or morally acceptable reasons for social and economic—as well as personal—positions which we actually hold on other grounds. Charles C. West points up this danger, for example, with reference to Christian attitudes toward communism. One task of Christian theology, he shows, is to confront the "good conscience" of the communists, who are convinced that they are exposing the self-deception or swindle

[15] *The Theology of Politics* (London: Oxford University Press, 1941), pp. 9-10.

of Christian faith, "with a witness which is not another system of ideas pretending to be objective truth and value while it in fact reflects and covers the interest of one social group." [16]

The MESTA questionnaire illustrates rather vividly at several points the actual functioning of economic and related factors in the social thinking of Methodists. On question 42, for instance, 20.4 per cent of all respondents reject socialized medicine because they believe "it would kill the individual initiative of doctors and the self-reliance of their patients"; 54 per cent take the less extreme position of advocating health insurance as the best way of meeting the costs of illness; and only 15.1 per cent think that "the co-operative employment of physicians by voluntary health associations would provide adequate care at lowest cost." The opinions registered in the Central Jurisdiction, representing an economic status much lower than that of the national average for Methodists, are quite different. Although 59.1 per cent favor health insurance, only 7.5 per cent voice specific opposition to socialized medicine, and the number of those endorsing the co-operative employment of physicians by voluntary health associations rises to 25.8 per cent. Also of interest is the fact that the number of "write-in" and "no response" replies is lower in this jurisdiction than in any other. Clearly mirrored in these results is the plight of people who are keenly conscious of their need for medical care which they cannot now afford.

A similar orientation appears in the responses to question 43 on labor legislation. Of the total group of respondents 29.3 per cent favor "right to work" laws and curbs on the power of labor unions, but only 16.7 per cent in the Central Jurisdiction support such legislation. Moreover, whereas only 14.2 per cent of the total want chiefly laws to protect labor's right to a union shop while limiting the right to strike in the public interest, 21.2 per cent of the Central Jurisdiction fall in this category. Again, only 3.4 per cent of all the replies seek mainly legislation designed to protect labor unions in provisions for collective bargaining and the like, but 6 per cent of the Central Jurisdiction take this position. Greater interest in the subject of labor legislation is also indicated in the Central Jurisdiction, where only half as many as in the total group (3.1 per cent vs. 6.2 per cent) make

[16] Communism and the Theologians (London: Student Christian Movement Press, 1958), p. 23.

no response to this question. Apparently, the more pronounced the economic need, the greater the concern for legislation and the greater the tendency to support legislation favorable to labor.

With reference to agriculture (question 44), the picture is similar. Nationally 9 per cent maintain that the federal government should "let the farmer care for himself and his soil," and 9.2 per cent go a little farther toward federal supervision, holding that the government should "concern itself only with soil conservation." Only 1.5 per cent and 3.1 per cent respectively of the Central Jurisdiction fall in these categories. At the other end of the scale, however, 69.7 per cent of Central Jurisdiction Methodists think that the government should "act to stabilize farm prices, control surpluses, and conserve the soil," in contrast to 47.5 per cent of the total group who are willing to go this far. Again, 7 per cent of the total number but only 3.1 per cent of the Central Jurisdiction make no reply.

Economic factors certainly shed much light also on the replies to question 41 on federal aid to public education. On a conservative-liberal scale 21.6 per cent of all respondents favor such aid "only if complete control remains with the states," 12 per cent "only if parochial and private schools are specifically excluded," 3.4 per cent if parochial and private schools receive only "such indirect aid as bus transportation," and 53.5 per cent "on the basis of need." In sharp contrast, the first three of these positions together command the support of only 15.1 per cent of Central Jurisdiction Methodists, 80.3 per cent of whom brush such considerations aside to favor federal aid to public education simply on the basis of need. Once more this jurisdiction produces the lowest incidence of omissions (3.1 per cent over against 5 per cent for the total), and only 1.5 per cent (in contrast to 4.5 per cent) write their own answers. It is safe to say that the experienced lack of educational opportunity has played a major part in these results. Yet this is so closely linked with the low economic status of the persons involved that the two factors reinforce rather than offset each other. Further, even though the power of the desire for equal educational opportunity rules out economic determinism, it no less than the economic factor represents a largely nontheological influence.

Regional as well as economic influences seem to be operative in the thinking of Methodists regarding public power projects like the

Tennessee Valley Authority (question 34). A total of 9.4 per cent of all respondents regard such projects as "a threat to our free enterprise economy," and 13.5 per cent question them "because they tax all our citizens to provide cheap electricity for a few." Over against this total of 22.9 per cent only 17.3 per cent of the Southeastern Jurisdiction and 15.1 per cent of the Central Jurisdiction, with the greatest number of its members in the southeast, take these two positions. At the other end of the scale, 59.7 per cent of the entire group favor public power projects, either because they greatly improve the nation's economic welfare (41 per cent) or because they "provide worthy experiments in the extension of democracy" (18.7 per cent). In the Southeastern and Central Jurisdictions, however, totals of 68.5 per cent and 68.2 per cent respectively express these opinions. Those who live closest to TVA and have greater opportunity for some direct share in its benefits are clearly more inclined than others to look favorably on such ventures.

In evaluating data like these it is important to ask whether there are variations of religious belief between the Central Jurisdiction and the total group which might indicate the operation of theological influences in the deviations noted. There is no basis for denying such influences. On the other hand, in many of the theological topics in the questionnaire there is pronounced harmony between the Central Jurisdiction and the others; and in the few cases where the percentages differ markedly there is no variation which can be correlated with that disclosed in the social questions just examined.

We can conclude only that in these instances economic and related factors are functioning significantly in the social thinking of Methodists. The evidence permits no conclusions, however, regarding the influence of these factors on religious beliefs, except to indicate that they do modify whatever effect religious beliefs have on social attitudes.

3. RACIAL INFLUENCES

Probably no area of human life demonstrates so unmistakably the power of extra-theological elements in the thinking and acting of Christian people as does that of race relations. The very presence within the Christian fellowship of problems centering in race is itself an illustration of that power. As Benjamin E. Mays pointed out in

183

an address to the Evanston Assembly of the World Council of Churches, there is no basis in the Bible or in ancient, medieval, or early Protestant church history for racial distinctions in the church of Christ. The setting up of racial barriers in the church is a modern development, dating only from the seventeenth century.

It was when modern Western imperialism began to explore and exploit the colored peoples of Africa, Asia, and America that the beginning of segregation and discrimination based on color and race was initiated. It was then that color was associated with "inferiority," and white with "superiority."

Under the impact of these social, economic, and cultural developments, Christians gradually took over the myth of racial superiority and inferiority even though the great weight of Biblical and post-Biblical Christian teaching was opposed to it.[17]

In the mid-twentieth century individual Protestants and their churches continue to condone and defend practices in church and society which are seriously out of harmony with their professed beliefs. The discrimination and segregation which characterize most Protestant churches today provide disturbing justification for the assumption of many sociologists that religion is "a function of culture." On this question George Eaton Simpson and J. Milton Yinger conclude:

Although the Protestant churches stress (1) the dignity and worth of the individual and (2) the brotherhood of man, the racial behavior patterns of most church members have not been substantially affected by these principles. With the exception of the financial support which white churches have contributed to Negro secondary schools and colleges, the Protestant denominations have given very little attention to the American racial situation.[18]

Noteworthy progress has been made in some quarters since these words were written in 1953. Present moves toward breaking the segregationist pattern compel some revision of Simpson and Yinger's judgment.

---

[17] "The Church and Racial Tension," *Christian Century*, 71 (1954), 1068.

[18] *Racial and Cultural Minorities* (New York: Harper and Brothers, 1953), p. 547. In this connection note the omission of any reference to the race question in the Social Creeds proclaimed by both the Federal Council of Churches and Methodist bodies in the first decades of this century.

However, some of them, stimulated in part by the famous decision of the United States Supreme Court in 1954 outlawing the segregation in the public schools, actually serve to underline the importance of nonreligious influences in the social attitudes of churches.

In 1946 the Federal Council of Churches adopted a statement renouncing segregation in its organizational structure and operation and inviting its member churches to join in working for "a non-segregated church and a non-segregated society." On June 11, 1952, the General Board of the National Council of Churches adopted a similarly strong position, viewing segregation based on race, color, or national origin as "a denial of the Christian faith and ethic which stems from the basic premise taught by our Lord that all men are created the children of God," and as "diametrically opposed to what Christians believe about the worth of persons." On December 5, 1957, the General Assembly of the National Council declared racial segregation to be "contradictory to the teaching of Jesus" and "contrary to the Christian principle, that all men are beings of worth in the sight of God." The assembly went on to reaffirm its renunciation of the pattern of segregation "both in the churches and in society, as a violation of the gospel of love and human brotherhood." It also declared segregation to be "bad economics, wasteful of human resources, detrimental to the development of a healthy political life, a grave obstacle to the development of our relationship and mission with churches in other parts of the world and to the establishment of world peace." Hence the General Assembly called on its member churches and their constituencies to work for the achievement as soon as possible of a nonsegregated society.

Yet segregation remains the pattern. There are important exceptions which are increasing in number. Some predominantly white churches are ready to integrate, but are prevented from doing so by the pattern of residential segregation which cuts them off from potential Negro members. But in the main segregation continues to prevail in the worship, membership, and fellowship of local churches; in the student bodies and faculties of many church-related colleges and universities; in the admission of patients, the staff membership of doctors, and the employment of nurses in church-controlled hospitals; and in the employment policies of other church institutions and agencies. The church has largely taken on the protective coloration of its environment.

A telling example of the way in which the pattern of segregation and discrimination, once established, operates to counteract the religious teachings of the churches which accept it is found in the involuntary transmission of a psychology of superiority-inferiority from one generation to another. In its statement of June 11, 1952, the General Board of the National Council of Churches observed that "children in our society, observing minorities as we segregate them, cannot easily escape the inference that such minorities are inferior." In the United States segregation as practiced "probably has more effect on the attitudes of the young than the formal teachings of the schools about democracy or of the churches about Christian brotherhood."

The extent to which cultural factors operate to guide the race relations of Christians and churches in other directions than those consistent with their professed theology finds typical illustration in The Methodist Church.

"The teaching of our Lord," affirmed the General Conference of 1956, "is that all men are brothers. The Master permits no discrimination because of race, color, or national origin." Asserting that the position of The Methodist Church, "long held and frequently declared, is an amplification of our Lord's teaching," the conference went on to make its own the words of the Episcopal Addresses of 1952 and 1956:

To discriminate against a person solely upon the basis of his race is both unfair and un-Christian. Every child of God is entitled to that place in society which he has won by his industry and character. To deny him that position of honor because of the accident of his birth is neither honest democracy nor good religion.

On this basis the General Conference insisted that "there must be no place" in the church for "racial discrimination or enforced segregation." Recognizing both progress toward but failure to attain this goal, the conference recommended that "discrimination or segregation by any method or practice . . . in The Methodist Church be abolished with reasonable speed."

186

Specific recommendations included the following: that all church institutions carefully restudy their policies and practices relating to race to make certain that such policies and practices are Christian; that Methodists in all their relationships work actively to eliminate racial discrimination; that churches in changing neighborhoods, instead of moving, prepare to receive members of all races as they become residents of their community; that better fraternal relations be sought at all levels between the Central Jurisdiction and adjacent or overlapping jurisdictions; that Methodists at national and international meetings provide for unsegregated accommodations for all races; and that the many racial and national groups which comprise the Methodist world fellowship be afforded unrestricted opportunity to participate in all the activities of the church.[19]

Legislatively, the General Conference of 1956 adopted a provision permitting any local church of the Central Jurisdiction to transfer to an Annual Conference in another Jurisdiction, with the approval of both Annual Conferences and both Jurisdictions concerned. The Conference also authorized the creation of a representative commission to make a thorough study of the jurisdictional system and recommend action concerning it to the General Conference of 1960.

These actions by Methodism's supreme legislative body represent forthright and vigorous efforts to harmonize the thinking and acting of Methodists in racial matters with basic Christian beliefs affirmed by the church. This process was carried forward by the national Methodist Conference on Human Relations held at Southern Methodist University, Dallas, in September 1959. Here 800 delegates adopted unanimously, for submission to the General Conference, a seven-point program for improved race relations, including open occupancy in housing, employment on the basis of merit, and provisions to increase fellowship and co-operation across racial lines. Bishop Roy H. Short of Nashville was chairman of the committee which drafted the report.[20] Meanwhile able Methodist thinkers are carefully examining the biblical and theological foundations of Christian race relations.[21] Such inquiries serve to confront the church with the religious implications of its racial practices.

[19] Discipline, 1956, par. 2026, pp. 723-24.
[20] Dallas Times-Herald, Sept. 4, 1959.
[21] Notable examples are Everett Tilson, Segregation and the Bible, and Waldo Beach, "A Theological Analysis of Race Relations," Faith and Ethics, ed. Paul Ramsey.

187

Yet there is abundant evidence that weighty cultural and regional forces retard change. The jurisdictional system itself is of course an outstanding example; it is at present unrealistic to expect it to be abolished by anything but a long and gradual process. Racial walls are crumbling here and there in the church's hospitals, homes, educational institutions, and other agencies, but the over-all pattern continues to involve segregation to a large extent. There are still Methodist theological seminaries which are prevented by the trustees of the universities to which they belong from admitting Negro candidates for the ministry. In 1952 Dwight W. Culver discovered that of the 361,585 Negro members of The Methodist Church in 330 districts which responded to a questionnaire, only 640 (.18 per cent) were in predominantly white but racially mixed local churches.[22] There is no evidence that this number has greatly increased. There are now a number of Negro pastors of predominantly white Methodist churches, and at least one instance (in the Southern California-Arizona Conference) where a white pastor serves a Negro congregation. Many pastors cross racial lines regularly in ministerial associations, and lay and clerical leaders work with fellow Methodists of other races in church-wide boards or local, state, or national councils of churches. Nevertheless, the vast majority of American Methodists carry on their church activities year after year without ever meeting face-to-face a Methodist Christian of another race, though there may be hundreds or thousands of persons of different racial backgrounds who are members of Methodist churches in their own communities.

It should be noted that environmental factors may work to reduce segregation as well as to reinforce it. The statement of the General Conference of 1956 already quoted cited the decisions of the Supreme Court as making necessary "far-reaching and often difficult community readjustments." The action of the court not only required adjustments in the behavior patterns of some Christians who were reluctant to make them; it also encouraged others to act in directions which they had previously been too timid to follow. For instance, the Baltimore Conference, meeting in June 1954, applauded the action of the Supreme Court taken only a few weeks earlier, deplored "the fact that the church has all too often trailed behind secular organizations

[22] *Negro Segregation in The Methodist Church* (New Haven: Yale University Press, 1953), pp. 143-44.

188

and powers rather than leading them on social issues," and proceeded to "call upon all Methodist educational institutions in our Baltimore Conference [including the college where the conference was meeting] to admit students without regard to race, color, ancestry, or national origin." The secretary was instructed to communicate the resolution to the presidents and trustees of all institutions involved.[23]

The results of the MESTA questionnaire offer convincing support for three conclusions: (1) that segregationist sentiment is by no means limited to the South; (2) that whether a professing Christian is a member of the majority or a minority race makes a decisive difference in his attitudes on racial issues confronting the church; and (3) that readiness on the part of the majority to lower racial barriers varies inversely in proportion to the size of the minority population.

The findings of question 28 speak so eloquently that the percentages are reproduced here *in toto:*

	Total	C[24]	NC	NE	SC	SE	W
Some races are inherently inferior, and are not entitled to equal rights and privileges with those of superior capacity	1.9	.0	2.6	.7	1.2	2.9	.4
Members of all races should have equal opportunities, but segregation is desirable to preserve racial purity	22.8	1.5	17.7	19.8	26.5	41.2	12.1
Members of all races should have the same opportunities, but present patterns should be changed gradually	52.3	16.6	56.3	55.7	50.0	40.6	59.4
All discrimination and enforced segregation based on race should be abolished	18.9	80.4	20.2	19.7	18.3	8.4	24.9

[23] *Minutes of the Baltimore Annual Conference,* 1954, p. 150.
[24] The alphabetical symbols designate, left to right, the Central, North Central, Northeastern, South Central, Southeastern, and Western Jurisdictions.

	Total	C	NC	NE	SC	SE	W
Write-in	2.2	1.5	1.8	1.9	1.9	4.5	1.4
No response	1.9	.0	1.4	2.2	2.1	2.4	1.8

The percentage of those asserting inherent racial inferiority and superiority may seem negligible, but the church can hardly rest content when 95 out of 5,020 of its members, in spite of all the Biblical teaching and scientific evidence to the contrary, still accept this doctrine. The wide disparity between the views of Methodists in the Central Jurisdiction and those of the respondents as a whole is so marked as to require no comment. Significantly, the only wide departures from the average upholding the segregationist position, except for the Central Jurisdiction, are the low percentage in the Western Jurisdiction, where the Negro population is lowest, and the high percentage in the Southeastern Jurisdiction, where it is highest. These jurisdictions also represent the extremes of gradualist sentiment among the predominantly white jurisdictions. Revealing is the contrast between the 80.4 per cent of the Central Jurisdiction who want racial segregation and discrimination abolished and the 8.4 per cent in the Southeastern Jurisdiction who take this position. Noteworthy also is the fact that none of the members of the Central Jurisdiction failed to answer this question; obviously the problem is one of deep concern to them.

Equally instructive are the replies to question 29 on "Race in the Organization of The Methodist Church," which are also given here in their entirety:

	Total	C	NC	NE	SC	SE	W
All jurisdictions, conferences, and churches should follow racial lines	14.5	1.5	10.2	9.1	15.5	34.1	6.4
The future status of the all-Negro jurisdiction and segregated Annual Conferences should be determined under permissive legislation	19.0	7.6	16.2	15.6	17.6	31.9	15.2

The all-Negro jurisdiction should now be abolished, and segregated

	Total	C	NC	NE	SC	SE	W
Annual Conferences and local churches should be gradually eliminated by permissive legislation	20.4	16.6	22.1	23.7	23.8	9.3	24.7
Racial segregation should be abolished at all levels	33.2	72.7	39.1	39.5	28.0	10.1	42.0
Write-in	3.6	1.6	2.2	3.4	4.7	6.5	3.0
No response	9.3	.0	10.2	8.7	10.4	8.1	8.7

The complexity of the problem and the difficulty of providing sufficient options in four statements may be reflected in the large percentages of write-in answers and omissions. Yet neither of these factors causes much trouble for Methodists in the Central Jurisdiction. As the people most concerned, they know what the problem is and where they stand regarding it. In view of this circumstance it seems likely that many of the nearly 10 per cent from the other jurisdictions who made no reply were either uninformed as to what the all-Negro jurisdiction is or insufficiently affected personally to care very much about the question. Either explanation would reflect at best a low degree of Christian social concern.

As in question 28, a sharp contrast appears between the scores of the Central Jurisdiction and those of the total group, except in the third position. Much greater is the spread between the Central and Southeastern Jurisdictions at all points. Revealing also is a comparison of the percentages of the Western with those of the Southeastern Jurisdiction. The former show a steady increase from the low of 6.4 per cent favoring complete segregation to the high of 42 per cent who want full integration. The picture presented by the Southeastern Jurisdiction is almost the reverse. Here there is a steady decrease from the high of 34.1 per cent for complete segregation to a low of 9.3 per cent for the third position, with a slightly higher number (10.1 per cent) favoring full integration. Again, white Methodists where the Negro population is smallest are much more favorable to the erasure of racial lines in the church than those where Negroes are most numerous. Obviously neither group is being guided mainly by purely religious or theological considerations.

Confirmation of the conclusions drawn from questions 28 and 29 is found in the replies to questions 48 and 49, which reflect the extent of Methodist participation in nonchurch organizations concerned with social problems. Of the total group, 16.7 per cent report participating regularly in the work of such organizations on the national level, while 17.2 per cent do so fairly often, 21.8 per cent seldom, and 18 per cent never. None of the predominantly white jurisdictions departs appreciably from this picture. In the Central Jurisdiction, however, 37.8 per cent report regular and 19.7 per cent fairly frequent participation in national organizations, while only 10.6 per cent take part seldom and only 9.1 per cent never.

The record of participation in nonchurch organizations concerned with social problems on the local community level is quite similar. Here the percentages are as follows:

	Regularly	Fairly Often	Seldom	Never
Total group	33.0	27.3	16.1	8.2
Central Jurisdiction	59.0	19.7	7.6	6.1

There is little variation in the percentages of the predominantly white jurisdictions. Interesting too is the fact that whereas 15.4 per cent of the total group made no response to this question, only 7.6 per cent of the Central Jurisdiction failed to reply. Clearly Negro Methodists show much more activity than white Methodists in organizations which seek a better society. Many, no doubt, are active members, nationally and in local chapters, of the National Association for the Advancement of Colored People. Apparently, when our personal and group interests are at stake we are concerned enough to organize and act together.

A similar orientation, though less pronounced, appears in the extent to which Methodists in different jurisdictions are willing to grant school teachers freedom to join "cause" organizations. Only a negligible percentage anywhere would deny this privilege entirely. Of the total number of respondents 8.6 per cent believe a teacher should join only those organizations approved by the institution employing him. However, only 3 per cent of the Central Jurisdiction take this position, whereas 16.9 per cent of the Southeastern Jurisdiction would favor this restriction. At the liberal end of the scale 70.4 per cent of the total affirm the teacher's right to join any social action organization which does not interfere with his effectiveness in teaching, and 12.1 per cent would allow the teacher to join any such organization— a total of 82.5 per cent upholding these two positions. The scores of the Central Jurisdiction in these categories are 81.8 per cent and 6.1 per cent respectively—a total of 87.9 per cent—whereas the Southeastern Jurisdiction percentages are 56.5 and 13.3 respectively—a total of 69.8 per cent. These differences are not great enough to justify sweeping conclusions, but taken with the other evidence they seem to indicate a more favorable attitude toward social action among those who are underprivileged because of race, and a somewhat less favorable attitude among those who possibly fear undesirable changes in the *status* quo if "cause" groups are not somehow restricted. It should be noted, however, that the questionnaire includes in its illustrations of "cause" organizations both the N.A.A.C.P. and the White Citizens' Councils.

In appraising data like these it is important to remember that the religious beliefs of Negro Methodists do not vary greatly from those of their white fellow members. Replies from the Central Jurisdiction to questions 1, 2, 3, 5, 13, 15, 16, 19, and 20 show almost complete uniformity with those from the other jurisdictions. Questions 8, 14, 17, and 18 reveal some variation from the average, but in the entire list of 20 questions the modal category for the Central Jurisdiction departs from that for the total number in only two instances—question 14, on the Christian's motivation for the good life, and question 17, on the responsibility of the church for social change. Even more significantly, the Central and Southeastern Jurisdictions, which differ most radically on the social questions just examined,[25] vary in similar ways from the other jurisdictions on a number of theological issues. Both find sin more deep-seated in human nature than do the others (4); both embrace a higher Christology (6); both espouse much more emphatically the view of the church as a Christ-renewed, Spirit-empowered community (7); and both give greater support to the traditional Methodist doctrine of the witness of the Spirit (11). Other instances of such covariance are questions 9, 10, and 12. Obviously regional factors are at work here. It seems clear that the differences in social thinking between Negro and white Methodists cannot

[25] See above, pp. 183 ff.

be traced to differences in religious belief, but are more soundly attributable to social and cultural factors.

C. Conclusions

In four sample areas we have discovered changes or variations in the theological thinking and the social beliefs and activities of Methodists which cannot be adequately explained unless a variety of non-theological factors are taken into account. Cultural factors affect religious beliefs as well as ethical and social judgments; they also modify the ways in which religious beliefs function in social thought and action. These influences are both positive and negative, serving sometimes to reinforce religious teaching and sometimes to undermine or counteract it. Unfortunately, they are negative often enough to justify the application to Methodists of John C. Bennett's observation: "The pressures of class interest, racial and ethnic prejudice, the national hysterias that have their periods of rise and decline distort the judgment and the conscience of people within the Christian community and outside." [26]

This is in no sense to forget the importance of the religious and theological factors which have been considered in the earlier chapters of this book. Many ambiguities have been discovered, and no mathematical calculation can be made of the precise effect of religious beliefs on the social concern of those who hold them. But clearly a great many Methodist individuals and groups definitely relate the positions they take on social questions to their basic Christian faith. Moreover, it is always in order to ask how much less enlightened the social attitudes of imperfect churchmen might have been, had those attitudes not been tempered with Christian teaching, however dimly understood or haltingly applied.

The truth seems to be that religious attitudes, beliefs, and practices on the one hand and social, economic, and cultural life and thought on the other function in reciprocal relation, each affecting the other in manifold ways. It must always be the concern of the Christian church to heighten the creative and redemptive influence of the former and to channel toward constructive ends the positive potentialities of the latter, while restricting the destructive, antisocial tendencies of both.

[26] *Christians and the State* (New York: Harper and Brothers, 1959), p. 21.

PART TWO

Proposals

CHAPTER SEVEN

Toward a Theology of Society

OUR INVESTIGATION MAKES PLAIN THAT MUCH OF THE THINK-
ing and acting of Methodists on social questions proceeds without
clear reference to any basic structure of religious conviction. Many
discussions of social problems and programs deal perceptively with
the ethical issues involved, but omit theological considerations entirely. Many other individual and corporate statements cite particular
Christian teachings in support of social positions, but seldom with
any indication that these doctrines are expressions or component parts
of a total Christian conception of society. Nor has there been much
exploration of the possible social implications of the Wesleyan doctrinal emphases, especially in the context of ecumenical theology.

In view of this situation, there is no occasion for surprise in the
ambiguities, inconsistencies, and cultural accommodations which we
have noted in Chapters Five and Six. To the degree that social
policies are formulated and decisions made without a specifically
Christian frame of reference, to that degree they are likely to reflect
the whims of individuals or the limited interests and partial perspectives of special groups inside or outside the church which are able
to command attention. Where there is little effort to root social objectives or methods of achieving them in a fundamental understanding of the Christian faith, the social ethic of the church easily absorbs
much of the social ethic prevailing in its surrounding culture, and
"Christian" standards become almost imperceptibly those of democracy, the Declaration of Independence, the American way of life, or
the like. If this happens, there is no good reason why Christians should
look to the church for special guidance as they make their decisions on
ethical and social questions. The absence of a central Christian orienta-

tion may also affect motivation sufficiently to account partially for the frequent failure of Methodists to express in action the social beliefs which they profess.

Some theology, or at least some basic point of view, is at the bottom of every form of social action. The question for Christians is therefore not whether they will have a theology or not, but whether their theology will be an unconscious, implicit, accidental, ill-defined, confused body of beliefs inadequately related to either the Christian gospel or the demands of daily life, or a carefully-wrought, integrated structure of conviction soundly rooted in the realities of Christian faith, and thus qualified to illuminate from the perspective of faith the intricate problems which face men in society. A theology of the latter type is one of the profound needs of The Methodist Church— and of Protestantism in general—today. The remainder of this book will be an attempt to suggest in broad outline one form which such a theology of society might take.

What is offered here can be little more than introductory. To lay complete theological foundations for a Christian social ethic would require a far more exhaustive treatment than present limitations of space allow. Many important questions must either be omitted entirely or examined only in a preliminary way. However, we can hope to indicate, in close relation to the descriptive study already made, some of the directions in which a more thorough discussion might move.

Obviously such a venture as this has an undeniably normative quality, in the sense that it seeks to develop certain emphases which the writer and his fellow researchers believe to be truly desirable for the church. But in no sense do these chapters pretend to set forth an official, definitive, authoritative, or all-Methodist conception of the theological bases of social thought and action. They are offered as a small contribution to the discussion of an urgent question, in the hope that they may help to stimulate other fuller inquiries. Out of such conversations may emerge a much closer approximation to what a Christian view of society should be than any statement now available.

In keeping with Methodism's ecumenical spirit and her position in the main stream of Protestant Christianity, we shall seek guidance primarily in the fundamental meaning of the Christian faith. Within this context we shall inquire what social implications may be found in the characteristic doctrinal emphases of John Wesley and historic Methodism. It would not be appropriate for members of one communion apart from others to proclaim as distinctive and superior its own particular conception of Christian social responsibility. On the contrary, it is appropriate and highly desirable that each communion should ask: "From our particular background and from our perspective within the Christian tradition, which aspects of truth concerning human society under God are we best qualified to illuminate? What has God given us to say and give to his church as a whole, and to the world to which we are all called to minister? What may we in turn receive from others which may be incorporated into a common Christian social witness?" Questions of this kind will therefore have a place in our search for a Christian social theology.

Our purpose will not be served if we simply list and expound the social implications of a series of relevant religious beliefs, such as those dealt with in Chapter Four. What is needed is rather a unified structure or configuration, a key-principle informing and vitalizing the whole organism of Christian thought concerning man's social relationships. Such an integrating center we shall now seek to discover and interpret.

A. The Search for a Foundation Principle

Christian faith arises initially as a joyous, grateful response to the redemptive action of God in Jesus Christ, and the life which results is the believer's continuing answer in trust, love, and obedience to God's manifold activity. Thus the ethical life of the Christian, as distinguished from that of others, centers in and issues from his relation to God, particularly to God as disclosed in the life, teachings, death, and resurrection of Jesus Christ. In such a relation the motivation for right living is the desire to serve him to whom we owe all; and the rightness of an attitude or act depends on the degree to which it represents a fitting response to the ways in which God has acted and now acts in human life.[1]

[1] In connection with this Protestant ethic of response the writer is indebted to the "Evangelical ethics" of H. Richard Niebuhr. See his penetrating chapter, "Evangelical and Protestant Ethics," in *The Heritage of the Reformation*, ed. Elmer J. F. Arndt (New York: Richard R. Smith, 1950), pp. 211-29.

According to Christian faith God's activities are infinitely rich and diversified, surpassing human comprehension. But in four discernible ways his deeds are peculiarly significant for the life of man on earth. He is constantly active as Creator and Sustainer of all existence, and upon his creative activity the very life of man constantly depends. He is the Lord of history and moral Governor of all human relations, acting in discipline and judgment to overthrow those ways of living which oppose his will and supporting those which fulfill it. He is the Redeemer of men and society, acting in suffering, reconciling, triumphant love to restore the relation broken by sin and to draw all men to himself. Finally, he is Strengthener, Life-giver, Sanctifier, seeking to empower his people and upbuild them in true holiness.

These four forms of activity can without distortion be viewed as essentially three, since judgment is involved in both the creative and the redemptive activity of God. The Creator and Sustainer is Sovereign of history and Judge of men; and the Redeemer, acting not vindictively but in sacrificial love, judges in order to redeem. This is in fact the interpretation adopted in the Christian doctrine of the Trinity. The threefold conception of God's unitary activity—as Creator, Redeemer, and Life-giver—may contribute greatly to our understanding of God's relation to human society.[2]

The whole life of man depends constantly on the energy of God, who in infinite wisdom and sovereign goodness creates, sustains, and orders his world, and summons men to act in responsible freedom to fulfill the creative potentialities he has given them. When they oppose his righteous will and choose their own self-centered way instead of his, he acts both in radical judgment, confronting them inexorably with the bitter consequences of their sin, and in forgiving love and healing power, seeking to deliver his erring children from their bondage to sin and death. But full deliverance is positive as well as negative; thus God acts as indwelling Spirit to re-create and make holy the life of men and society, and to deepen love and advance true community among men and between men and God.

Creation and redemption are often linked as grounds of social con-

---

[2] During World War II this trinitarian conception provided the foundation of a discerning study of the church and war by a commission of Christian scholars, *The Relation of the Church to the War in the Light of the Christian Faith* (Federal Council of the Churches of Christ in America, 1944).

cern. In Christian teaching, as we have already noted in Chapter Four, men are summoned to seek each other's welfare and a just social order because all men are children of one Father, and because all persons are objects of God's redeeming love manifest in Christ. Eric Baker, British Methodist theologian, has stated these two closely related motifs with simplicity and effectiveness in declaring that "men are one because God made them all and Jesus died for all." [3]

It is very easy, however, to overemphasize the distinction between these two phases of the divine activity, and that between each of them and the work of God as Holy Spirit. The intimate relation between creation and redemption in Christian thought appears in the way in which traditional theology has conceived of the eternal Logos, Word, or Son not only as incarnate in Jesus Christ for human redemption, but also as in some sense participating in the work of creation. Paul sounded a frequently recurring note when, in writing to the Colossians of God's "beloved Son, in whom we have redemption, the forgiveness of sins," he added immediately: "He is the image of the invisible God, the first-born of all creation; . . . all things were created . . . through him and for him. He is before all things, and in him all things hold together" (Col. 1:14-17).

Similarly, the activities ascribed to Son and Spirit in Christian thought cannot be sharply separated, but overlap. As Cyril Richardson has pointed out, both terms focus attention on God the Related rather than God the Beyond. They speak of God in his relation to the life of man, as distinguished from God in his ineffable, transcendent glory.[4] Both are concerned with what God does among men to reveal himself and to inspire, renew, re-create, and sanctify human life.

Historic Christian faith has always recognized this underlying unity in the manifold activity of God. It has also tended strongly to interpret the divine activity primarily from the standpoint of redemption— without in any sense obscuring or devaluating the other aspects of God's work. While continually viewing man as the creature of God, Christianity has had to reckon with the fact that he has in rebellious pride distorted the divine image in which he was created and broken the fellowship with his Creator, hence stands in need of salvation. It is creation as spoiled by sin that figures mainly in the gospel.

[3] *The Faith of a Methodist*, p. 13. London. The Epworth Press, 1958.
[4] *The Doctrine of the Trinity* (Nashville: Abingdon Press, 1958), pp. 13-27, 141-49.

Further, the redemption begun in Jesus Christ needs to be completed and fulfilled, and the work of the Holy Spirit is always seen as enlarging, empowering, deepening, and making holy the lives of those who have been made new creatures in Christ Jesus. Thus God's total redemptive activity seeks the restoration and fulfillment of his purpose in creation.

There is no question about the centrality of salvation in Christian theology. This is what the New Testament is all about! The gospel is the good tidings of what God has done and is doing for the salvation of mankind. The book that tells this joyous story is most properly designated the New Covenant—a covenant offered by the grace of him who wrought in Christ to reconcile the world to himself (II Cor. 5:19). It tells of one who was called Jesus because he was to save his people from their sins, and who was anointed

> to preach good news to the poor . . .
> to proclaim release to the captives
> and recovering of sight to the blind,
> to set at liberty those who are oppressed,
> to proclaim the acceptable year of the Lord.
> —Luke 4:18

Moreover, the Christian faith and life which we have described as called forth by the prior action of God are centrally man's answer to the saving work of God. The deepest springs of gratitude, repentance, and commitment are touched by man's awareness of the rejection which his sin has deserved and of the costliness of the undeserved love which has acted to redeem him. The most profound interpretation of the Christian ethical life sees it as the thankful, faithful, loving response of those who have been saved by divine grace.

It is highly instructive to note the way in which the Letter to the Ephesians makes precisely this connection. First the author describes how Christ's death on the cross has wrought the reconciliation of men to God, and of Jew and Gentile to each other:

In him we have redemption through his blood. . . . God, who is rich in mercy, out of the great love with which he loved us, even when we were dead through our trespasses, made us alive together with Christ. . . . By grace you have been saved through faith; and this is not your own doing, it is the gift of God. . . . In Christ Jesus you who once were far off have been brought near in the blood of Christ. For he is our peace, who has made us both one, and has broken down the dividing wall of hostility . . . that he might create in himself one new man in place of the two, so making peace, and might reconcile us both to God in one body through the cross, thereby bringing the hostility to an end. . . . Through him we both have access in one Spirit to the Father.

—Eph. 1:7; 2:4-5, 13-16, 18

The at-one-ment which God has effected in Christ then becomes the basis of a stirring appeal to Christians to offer to God lives marked by a love akin to his:

I therefore . . . beg you to lead a life worthy of the calling to which you have been called, with all lowliness and meekness, with patience, forbearing one another in love. . . . Be renewed in the spirit of your minds, and put on the new nature, created after the likeness of God in true righteousness and holiness. Therefore, putting away falsehood, let everyone speak the truth with his neighbor, for we are members of one another. . . . Be kind to one another, tenderhearted, forgiving one another, as God in Christ forgave you. Therefore be imitators of God, as beloved children. And walk in love, as Christ loved us and gave himself up for us, a fragrant offering and sacrifice to God.[5]

—Eph. 4:1-2, 23-25, 32; 5:1-2

"You are not your own," writes Paul to the Corinthians; "you were bought with a price. So glorify God in your body" (I Cor. 6:19-20). The Johannine message is the same: "In this the love of God was made manifest among us, that God sent his only Son into the world, so that we might live through him. . . . Beloved, if God so loved us, we also ought to love one another. . . . We love, because he first loved us" (I John 4:9, 11, 19).

In passages like these the authors do not deny or even ignore their status as creatures of God or their dependence on his continuing creative action. Yet the reality which primarily motivates the good life and more than anything else determines its quality is the experience of being forgiven and given a new start by the mercy of God displayed in Jesus Christ. Nor do such statements overlook the abid-

[5] Italics mine.

203

ing presence of God as indwelling Spirit of holiness. In fact, the very nature of the redemption begun in Christ requires that the redeemed go forward in constant reliance on the power of God, "strengthened with might through his Spirit in the inner man" (Eph. 3:16). Salvation is not a once-for-all occurrence, but a continuing, growing, deepening experience in which the recipient responds daily to new manifestations of divine grace with new commitments and new acts of love.

Rooted in God, salvation thus comes to full flower in the life of righteousness and love toward God and all whom God loves. This means that salvation is for truly Christian faith inevitably social. Men do not live alone, and they cannot be saved in isolation. They must be saved as whole persons, and this means as persons-in-community, with all manner of interlocking connections. It is amid these connections, and related to other individuals in the manifold activities of daily life, that persons express the range and depth of their grateful response to God's forgiving and transforming love.

This aspect becomes especially clear when we consider the indispensable role of the church in salvation as portrayed in the New Testament. The good news is proclaimed by the church, and he who responds enters "the household of God," the community of those who have previously heard and answered the divine call. It is within this closely knit fellowship, "the body of Christ," that salvation is fulfilled. Its members are summoned to use their God-given talents to build up the body in love, that they may "all attain to the unity of the faith and of the knowledge of the Son of God, to mature manhood, to the measure of the stature of the fullness of Christ." Nourished and strengthened by Christ, the head, they "grow up in every way into him" (Eph. 2:19; 4:1-16).

But the church cannot be the church of Christ and live in isolation from society. As his body it is called to carry on his work in the world. It is a redemptive as well as a redeemed community. As Paul declares, the God "who through Christ reconciled us to himself . . . gave us the ministry of reconciliation" (II Cor. 5:18-19). This is the mission of the church, and all its members have a share in it. But they can fulfill it only as they participate freely and responsibly in the life of society. They are called to witness where they are to what God has done and is doing to restore men to their true relation to him and to each other. In their own lives they are to be his agents, carrying for-

204

ward the work of Christ in reconciling man with God and man with man.

Thus the very nature and mission of the church in the redemptive purpose of God give it a profound social significance. Its oneness in Christ, stressed not only in Ephesians but throughout the New Testament, leaves no room for economic, national, or racial divisions which destroy community. Since the church is called to preach the gospel of salvation to all men, all men are potential members; hence it is committed in principle to the abolition of such divisions. Further, in the process of fulfilling its task it introduces men into that common relation to a saving God which is the only sure foundation of true community.

The social relevance of the church as the redemptive body of Christ becomes still clearer when we notice the nature of the love which it is called upon to practice and spread. In the New Testament true agape [6] is not merely a relation between two individuals, but a koinonia[7] love, involving the profound fellowship of those who "in Christ" share his "unsearchable riches." Such love binds persons together in a community of interlocking relationships deeply rooted in the activity of the Holy Spirit. Under its influence individuals lose their private selves only to find them enriched and fulfilled in communion with God and other human beings. A church which knows the meaning of koinonia love will not be content simply to tell the good news to others; it will rather seek to share with them in intimate community the fullness of the forgiving, transforming love of God. This cannot be done when men's "spiritual" needs are separated from their occupational, economic, recreational, social, and political concerns. A church motivated by koinonia love will extend as widely as possible, and in all human relationships, the faith for which "there is neither Jew nor Greek, there is neither slave nor free, there is neither male nor female; for you are all one in Christ Jesus" (Gal. 3:28).[8]

The New Testament contains no blueprint for a Christian social order. Indeed, so convinced were most of the first Christians of the

---

[6] See John 17; I Cor. 12 and 13; I John.

[7] The Greek word used in the New Testament to designate the deep inner spirit of fellowship or communion which binds together in love those who compose the church.

[8] Here the writer is indebted to the interpretation of L. Harold DeWolf, mentioned above, p. 138.

imminent end of the world and the early inauguration of God's New Age that sweeping changes in the structure of earthly society must have seemed to them relatively unimportant. As a minority group with little political or economic power they also were in no position to initiate or carry through such changes. Hence they made no frontal attack on institutions like slavery, war, or Roman imperialism. Even so, the leaven of the gospel worked quietly but powerfully within the Christian fellowship to establish a new pattern of family relations and to obliterate all the false barriers of race, nationality, sex, and social status.[9]

The situation of Christians today is quite different. We do not expect the early end of the world—unless it be accomplished by the folly of man through nuclear war. Unlike our first-century ancestors, among us are many who hold positions of great responsibility in the political, economic, and social life of our time, and in most Western countries even the lowliest Christian has some voice. In America the opportunity for Christian people to shape the life of society is very great. But the gospel of redemption committed to us is the same as that which the New Testament writers proclaim. We have therefore a clear mandate to explore and explicate the revolutionary implications of our faith in terms that are relevant to our own day.

The nature of society itself, especially its interdependence, strongly reinforces the inner demand of the gospel that it be related to the total life of the human community. Though, strictly speaking, only individuals can sin or do the right, in a profound way good and evil in men's group relations are collective in nature, not merely the sum of the good and evil deeds of individuals. Thus society, too, stands in need of redemption. Moreover, individuals may be either corrupted or benefited by their group involvements. Therefore, even a Christian concern limited to the salvation of individuals would have to seek the improvement of the environment in which they live and grow. Hence Christians are obliged, as Paul A. Carter affirms, "to act directly upon the social order and work for its reconstruction, as a part of their religious responsibility to their fellow men." [10]

[9] See, for example, Acts 2:5-11; 10:1–11:18; Gal. 3:26-29; Eph. 5:21–6:4; Col. 3:11.
[10] *The Decline and Revival of the Social Gospel*, New York, Columbia University Press, 1956, p. 5.

Clarence Tucker Craig relates this responsibility quite directly to the salvation wrought when men respond to the redemptive action of God. Those who are redeemed by God's grace, he writes,

are *required* to respond by a life in the Spirit which is well-pleasing to him. This will involve a corporate response in the social and political areas, for a salvation which does not eventuate in changes in these areas as well as in purely personal relations stopped short of full realization.[11]

A significant ecumenical recognition of the social nature of the salvation proclaimed in the gospel appears, for example, in one of the reports of the Conference on Church, Community, and State held at Oxford in 1937. Section III on "The Church and the Economic Order" declared, "We must love our fellow men because God loves them and wills to redeem them." With this background it insisted that

the message of the gospel is not addressed . . . to the individual alone. Christianity is emphatically a social religion. Its teaching is directed to men not as units isolated from their fellows but as members of groups and communities. . . . It asserts that the relations of men to one another are part of their relation to God. . . . It is clearly the duty of Christians, therefore, to test by the canons of their faith not merely their individual conduct and the quality of their private lives, but also the institutional framework of organized society.[12]

B. A Social Theology of Salvation

In the foregoing discussion we have been led to a theology of salvation as the foundation of a dynamic Christian social ethic. The social concern of the Christian is implicit in and an outgrowth of his experience of redemption, and the social task of the church is part of its ministry of reconciliation. The steps leading to this conclusion might be summarized as follows:

1. From the perspective of Christian faith, the mighty acts of God center in what he has done and is doing in love to redeem sinful men and fulfill his purpose in creation.

[11] "A Methodist Contribution," *Biblical Authority for Today*, ed. Alan Richardson and Wolfgang Schweitzer, p. 53.

[12] J. H. Oldham (ed.), *The Oxford Conference: Official Report* (Chicago and New York: Willett, Clark & Co., 1937), pp. 76, 92.

2. Christian faith and life, including the ethical life, are man's grateful, repentant, loving response to God's saving grace.

3. The salvation thus made possible finds fulfillment as men empowered by God grow and deepen in love toward God and all whom God loves.

4. Salvation is inevitably social, involving persons in their wholeness, inter-related with other persons in manifold ways.

5. Salvation is realized within the fellowship of a redeemed and redeeming community, the church, which is called to a ministry of reconciliation of man with God and man with man.

6. Both the inner nature of the gospel and the interdependence of society require the church so commissioned to seek the redemption and transformation of the total life of man, corporate and institutional as well as individual.

This conception has been derived directly from an examination of the nature of the Christian faith. However, it is implicit in and binds together the six Protestant ecumenical doctrinal emphases which Methodists have cited as major grounds of social concern.[13] The Bible recounts above everything else the acts of the God who "has visited and redeemed his people" (Luke 1:68), and the ethical as well as the religious teachings of Jesus all aim to relate people to God's saving power. God's universal fatherhood, righteous sovereignty, and reconciling love are all summed up and expressed in God's work as Redeemer of men. The deepest ground of the real worth of persons is that God not only created them for fellowship with himself but acts at infinite cost to overcome their sinful estrangement. The social significance of salvation is immeasurably heightened when the whole Christian message is regarded as the gospel of redemption. The love which is the norm of the Christian ethical life is called forth by the saving love of God manifest in Christ. The kingdom of God takes on deepest meaning when it is related to the purpose of God to redeem and fulfill human history, and to the consummation of that purpose at the end of history. The social task of the church is most fully understood when it is conceived as part of a total ministry of reconciliation which continues God's redeeming work in Christ for all mankind.

It is likewise clear that a social ethic organized around salvation

[13] See above, Chapter Four.

is ideally qualified to serve as a theology of society for Christians in the Wesleyan tradition. The main drive of John Wesley's ministry was his concern for the redemption of men, and the heart of his controversy with his administrative superiors and many of the parish priests of the Church of England was his conviction that they were recreant to their obligation to preach the gospel of God's saving love to multitudes desperately in need of it. This is why he dared to "look upon all the world" as his parish.

Thus far I mean, that in whatever part of it I am I judge it meet, right, and my bounden duty to declare, unto all that are willing to hear, the glad tidings of salvation. This is the work which I know God has called me to; and sure I am that his blessing attends it.[14]

In Wesley's view the church is called to be the agent of God in the salvation of the world, spreading "scriptural holiness" and building up persons in love toward God and man. Nothing that obstructs that task is sacrosanct; everything that advances it is acceptable.

This basic concern found harmonious expression in Wesley's characteristic doctrinal emphases: sinful man's need of repentance (the porch of religion); justification by grace through faith, universally available and personally experienced (the door of religion); and holiness—sanctification and perfection (the house of religion). As we have seen,[15] these doctrines are integrally related in Wesley's thought in what may accurately be called his theology of salvation.

Hence a conception of Christian social responsibility which centers in the gospel of redemption has a built-in point of contact with Wesleyan thought. It may also provide a perfect medium for working out the social implications which were clearly present in Wesley's teachings but which Wesley himself never fully developed.

There are thus three good reasons for believing that in the concept of redemption we have found the key principle for a sound theology of society. (1) A social theology centering in salvation broadly interpreted will be true to the deepest meaning of the Christian gospel, which calls on men to respond in trust to God's redemptive work for mankind. (2) It will provide an integrating center for the ecumeni-

[14] "To James Hervey," Letters, I, 286.
[15] See above, pp. 204 ff.

cal doctrines which Methodists and other Protestants have actually regarded as socially significant. (3) Finally, it will build on and develop the major emphasis of the Wesleyan tradition itself.

One other consideration, practical as well as theological, suggests the wisdom of the orientation suggested. Among many Christians there has been a strong tendency to regard evangelism and social action as separate if not opposed concerns. As a result, much evangelism has proceeded with little conception of the reality and seriousness of men's social sins, and little or no awareness that Christian commitment involves the acceptance of social responsibility. On the other hand, much social action has ignored the pervasive sway of individual sin in the social evils it attacks; forgotten the need for personal transformation; urged men to act rightly without relating them to the power of God, apart from which they cannot act rightly; or treated symptoms without penetrating to basic causes. The Methodist Church of Canada, apparently perceiving the fallacy of this separation, performed both activities through one Department of Social Service and Evangelism. Similarly, the United Church of Canada, formed in 1925 by a merger of Congregationalists, Presbyterians, and Methodists, has one Board of Evangelism and Social Service. A comparable sense of the oneness of the two tasks is profoundly needed in our other Protestant churches today, however that oneness may be expressed in board structures. A strategic contribution to the development of such an awareness can be made by a social theology basically concerned with the salvation of whole persons in all of their interlocking relations with each other.

CHAPTER EIGHT

The Meaning of Social Redemption

HAVING FOUND FIRM FOUNDATIONS FOR A CHRISTIAN SOCIAL ethic in a theology centering in salvation, we have now to ask what kind of superstructure may soundly be built on such a foundation. Two types of questions press for answers. First, just what is meant by a redeemed society? In comparison to the salvation of an individual, what does it mean for a society to be "saved"? What clues may we find in a theology of salvation to the nature of the social order we should seek? What are sound Christian goals for society?

Secondly, to what degree are such goals attainable on earth? In what sense, if any, can there be such a reality as a Christian society? How should Christians think and act in order to exert a redemptive influence in society? What guidance may we find in the Christian faith for right decisions on social questions? How does the Christian form ethical judgments? How can we discover sound norms or principles which are applicable to present-day social problems? What is the social responsibility of the church?

These two types of questions will be considered, respectively, in the present chapter and the one to follow. Problems as complex and important as these, eliciting widely diversified answers, demand far more thorough examination than is possible within the limits of this volume. The discussion will attempt to point certain directions in which Christian thought may appropriately move with respect to the theological issues underlying the moot questions. More than this, however, it cannot hope to do. It will be impossible, for example, to undertake any careful criticism of alternative positions. The most that can be expected is some clear indication of the directions which may soundly be taken, in the context of the doctrinal emphases already examined, by a socially oriented theology of salvation.

A. What Is Social Salvation?

Negatively, salvation involves primarily deliverance from sin. Adequate understanding of its meaning, therefore, depends partly on a clear notion of the nature of sin. In the individual, sin may be broadly defined as any attitude or action which is contrary to the will of God. Within the large area encompassed by this definition we may distinguish five concentric circles, marked, from center to circumference, by steadily decreasing measures of personal choice and responsibility. Sin may be (1) conscious, voluntary disobedience, in thought or deed, to the known will of God; (2) failure to keep the basic attitude and purpose of one's life in harmony with the divine will; (3) attitudes and actions so inextricably intertwined with those of other persons that the extent of one's real responsibility is impossible to trace; (4) decisions made in situations in which every possible choice inevitably involves for the spiritually sensitive person some conscious violation of the will of God; and (5) unconscious, unrecognized, unsuspected departures from the divine purpose.

Since the wrong involved in the fourth and fifth of these areas is unavoidable and therefore implies no personal guilt, some thinkers would prefer not to designate it as sin. However, it is materially though not formally sinful, and it involves circumstances from which and in which men desperately need to be saved. Hence the term sin seems an appropriate designation. All of the choices mentioned involve some alienation of man from God and some hindrance to the fulfillment of God's perfect will for his children. Hence all constitute occasions where a change is profoundly needed. This change is salvation.

Salvation is deliverance from the guilt and power of sin to a life of righteousness in filial fellowship with God, begun and advanced in this world and deepened and enriched in the life to come. It is victory over those ways of thought and life which separate us from God and our fellows. It involves the restoration of inner harmony, the re-establishment of right human relations, and reconciliation with God.

Salvation has also a broader meaning, including deliverance from many experiences which may not entail sin in the individual who suf-

212

fers them, though they may be caused partly by the sins of others. For example, persons need to be saved from fear to faith, from despair to hope, from death to life. They need to be delivered from physical and mental illness to health, from poverty to the satisfaction of material needs, from ignorance to wisdom and ethical discernment.[1] While redemption from sin remains central in the gospel, salvation in the fully Christian sense includes deliverance from evils like these as well.

Greater concreteness is imparted to the concept of salvation when it is related to its Hebrew counterpart, the Arabic root [2] of which means simply *room*. Thus to be saved means literally to have space enough to move around in without restriction. The psalmist sings gratefully:

> Into thy hand I commit my spirit;
>   thou hast redeemed me, O Lord, faithful God.
>
> . . . .
>
> [Thou] hast not delivered me into the hand of the enemy;
>   thou hast set my feet in a broad place.[3]

This connotation was peculiarly relevant to the experience of the Hebrew people, with their history of long years of confinement to narrow territories during the bondage in Egypt and the captivity in Babylon. But it is hardly less applicable to those enslaved by sin, captive to the self-centered passions of their own hearts. It is not accidental that Christians call Savior one who came that man might have abundant life. The saved life is the life that is free, spacious, roomy, unhampered, because it is opened to and controlled by the purposes of him in whose will is perfect freedom. "In some germinal and rudimentary form," wrote Walter Rauschenbusch, "salvation must turn us from a life centered on ourselves toward a life going out toward God and man." [4]

---

[1] See Luke 1:46-55, 67-79; 4:16-21.

[2] wesa‘; Hebrew, yesa‘.

[3] Psa. 31:5, 8, Revised Standard Version. The King James Version of verse eight reads:
> "[Thou] hast not shut me up into the hand of the enemy:
>   thou hast set my feet in a large room."

[4] *A Theology for the Social Gospel* (New York: The Macmillan Company, 1918), p. 98.

The term redemption has a similar import. Ancient family law provided that if a person was sold into slavery, his nearest male relative should if possible buy his freedom and thus restore the solidarity of the family. This kinsman was called the redeemer. In view of the intimate covenant relation between God and Israel, it was natural that the term should be broadened and applied to God, who acted to free his enslaved people. Redemption therefore connotes, negatively, deliverance by divine action from bondage to sin; and, positively, forgiveness, reconciliation, and freedom for a new life in the strength of God.

These interpretations of sin and salvation for the individual cannot be literally or rigidly carried over to society, but they do make clear in broad outline what is meant by social sin and social redemption. Since man is inherently a social being, each individual is enmeshed in intricate interconnections with other individuals and in manifold group relationships. Groups, however, have no existence apart from the individuals which compose them. All so-called social sins are therefore ultimately the sins of individuals, and their evil consequences come to a focus in the lives of individuals.

Nevertheless, there is a more-than-individual quality in social sin. The term refers to attitudes and actions which are shared by the persons who compose a group and which are opposed to the will of God for the members of that group and other groups affected. Such joint participation heightens the injurious results of collective sins, creates the impression of impersonal causation, and makes it easy for individuals to disclaim personal responsibility. Any sanctioning by one group of conditions or actions which impair fullness of life for the members of other groups is social sin. Instances which come readily to mind are war; discrimination on the basis of race, color, religion, social status, or national origin; misuse of natural resources; abuse of political power; denials of opportunity for useful work, favorable working conditions, and fair income; and connivance in or passive acceptance of conditions which breed crime, delinquency, disease, and ignorance; and indifference to various forms of preventable evil.[5]

Social salvation, then, is the deliverance of groups, and of society in general, from the conditions, attitudes, and activities which blight life and obstruct the divine purpose; and the establishment of group

[5] See below, pp. 59 ff.

relations which express and encourage the concern of persons for each other's welfare, make possible the realization of their highest potentialities, and facilitate their entrance into a transforming experience of the love and power of God. In short, social salvation consists of those changes in social conditions and group attitudes and actions which further the salvation of individuals in relation to each other. Furthermore, just as individual salvation is not a once-for-all accomplishment, a static, finished condition, so social redemption is a process rather than a state. Groups and societies are not so much saved as put on the way to salvation or in process of being saved.

B. Social Repentance

We have previously seen[6] that in John Wesley's theology repentance, faith, and holiness are respectively the porch, the door, and the house of religion, or, more specifically, of salvation. These three aspects are so basic in the Christian account of individual redemption that they provide a natural framework for the development of a doctrine of social salvation. We shall not expect any exact correspondence between the redemption of the individual and that of society. The former must not become a Procrustean bed into which the latter is forced. But clarification should result if we ask what each of the three Wesleyan—and ecumenical—emphases means with respect to the salvation of the group life of mankind. A slight modification of Wesley's scheme also seems in order. A sense of sin and the repentance which results are more than the porch of salvation; they constitute also an actual entrance into the experience. Further, justification by grace through faith is more than the door; the need for new experiences of forgiveness as well as repentance continues throughout the earthly life of the Christian. Hence we shall think of repentance as the door of salvation and of justification by faith and sanctification as two adjoining rooms in the house to which the door leads.

What does it mean for a group or a society to repent? Strictly speaking it is only individuals who sin, and therefore only individuals can repent. Nevertheless, social repentance has a valid meaning of its own. The term refers to the remorseful repudiation, by groups of

* See above, pp. 59 ff.

individuals, of sins against other groups—shared attitudes and acts which injure other persons because of their membership in an affected group.

Such an experience is the first condition of social salvation and the first step toward its realization. Neither individuals nor groups can be redeemed unless they are aware of their need of redemption. This involves repentance. Yet such a spirit is notoriously lacking in most groups, even those composed predominantly of professing Christians. As Reinhold Niebuhr vividly pointed out in *Moral Man and Immoral Society*,[7] human social relations are even harder to moralize than those of individuals, because actions undertaken by groups readily take on an impersonal character in which individual responsibility is hidden, because direct casual connections are much harder to trace, because group relations afford more scope for the operation of unfettered pride, and because groups find it easier to rationalize their self-centered motives and pretend that they are nobler than they actually are. This makes all the more imperative a clear-sighted acknowledgment of the great gap between the divine intention for society and the concrete actuality of men's group relations.

Some of the more obvious social sins which call for repentance have already been mentioned.[8] However, the Christian conscience needs to be sensitized also to the less flagrant sins of omission and hidden involvement in evil which beset all men. Precisely because these are easily overlooked, they offer insidious encouragement to self-righteousness on the part of average church members. Three forms assumed by these departures from the divine will may be listed here.

1. Acquiescence in or indifference to evils for which we share responsibility. By inertia if not outright opposition we prevent needed changes in the *status quo*. In self-centered pursuit of private ends or limited group goals, we fail to see injustices from which we indirectly profit. We tacitly approve, by failing to oppose, social policies and practices which entail suffering for other people. Unquestioningly we share—through dividends on our life insurance policies if in no other way—in the gains of corporations whose names we do not know and of whose advertising practices and labor policies we are completely

[7] New York: Charles Scribner's Sons, 1932.
[8] See above, pp. 214 ff.

ignorant. In our complex economic order, how many individuals have the time or ability to check carefully the ethics of the business firms whose profits help to make possible the interest on their savings accounts? We accept uncritically the materialistic, competitive standards of success of our sensate culture. We fall easy prey to the advocates of "planned obsolescence," unmindful of the temptations this involves for many to spend on the latest model money which might otherwise advance some social cause, strengthen the benevolent work of the church, or start a daughter in college.

Finding it difficult to keep informed on world affairs and even harder to form judgments in the light of our Christian convictions, we passively if not actively approve almost any foreign policy which our government may pursue. We raise few questions about an economic prosperity made possible in considerable measure by colossal military expenditures. In a manner unworthy of our professed faith in a universal God, we accept a black-white picture of East and West, readily believing the worst about the Soviet Union while pretending that our own country can do no wrong. Keeping silent in the face of a bitter race with Russia in the production and testing of hydrogen bombs and intercontinental missiles, we contribute to the nationalistic bravado and the building up of tensions which lead toward war.

2. Insensitivity to the problems, needs, and aspirations of members of minority groups or other less fortunate members of society. How many white persons really grasp the full meaning of the rebuffs and indignities experienced daily by Negroes, North and South, as they face the ordinary human problems of getting an education, finding a respectable place to live, locating a job consonant with their training and abilities, gaining access to recreational facilities, and simply securing enough to eat and wear on the low incomes from the types of work open to most members of their race? We enjoy the quality and convenience of modern frozen and canned foods, but seldom think of the drab existence of the migrant laborers whose work is often indispensable to the production of such foods—their rootlessness and lack of any stable community life, the absence of adequate educational and religious opportunities for their children, their substandard housing.

We open a neatly-packaged shirt from the department store and casually note the paper slip with its memo, "Pressed by No. 59," or

"Inspected by No. 378," with hardly a thought for those who, as numbers rather than persons, work year after year at monotonous assembly-line tasks. We all benefit from the hard, dirty, dangerous work of coal miners, whether directly from the comfort of buildings heated by coal or indirectly from the products of factories where coal is the source of power. How vividly do we remember these things when attempting to weigh the issues of a miners' strike for better wages, working conditions, pensions, or the like? We read of the bitter plight of Arab refugees or of poverty in underdeveloped countries, but are seldom moved to action to improve such conditions. When economic aid to other lands is up for consideration, we are likely to ask first whether these people are on our side in the cold war, or how much such aid will raise our taxes. We lack the imagination to put ourselves in others' places, to "sit where they sit" and see life from their perspective.

3. The easy assumption of superior worthiness on the part of the more favored members of society. The privileged easily dull their consciences in the presence of glaring inequities by convincing themselves that their opportunities are due to righteousness or industry exceeding those of other men, and that the disadvantages of others are always traceable to their own laziness, improvidence, or irresponsibility. From a truly Christian perspective, however, we are all unworthy of what we have received. When we have done all, we are still unprofitable servants who fall far short of a response really in keeping with the matchless bounty and grace of God. Whether our abilities are small or great, they are all gifts of God, and they are not awarded on the basis of desert. It ill becomes respectable citizens to make invidious comparisons between themselves and others regarded as enemies of society. Many of us are what we are partly because acquisitive or otherwise antisocial tendencies within us have had small opportunity for expression, while in others similar tendencies, offered fuller scope, have found outlets and produced destructive social consequences. In such circumstances the appropriate Christian mood is not "I thank thee, God, that I am not as other men," but "There, but for the grace of God, go I," and "God, be merciful to me, a sinner."

These and other occasions for repentance are by no means confined to society outside the church. Examples of each of them may be found within the ongoing life of Christian congregations themselves. As Reinhold Niebuhr said in addressing the Oxford Conference on Church, Community, and State in 1937:

The tragedy of our time is not that the church has to face a pagan and secular world. This has always been so. The tragedy is that too often we have had only a pagan and secular church with which to face that world.[9]

As has frequently been noted, the major Protestant denominations have become mainly middle-class institutions, numbering in their membership relatively few persons who earn their livelihood by manual labor. Only 4.4 per cent of the respondents to the MESTA questionnaire on "The Beliefs of Methodists" listed themselves as operatives (2.3 per cent), domestics (.2 per cent), service workers (1 per cent), and farm laborers and laborers (.9 per cent). This situation should prompt some serious questioning among Methodists. Why are not larger numbers of these groups in our membership? Why are they not interested in the church? Do they feel with some justice that the church is not interested in them? How sympathetically can the church understand their problems when it numbers so few of them in its ranks? What are church members doing to gain such understanding and to overcome the estrangement between labor and organized religion?

About three years ago a Methodist church in New England with two Negroes in its congregation staged a black-face minstrel show, under the leadership of its director of music and with the approval of the pastor and the committee on music and worship. When questions were raised regarding the ethics of such a performance, with particular reference to the possible affront to the self-respect of Negro people in such stereotyping of their race, few members of the official board or the congregation saw anything wrong with the project. To most it was simply innocent fun. Could it have seemed so if they had had sufficient imagination to see it from the perspective of a sensitive Negro?

The sharp contrast in the economic status of white and Negro ministers in The Methodist Church should occasion shame and contrition on the part of the entire white majority. For the conference

[9] Allan Knight Chalmers, *High Wind at Noon* (New York: Charles Scribner's Sons, 1948), p. 164.

219

year 1958-1959 the ministerial salaries reported by nine typical all-Negro conferences averaged only 44.5 per cent as much as those of the nine all-white conferences in the same regions, hence with the same living costs. The pension rates for the retired ministers of the Negro conferences in the same year were on the average only 31.5 per cent of those of the white conferences.[10] These glaring inequalities are of course not intended or desired by The Methodist Church, but are rather a reflection of the lower economic status of Negro people in general. Yet they are particularly indefensible when they occur within the fellowship of the church and its ministry, and when there is no concerted effort in the church as a whole to lift the economic level of its Negro pastors. With sufficient concern and creative imagination Methodists could use their connectional machinery to advance practical brotherhood among their ministers.

Widespread repentance related to social evils like those mentioned can open the door to social salvation. It does this by changing the attitudes of those who repent, exposing them to the forgiveness and healing of God, and arousing them to action empowered by God and committed to changes harmonious with his will. Once we genuinely acknowledge, in humility and contrition, our involvement—even largely unavoidable involvement—in social injustices, we are ready

White Conferences			Negro Conferences		
	Salary	Annuity Rate		Salary	Annuity Rate
Baltimore	$5,564	$62.00	Washington	$2,934	$29.00
Florida	5,341	60.00	Florida	1,880	15.00
Little Rock	5,651	48.00	Louisiana	2,776	17.00
Louisiana	5,197	54.00	Mississippi	2,225	10.00
Mississippi	4,610	43.00	North Carolina	2,834	22.00
North Carolina	5,026	50.00	South Carolina	2,363	18.00
South Carolina	5,593	55.00	Tennessee	1,907	14.00
Tennessee	5,036	48.00	East Tennessee	1,778	11.00
Texas	6,085	58.00	Texas	2,609	14.50
Average	5,345	53.10	Average	2,368	16.72

(*Pensions in The Methodist Church*, January 1959, pp. 31, 34.)

[10] With the exception of the Baltimore Conference (Northeastern), the white conferences are located in the Southeastern and South Central Jurisdictions. However, comparisons of northern and western conferences with Central Jurisdiction conferences would reveal substantially the same inequalities. The Baltimore Conference is also a slight exception to the "all-white" designation, since it includes one Negro minister serving a predominantly Negro congregation. A minister's annual pension is computed by multiplying the annuity rate by the number of years he has served as a conference member. The figures, which do not include housing, are as follows:

to recognize the rights of other persons in relation to us. We gain a greater appreciation of the concerns and problems of others, and this becomes a basis for reconciliation between groups. Once we realize that we ourselves stand in need of redemption, we are enabled to reach out toward others not primarily in judgment or hostility, but in saving concern. When we then go on to experience the redemptive love of God, we know that others who have rejected his ways may have a like experience. As Clyde A. Holbrook has shown, if by faith "we see ourselves created, judged, and redeemed by God's love in Christ, we cannot reject those who obstruct in the highest degree God's will to community." [11] Repentance thus opens the way to the attitude which welcomes and seeks change within and without, and to the spirit and power which make it possible.

C. Social Implications of Justification by Faith

Indispensable though it is, repentance is only the door to salvation. He who passes through it receives in faith the free gift of God's forgiving grace. Confronting one who treats him as righteous in spite of his sin, he gives up trying to merit forgiveness by his own deeds and yields himself to God in complete trust. Surrendering his pretensions of independence, he joyously accepts his dependence on God, and God replaces self as the center of his life. Once he begins to operate from this new center, all is different.

As we have previously seen, the entire ethical life of the Christian in society is a grateful response to the activity of God in his behalf which comes to a focus in his reconciliation with God through Jesus Christ. We have now to examine somewhat more in detail the social significance of this relationship. Three main aspects call for particular mention.

1. The awareness that we are reconciled to God in spite of our unworthiness releases us for positive and courageous action in the world as God's children. In true faith we acknowledge that we are sinners, that we are unable to do anything to merit forgiveness, and that God nevertheless forgives us by sheer grace. There is thus no need to defend ourselves for not being better than we are, or to try to show by comparing ourselves with others that we are better than

[11] *Faith and Community: A Christian Existential Approach,* (New York: Harper and Brothers, 1959), p. 134.

they. Saved from both self-righteousness and despair, and experiencing now the mercy of God rather than his judgment, we are moved to act in spite of our own weaknesses and the obstacles that confront us in society. This frees us for a much higher type of morality than was possible before.

Living from our new center in God, we are enabled to be instruments of his love. In this new relationship our lives become fruitful in disinterested service. No longer needing to direct our love anxiously toward ourselves, we can now freely reach out in love toward others. All our actions are performed, as Luther said, "simply to please God thereby," and God is most pleased by self-forgetful concern for our neighbor expressed amid the demands of men's common life.

This changed orientation also prevents us from avoiding responsibilities because we fear our decisions will not be right, and from vain regret because in retrospect we feel we should have acted differently. Conscious of ourselves as sinners and yet as accepted by God, we can face humbly the incompleteness of our commitment, the impurity of our intentions, and the deficiencies in our wisdom and strength, and act according to the best light we have. We are justified not by our impeccable judgment or our perfect righteousness, but by faith in God. This awareness, as Alexander Miller declares, "encourages us to believe that the erroneous decision . . . is not wasted if it is taken in faith, but is built into a divine structure of activity that is wider than our vision and wiser than our devising." [12]

2. The stress on the grace of God received in faith gives strength for affirmative action in society because it grounds the ethical imperative in the divine indicative. It sees what God requires of man always in the context of what God is, has done, and is doing.

According to Emil Brunner in his monumental work, The Divine Imperative, the new life of the Christian is "life in the Divine indicative (mood), instead of in the imperative"; it is lived "in dependence upon God, not in search for God." "The Good," therefore, "is that which God does, not that which man does." [13] Nevertheless, for Brunner the actual content of Christian ethics remains "the divine imperative." Paul Lehmann, dissatisfied with so large a place for the

---

[12] From: The Renewal of Man, by Alexander Miller. Copyright 1955 by Alexander Miller. Reprinted by Permission of Doubleday & Company, Inc., p. 114.
[13] The Divine Imperative (New York: The Macmillan Company, 1937), p. 77.

imperative, insists that an ethic based on God's self-revelation in Christ will be concerned more with the divine indicative than with the divine imperative.

The primary question for Christian ethics, according to Lehmann, is not, "What does God command?" but rather, "What does God do?" An indicative ethic does not rule out ethical demands, but insists that "they acquire meaning and authority from the specific ethical relationships which precede and shape these demands." Christian ethics is a disciplined effort to answer the question, "What am I, as a believer in Jesus Christ, and a member of his Church to do?" In Lehmann's judgment the answer is, "I am to do what I am"— one redeemed by Jesus Christ into the fellowship of the covenant community. "Speaking the truth in love, we are to grow up in every way into him who is the head, into Christ, from whom the whole body . . . makes bodily growth and upbuilds itself in love" (Eph. 4: 15-16). In the koinonia [14] of the church, Christians are summoned to be in word and act what they are.[15]

To the present writer this interpretation draws too sharp a contrast between the indicative and the imperative. The extreme subordination of the latter to the former can easily result in vagueness regarding the actual content of the imperative. Moreover, indicative ethics does not really succeed in subordinating the imperative as much as may appear on the surface. It avoids the use of terms like ought, should, duty, obligation, and the like, but it cannot avoid implying them in the words used. What does it mean, for example, to say that as Christians we are to be or do what we are? Is not this simply another way of saying: "Fulfill your true meaning and destiny; be what you ought to be as a member of the community of faith; live as becomes those who through Jesus Christ have been reconciled to God"? If this is approximately what is meant, then the imperative retains a quite important position, though under another name. Even the Book of Ephesians, rightly cited by Lehmann as a major Biblical foundation for indicative ethics, is full of imperatives, though they all presuppose the Christian community and reflect the manner of life characteristic of that community.

[14] See above, p. 221.
[15] "The Foundation and Pattern of Christian Behavior." John A. Hutchinson (ed.), Christian Faith and Social Action (New York: Charles Scribner's Sons, 1953), pp. 100-108.

Nevertheless, this underlining of the indicative calls attention to an exceedingly important aspect of Christian ethics, social as well as individual. It properly excludes any suggestion that the Christian life is chiefly the fulfillment, by strenuous human endeavor, of certain codes or standards of conduct prescribed by the divine Law-giver. More importantly, it makes plain that underlying and supporting all that the Christian in gratitude attempts to do and be is the reality of what God has done and is doing. It reminds us that our feeble efforts to increase justice and love among men are not ours alone, but embodiments of the spirit and manner in which God himself acts in his world. We are called to "be imitators of God" not externally, as high jumpers trying hopelessly to equal the record of the champion, but "as beloved children" (Eph. 5:1) who seek to express as far as trustful children can the love which upholds them, forgives them when they stray, and binds them together in their Father's house. We are summoned to "walk in love, as Christ loved us and gave himself up for us" (Eph. 5:2).

All that Christians do in the direction of personal or social righteousness is done in the context of the divine grace. "To make our decisions in faith," writes H. Richard Niebuhr, "is to make them in view of the fact that the world of culture—man's achievement—exists within the world of grace—God's Kingdom." [16] In that grace, moreover, are infinite possibilities for renewal and reconciliation, so that those who live supported by it need not lose heart even in situations which appear quite hopeless. Thus, a social ethic which moves to what ought to be from what is, when "what is" is the love and redemptive activity of God, has at its disposal an immeasurable reservoir of power for effecting the changes in society which Christian goals demand.

3. An ethic which roots in the believer's grateful, trustful response to the redemptive act of God in Christ is inherently social. The faith through which we are saved is called forth within a faithful community, the church, to which God has entrusted the good news. The redemption of the individual begins and continues within a redeemed and redeeming fellowship. As Paul Lehmann suggests, Christian ethics is koinonia ethics.[17] If, therefore, our response to God's reconciling

---

[16] *Christ and Culture,* (New York: Harper and Brothers, 1950) p. 256.
[17] *The Foundation and Pattern of Christian Behavior,* pp. 102-9.

love is authentic, it occurs among a people whose lives are closely enmeshed with each other. Thus when we ask, "What are we, undeserving recipients of the divine grace, to do?" the question unavoidably concerns the action we are to take as members of the community, the body of Christ.

But this action cannot be confined within a closed circle. The new community itself is thrust into the larger community of the world and given a redemptive mission to perform there. Those who have received mercy, writes the author of I Peter, are "a chosen race, a royal priesthood, a holy nation, God's own people, that you may declare the wonderful deeds of him who called you out of darkness into his marvelous light" (I Peter 2:9-10). That light, the New Testament makes unmistakable, is meant for all mankind. The very universalism of the gospel forbids the erection of any boundaries whatever to the Christian's outreach toward his neighbor. God so loved the *world*. We are called to love not only *because* he first loved us, but *as* he first loved us—sacrificially and unrestrictedly.

Nor is Christian action, either within the smaller community that is being redeemed or in the larger community to be redeemed, directed toward purely "spiritual" ends without reference to the earthly realities of man's daily existence. Not only is neighborliness in Luke 10:29-37 defined in terms of mercy extended to those in need without regard to race, nationality, or religion, but the need is a physical one resulting from a frequently recurring social situation. Similarly, the great eschatological parable of the sheep and the goats in Matthew 25 interprets service to Christ in terms of feeding the hungry, clothing the naked, and caring for the sick and imprisoned. Clearly, to be reconciled with God through faith in Christ means to be so closely identified with those whom God also loves and seeks to redeem that their needs at all levels are the object of our intimate concern.

Both the interpenetration of the two communities and the need for material embodiment of Christian social concern are aptly stated in the words of Alexander Miller:

The community of the justified men, in whom the circle of self is broken, is the community of those who, being "righted" with God, are set in a relation of joyous obligation with all "the brethren for whom Christ died." This new solidarity implements itself first within the *koinonia*—"neither

225

counted any man aught that he possessed to be his own"—but it shortly runs out into political concern and the care of the state, as soon as it becomes manifest that the community of love must coexist with the communities of law, and that the feeding of the hungry and the care of the poor is a political act.[18]

Individuals who are truly justified by faith are released and empowered for positive Christian action in society. But we are thinking of social salvation—the deliverance of society from those factors which obstruct the purpose of God and the establishment of relationships which fulfill that purpose. To what extent can society itself be justified by faith? Obviously not in any literal sense. Groups as such, lacking personal consciousness, cannot be aware of being treated as righteous by God in spite of their sin, nor respond as may individuals in grateful trust and service. But the persons who compose them can have these experiences. When this happens to a considerable number, or even to a few whose changed lives leaven the entire lump, a group may become a redemptive agent in relation to other groups. Under the leadership of Martin Luther King and others, the Montgomery Improvement Association was saved from bitterness to love, became veritably a new community, and brought a larger outlook and a changed attitude to many outside its ranks.[19]

D. Social Holiness

Christians are not only forgiven sinners; they feel themselves "called to be saints" (Rom. 1:7; I Cor. 1:2). They are not content to be restored by grace to the divine favor; they endeavor to grow into the divine likeness. They not only rejoice in their deliverance through Christ from the power of sin; they devote themselves positively in the power of God to the life of true righteousness in obedience to his will. "Strengthened with might through his Spirit," they seek to attain "to mature manhood, to the measure of the stature of the fullness of Christ" (Eph. 3:16; 4:13). Faith is not only the human channel of divine pardon; it also "works by love" (Gal. 5:6) to produce what Wesley called inward and outward holiness.[20] Thus to

[18] *The Renewal of Man* (Garden City, N. Y.: Doubleday and Company, 1955), p. 106.

[19] See Martin Luther King, *Stride Toward Freedom; The Montgomery Story* (New York: Harper and Brothers, 1958).

[20] See above, p. 54.

226

justification is added sanctification. Both are included in the full reality of Christian salvation:

> He died that we might be forgiven,
> He died to make us good.[21]

1. THE VALIDITY OF CHRISTIAN CONCERN FOR PERSONAL HOLINESS

Most theologians who stress justification by faith as the foundation of Christian ethics allow little or no place in their conception of the Christian life for the desire for holiness or perfection.[22] In fact, H. Richard Niebuhr views concern for perfection in conduct as an aspect of the defensive, narrow, negative, self-conscious, and uncreative morality which he finds opposed to evangelical ethics.[23] Such doubt regarding the legitimacy of Christian perfectionism has a sound basis in the history of the church. Those Christians who have made holiness their central emphasis have often embraced in fact a doctrine of justification by works, assuming that salvation is won through man's rigorous obedience to precise codes of moral law. They frequently oversimplify the meaning of sin and underestimate its depth and power. In self-centered pursuit of their own salvation, they readily succumb to both sanctimonious pride and social irresponsibility.

But faults like these are not inherent in the desire for holiness of life. It need not be linked with a legalistic conception of righteousness or faith in man's own ability to save himself. It can be and often is an integral part of the grateful, trustful response of the redeemed person to the gracious act of the God who has saved him. As the undeserving recipient of such bounty, he is not satisfied simply to accept the fact of his forgiveness, but wants to give *his utmost* in love and service. This he can do in humility, self-forgetful regard for others, and constant reliance on God.

Actually, without this dimension an ethic of justification by faith is in danger of encouraging a form of moral indifference and a quality of life not higher but lower than that of the Pharisaic legalists.[24] Protesting his own unworthiness, the believer may easily make it a basis for surrendering any expectation of real growth in Christian

[21] Cecil F. Alexander.

[22] For example, Emil Brunner, Paul Lehmann, Alexander Miller, H. Richard Niebuhr.

[23] "Evangelical and Protestant Ethics," *The Heritage of the Reformation*, ed, Elmer J. F. Arndt, pp. 217-18.

227

character, or any real challenge to social sin, and resign himself to a mediocre level of attainment. In this context the summons of an indicative ethic to the Christian to "do what he is" may be distorted to rationalize his becoming no better than he now is.

The Christian ethical life comes to finest flower only when it is cultivated; and the cultivation involved in disciplined human effort grounded in God's grace is no more man-centered than that of the gardener who, relying basically on mysterious powers not his own in sun and soil and seed, nevertheless plants, fertilizes, and tills to secure the best attainable results. It is God who gives the increase, but Paul and Apollos must still plant and water, religiously and ethically as well as horticulturally.

Whatever terms may be used to describe it, the element of active striving for the highest possible fulfillment cannot be eliminated from the Christian life without ignoring a constant refrain of the New Testament writers. The Sermon on the Mount, calling on citizens of the kingdom to be perfect as God their Father is perfect (Matt. 5:48), is far from an isolated instance.

Paul, exponent *par excellence* of justification by faith, constantly summons the redeemed to bring forth the fruits of faith in Christlike living. After telling the Romans in the strongest possible terms that Jew and Gentile alike are saved only by the unmerited mercy of God received in faith, he proceeds to draw the ethical conclusion:

I appeal to you therefore, brethren, by the mercies of God, to present your bodies as a living sacrifice, holy and acceptable to God. . . . Be transformed by the renewal of your mind, that you may prove what is the will of God, what is good and acceptable and perfect.—Rom. 12:1-2

He informs the Colossians that he proclaims Christ "that we may present every man mature in Christ. For this I toil, striving with all the energy which he mightily inspires within me." He also conveys to them the greeting and earnest prayer of Epaphras that they "may stand mature and fully assured in all the will of God" (Col. 1:28; 4:12). He upbraids the Corinthians for not building rightly on the foundation of Jesus Christ. "Do you not know that you are God's

[24] For a balanced recognition of the dangers in both moralism and a subordination of the claims of morality, see John C. Bennett, "Morality and Moralism," *Union Seminary Quarterly Review*, XI, No. 4 (May 1956), 39-41.

temple and that God's Spirit dwells in you? . . . God's temple is holy, and that temple you are." (I Cor. 3:16-17.)

We have found in the Letter to the Ephesians the classical New Testament interpretation of the Christian ethical life as a thankful response to the redemptive action of God in Christ. It also summons the Christian unequivocally to a life of holiness. Here the church is called to grow into "a holy temple in the Lord," by whom individual Christians are "built into it for a dwelling place of God in the Spirit." God has chosen us "before the foundation of the world, that we should be holy and blameless before him." Therefore we are to "put on the new nature, created after the likeness of God in true righteousness and holiness" (Eph. 2:22; 1:4; 4:24; cf. 3:19-20; 4:1-3).

In giving similar counsel the writer of I Peter has enough respect even for the law to take his cue from Leviticus 11:44-45. Calling on his readers to be "obedient children," he counsels them: "As he who called you is holy, be holy yourselves in all your conduct." Those who "grow up to salvation" are to be built into "a spiritual house," "a holy priesthood to offer spiritual sacrifices acceptable to God" (I Peter 1:14-15; 2:5; cf. 2:9-10).

The Epistle to the Hebrews sees in the suffering of Christians the discipline of the Lord, "that we may share his holiness." But like the other passages it grounds the whole life of the believer in the gracious activity of God. The closing prayer is that the God of peace may equip those who read with everything good that they "may do his will," working in them "that which is well pleasing in his sight" (Heb. 12:10; 13:20-21).

The Johannine Epistles do not mention holiness, but they have much to say of that love which is the redeemed man's answer to God's love for him. The normative expectation is that Christians will so abide in the love of God that his love will be "perfected" in them (I John 4:7-21).

These passages, typical of many which might be cited, are in no sense antagonistic to the ethic of justification by faith. In fact, they presuppose it. All of the appeals for holiness in the New Testament are predicated on man's constant dependence on God, and see the good life as the fruit of a redemptive relation to him. However, they do not expect the fruit to remain green, but rather assume that, carefully tended, it will ripen and grow to maturity. They take for granted that those whom God has redeemed will give to him their best. As new creatures in Christ Jesus they cannot be content with mediocrity; rather they earnestly desire to be made as nearly perfect in love as their finite limitations will allow. Aware that only God knows where those limits are, they seek to place themselves completely at the divine disposal. To co-operate with God's intent, that we should in his strength obey his holy will, involves no more reliance on man for salvation than to accept in trust his forgiving grace. Redemption in its fullness involves both justification and sanctification, and both are centrally acts of God to which men respond in gratitude, trust, and love. In the New Testament perspective, therefore, to set an ethic of faith over against an ethic of perfection involves a false opposition. Truly evangelical ethics includes both.

To stress the validity and authenticity of Christian striving for holiness of attitude and life does not mean in any sense to gloss over the glaring imperfections of man or the stark reality of human sinfulness. It does mean to cherish real faith in the positive possibilities for growth in love open to those who, "rooted and grounded" in the love of God (Eph. 3:17) and upheld by the koinonia of the Christian community, reach out responsibly toward the larger circle of their fellow men. It does not mean belief in the attainment of a finished state in which all possibilities are exhausted. It does mean, as Eric Baker declares, the conviction "that no limit whatever can be set to what God can accomplish in and through the believer." [25] This conviction is an important part of the New Testament message. It played a prominent role in the radical Protestant movements of the sixteenth century. It has been a major emphasis of the Wesleyan heritage. In these days of conventional and often anemic Christianity, its rediscovery, reassertion, and demonstration could go far toward revitalizing the Christian witness.

2. The Social Extension of Holiness

If salvation is to be social, the holiness of life which fulfills it cannot stop with the individual, but must extend to all aspects of society. Unfortunately John Wesley, in spite of his strong insistence on sanctification and perfection as normative goals for the individual Christian, never developed the social implications of his doctrine. Nor

[25] The Faith of a Methodist, p. 42.

has this been done by later Methodism as a whole, although in the twentieth century, especially in the early decades, many Methodist voices have appealed eloquently for the sanctification of the whole of life.

Ironically, the distortions of sanctification among its most euthusiastic advocates, in and out of Methodism, have generated widespread skepticism even concerning the desirability of personal holiness. As extensively interpreted and practiced, holiness has become identified not with the healthy, outgoing righteousness and growing, transforming love portrayed in the New Testament, but with a smug, self-righteous, static, ingrown piety. This kind of religion is not encouraged but opposed by the New Testament writers, and a major concern of the gospel is to free men from its stifling influence. Moreover, it defeats its own purpose. The individual is bound to his social environment by intricate interconnections which affect him intimately at every point. Even a realistic concern for his own purity would require him to be equally concerned for the purity of those who constantly affect him for good or ill.

While the holiness sects have diverted men's attention from their responsibilities in the world, strong pressures have often operated in mainstream Protestantism to hallow the world largely as it is. Charles C. West writes perceptively: "It is the disgrace of Christian theology that Marx found in it, not the Gospel of good news to the whole man, body and soul, especially to the humble and the poor, not the promise of the coming of an already arisen and ruling Christ, but only the division of body from spirit, the hope of a spiritual eternal life, and the neglect or the sanctification of the material arrangements of this world." [26] An informed Christian faith will be no more interested in the glorification and preservation of the *status quo* than in evading responsibility for changing it. Such a faith will seek not to call society holy in the name of God, but to make it holy by the power of God.

Quite apart from the need of avoiding the perversions mentioned, the extension of concern for holiness to the corporate life of man is supported by weighty positive considerations.

1. Sanctification in the scriptural sense means more than anything else the divine activity by which men are "made perfect," or grow toward maturity, *in love*. Thus a sanctity which concentrates on

[26] *Communism and the Theologians*, p. 331.

231

one's own unblemished purity while forgetting one's responsibilities to other persons is inherently contradictory. Since the appropriate response to the redemptive, self-giving love of God is a human love which also gives itself for the sake of others, and since the lives of those we are called to love are inextricably involved in all manner of corporate relationships, an effective ministry to them requires the vigorous endeavor to harmonize those relationships as fully as possible with the intention of God.

2. God's redemptive purpose, which the church is commissioned to serve, embraces the totality of man's existence. The covenant between God and Israel called on the people as a whole to be a holy nation, fulfilling the commands of a righteous God. The great Old Testament prophets repeatedly interpreted this holiness in corporate terms; it concerned all the political, economic, judicial, and familial relationships of the Hebrew people. When the covenant was broken and national disaster resulted, the promises of redemption in the Messianic prophecies, notably those of Isaiah, were cast in strongly social terms. These passages envisaged a new society, marked by the righteous government of a divinely endowed king, the ordered, godly living of people united in mutual helpfulness, and freedom from oppression and war (Isa. 9:1-7; 2:2-5; Micah 4:1-4). Under the rule of the Anointed One even ordinary citizens were to be, as it were, anointed: "... the Spirit is poured upon us from on high" (Isa. 32:15). Then justice would prevail in wilderness and fruitful field alike, and the result of righteousness would be peace (Isa. 32:15-18). The universalistic vision of Second Isaiah extended this redemption to all peoples.

The coming of Jesus Christ, proclaimer of the new covenant and fulfiller of the Messianic hope, was heralded in similar terms. Through him God would deliver his people from fear to "holiness and righteousness," and guide their feet into the way of light and peace (Luke 1:68-79). The central concept in the synoptic gospels is a social one—the kingdom of God. Significantly, in the Lord's Prayer the petition that God's name may be hallowed is followed immediately by the prayers for the coming of the kingdom and the doing of his will, which in effect interpret and amplify the earlier petition. According to the Fourth Gospel it is "the world" which is to be saved through Christ (John 3:16-17; 16:33; 17:15-18).

The outpouring of the Holy Spirit at Pentecost, a deeply corporate experience, was the sign of a new age. Two immediate consequences of the Pentecostal experience are particularly noteworthy: "the company of those who believed were of one heart and soul," and they were moved to pool their material resources and share them with each other according to need, so that "there was not a needy person among them" (Acts 2:44-47; 4:32-37). Such was the transforming effect of a direct encounter with the holy God.

It is worth noting that both the Messianic hope and the Pentecostal event were strongly eschatological in orientation, announcing the coming fulfillment of the end of history and the consummation of the divine purpose. But this served to strengthen rather than to undermine their reference to the totality of man's life, since the consummation expected involved the radical transformation of society.

If the church's redemptive ministry is to be worthy of its Biblical sources, it must seek the sanctification of the total life of man. Further, since amid the complex interconnections of modern culture it cannot fulfill its mission without the co-operation and utilization of agencies outside the church, it must be concerned with the transformation of those agencies.

The First Assembly of the World Council of Churches was keenly aware of this responsibility when it summoned Christians and Christian congregations everywhere, in new commitment to the Lord of the church, to

seek together, where they live, to be His witnesses and servants among their neighbours. We have to remind ourselves and all men that God has put down the mighty from their seats and exalted the humble and meek. We have to learn afresh together to speak boldly in Christ's name both to those in power and to the people, to oppose terror, cruelty, and race discrimination, to stand by the outcast, the prisoner and refugee. We have to make of the Church in every place a voice for those who have no voice, and a home where every man will be at home. We have to learn afresh together what is the duty of the Christian man or woman in industry, in agriculture, in politics, in the professions and in the home. We have to ask God to teach us together to say "No" and to say "Yes" in truth. "No", to all that flouts the love of Christ, to every system, every program, and every person that treats any man as though he were an irresponsible thing or a means of profit, to the defenders of injustice in the name of order, to those who sow the seeds of war or urge war as inevitable; "Yes", to all that conforms to the love of Christ, to all who seek for justice, to the peacemakers, to all who hope, fight, and suffer for the cause of man, to all who—even without knowing it—look for new heavens and a new earth wherein dwelleth righteousness.[27]

3. The same conclusion is implicit in another central Christian doctrine, the incarnation. God's act in incarnating himself on the plane of history in Jesus Christ imparts a sacred meaning to the whole realm of the human, the material, and the earthly. Where do we most clearly behold God's glory, full of grace and truth? In one who, born in the rudest surroundings, lived a real physical life; mingled freely with fishermen, farmers, tradesmen, artisans, lawyers, and tax-collectors; spoke to them of God in terms of sheepfold, field, lake, hillside, marketplace, and home; fed the hungry and healed the sick of body and mind; used ordinary bread and wine to represent the sacrificial love of God embodied in his own life and death; and went to the cross between two thieves. The common life of men thus emerges not as a realm apart from the life of the spirit, but as a sphere in which God is directly and peculiarly interested and in which he is to be made known.

In World War II St. Nicholas Parish Church, standing above the Mersey River at Liverpool, England, was badly damaged by bombs. Formerly those who entered it had to turn their backs on the market-place, the harbor, and the wheat ships anchored there, and then found themselves facing the communion table in semidarkness at the far end. After the war, as George MacLeod graphically tells,[28] a prefabricated hut was built on the ruins, facing the other way. What had been the porch became the sanctuary, and the tall doors became windows which without stained glass afforded an unobstructed view of marketplace and river. Communicants then saw the bread of the common meal on the holy table in the same frame of reference as the wheat produced in man's common life. A living church which is fulfilling its mission will see all life in just such a setting, where worship gives new meaning to work and work brings deepened reality to worship. It is called, in ways suited to its capacities, to incarnate the reconciling and trans-

[27] *The First Assembly of the World Council of Churches*, ed. W. A. Visser 't Hooft (New York: Harper and Brothers, 1949), p. 10.
[28] *We Shall Re-build* (Glasgow: Iona Community Publishing Department, n.d.), pp. 12-14.

forming love of God amid the ordinary relations of men in society.

Charles A. Coulson, British atomic scientist and a Methodist, has applied this conception to man's use of atomic energy. Speaking before the Ninth World Methodist Conference at Lake Junaluska, North Carolina, in 1956, he asserted that understanding of "the significance of the material order" and "the real meaning of the Incarnation" require the recognition that God himself is concerned with a fair and reasonable distribution of atomic power. Genesis I and Psalms 24:1 affirm that the whole universe belongs to God, and according to Ephesians 1:10 the purpose of God as set forth in Christ is "to unite all things in him, things in heaven and things on earth." The emphasis here, declared Coulson, is on things, not people. "The order of nature carries meaning . . . and this meaning is bound up with the nature of God." Therefore increased knowledge of the physical universe involves fuller knowledge of God, and "all true scientific study is a religious activity."

This means that man's new-found knowledge of the atom is a sacred trust. "The uranium is not ours—the Christian will see it as God's. Seeing it thus, he will endeavor to use it only in ways that will incarnate and realize God's purpose of a full life for all His children." [29]

When holiness is socially as well as personally understood, and when it is dynamically rather than statically interpreted as a process and not a condition, we may even be permitted to speak soberly of "entire sanctification." The words of Benjamin Hellier, a nineteenth-century British Methodist theologian, are equally relevant today:

Entire sanctification means the sanctification of everything. The sanctification, for example, of the daily work; that is, doing it to the Lord, and, therefore, doing it as well as we can. If a ploughman be entirely sanctified, he will plough a straight furrow—or at least try his best to do so. If he be a mason, he will put no bad work into his walls; if a doctor, he will care more about curing his patients than about getting large fees; if he be a minister of religion, he will strive to serve the people of his charge to the utmost of his ability. . . . Entire sanctification means simply this: spending all our time in the Lord's service; making our religion our life, our life our religion.[30]

[29] "Nuclear Knowledge and Christian Responsibility," *Proceedings, Ninth World Methodist Conference*, 1956, ed. Elmer T. Clark and E. Benson Perkins, p. 235.
[30] Eric Baker, *The Faith of a Methodist* (The Epworth Press, 1958), p. 32.

CHAPTER NINE

From Theory to Reality

THE CENTRAL SOCIAL GOAL OF THE CHRISTIAN IS A REDEEMED society. This involves, negatively, the release of persons from all those aspects of their group relations which corrupt life, obstruct personal growth, and hinder the divine purpose; and, positively, the establishment among groups of relations which promote the maximum concern of persons for each other's welfare, further the realization of their highest potentialities, and facilitate their communion with and service of God. Actually, since society is always changing, its redemption is not a fixed state, but a continuing process, so that society or any group within it can be described as being redeemed when changes are occurring which advance the goals named.

From the standpoint of the three aspects discussed in the preceding chapter, redemption takes place to the degree that the members of any group (1) recognize, repentantly admit, and move to change those attitudes and actions of the group which have hurt the members of other groups; (2) see themselves and their group as the unworthy objects of the mercy of God, commit themselves trustfully to his grace, and so are freed from the compulsion to maintain the claim of their own group to superior righteousness or special status; and (3) strive in the power of God to fulfill his righteous will through a love which seeks actively, in all the ways available, the reconciliation of man with man and the highest welfare of all members of other groups as well as their own.

Crucial in this interpretation is the phrase, "to the degree that." Obviously no historical or contemporary group, large or small, comes anywhere near a complete fulfillment of these conditions. Most groups, secular in orientation and composed of many members who are not

Christian or even religious in outlook, seek purposes which are not consciously related to God or his will. Even avowedly Christian groups as groups often seem to illustrate the need for redemption more than the reality of it. As Harry Emerson Fosdick said years ago, they are part of the problem rather than its solution. Instead of leaven, they are part of the lump. This being true, can we realistically expect society, or any group within it, to fit the picture painted to such a degree that we can honestly speak of it as in process of redemption? Is social salvation really attainable in any sense worthy of the name? Or are those who think in such terms naïvely optimistic, indulging in an idle dream?

Sweeping reforms and improvements in human social relations are urgently needed if multitudes of persons are to have an opportunity for fullness of life. Injustices cry out to be righted, and people the world over are restive under the pressure of vast unmet demands. At a deeper level, men are alienated from each other and from God. But powerful inertias impede change, and formidable influences, personal and social, oppose it. Is there any sound basis for belief in the possibility of the correction of social wrongs, the reconciliation of group differences, and a genuine reordering of the life of society?

A. The Possibility of Social Redemption

History, contemporary society, and human nature afford inescapable and convincing evidence of the enormous difficulties involved in the solution of social problems. Six major aspects of this evidence may be cited here.

1. Fundamental is the manifest sinfulness of man, which is powerful in individuals and compounded as they function in social relationships. As Reinhold Niebuhr has convincingly shown, sin affects not only our worst acts but our best ones also, since even our noblest deeds are tinctured with self-centered motives and susceptibility to group pressures. No amount of improvement in social institutions will render them immune to the destructive influence of the self-seeking of individuals who use them as instruments of personal power. Moreover, human beings are remarkably skillful in devising plausible explanations by which they convince at least themselves of the moral purity of acts which an unbiased judgment would regard as highly questionable. By such rationalizations we obscure from ourselves and the groups we sway the true extent of our departures from rectitude, and

237

justify the tenacity by which we resist change which threatens our inflated self-esteem. Appeals for policy changes for the sake of human welfare have small effect on those who are sure that their policies already have the true good of mankind at heart.

2. The problem is immensely complicated by the weight of our social inheritance. Never do we face a social question with complete freedom to decide on a course of action purely in terms of the ideal. Many issues are colored and blurred by a long accumulation of prejudices, rivalries, hostilities, and fears which guarantee that any decision reached will fall short of objective rightness. In the struggle over West Berlin the West has far less freedom than it would have had if there had been no Potsdam Agreement; and the Soviet Union, suffering from a mind-set of ingrained suspicion, produced partly by years of nonrecognition and rebuffs by non-Communist nations, can form no judgments which are uninfluenced by her desire for the status of a great power.

For some years Boston's base for real estate taxation has dwindled, as more land has passed from income-producing use to ownership by public, educational, or religious agencies, while at the same time governmental costs have sharply risen. But little has been done to face the problem forthrightly. So the city felt forced to set the tax rate for 1959 at $101.20,[1] well aware of the hardship this would involve for some people, the economic handicap it would impose on business, and its deterrent effect on new enterprises considering Boston locations, yet equally conscious that a lower rate would mean either seriously curtailed public services or deficit financing which would invite future disaster. The walls of the past are strong and high, greatly circumscribing the range and quality of possible choices.

3. Similarly, the manifold interconnections of our present social environment are often so intricate that any decision that is open entails some social evil. Many inadequate bills are approved by high-minded legislators or signed by president or governor with grave misgivings, simply because with all their limitations they do include essential provisions, and because less objectionable legislation has no chance of being enacted. The conscientious soldier and the conscientious objector to military service both face bewildering moral

---

[1] Requiring the payment of this amount for each $1,000 of assessed valuation.

dilemmas: the former because of the agonizing knowledge that he is co-operating in training designed to make him an efficient killer of his fellow men; the latter because his chances to oppose the enemies of his country in nonviolent ways are so limited, because he is seldom called upon to make sacrifices for his country as great as those expected of the armed combatant, and because he can never avoid, as long as he goes on living and paying taxes, at least indirect contributions to war preparations. Gandhi's nonviolent methods brought new self-respect and improved economic status to the poverty-stricken people of India, partly by teaching them to weave their own cloth on hand looms, but not without a boycott of British-manufactured goods which brought unemployment and suffering to textile workers in Great Britain. Such is the ambiguity which often confronts us as we try to act responsibly on social questions.

4. Further confusion arises from the clash of group interests. Among nations which differ in size, location, culture, natural resources, and technological advancement, conflicts are inevitable, and solutions which are both fair and acceptable to all parties are exceedingly difficult to find. Within a given country not only do labor and management represent different orientations, but unions vie with each other for power, and business interests of different sections compete for markets and raw materials. Low tolls on the St. Lawrence Seaway are a boon to midwestern commerce, but a threat to New England shipping. In such situations compromises of conflicting demands— and of the claims of ideal justice—are inevitable.

When the economic aims of large-scale social groups collide, the nearest attainable approximation to justice would seem to come through the pursuit of enlightened self-interest by each group. But even this is often far more than can be realistically expected at present. Self-interest by its very nature resists the demand for consideration of broad contexts and long-range advantages, and even such enlightenment as comes is easily lost when situations and leaders change and competition stiffens.

In 1944 one lay member of the Methodist General Conference, representing an Annual Conference in the Northeastern Jurisdiction, was a lawyer who in his own city had long been active, as a participant and as legal counsel, in groups supporting real estate covenants, signers of which agreed not to sell or rent their property to Negroes. At the

General Conference he voted for a resolution stipulating that future General Conferences could be held only in cities guaranteeing freedom from racial discrimination in living accommodations. Asked on his return how he reconciled the discrepancy between his actions in Kansas City and those in his home city, he replied: "There I was acting in my Christian capacity; here I am acting in my legal capacity." The incident highlights not only the dualism which often character-izes Christians in their professional or occupational relationships, but also the complexities and difficulties which confront them as they try to reconcile the conflicting expectations and demands of the groups to which they belong.

5. The largely impersonal nature of most social relationships greatly complicates the task of ordering them in accord with Christian love. This is partly because we cannot adequately visualize the real needs and living concerns of people whom we have never met and cannot know, so that real interest in others is likely to vary inversely with the distance between them and us. It is also due to the fact that social organization best promotes human well-being by provisions for safe-guarding equally, as far as possible, the interests and rights of all. This involves a large element of coercion, particularly when political authority operates through law to restrain possible offenders and punish violators.

Thus it becomes extremely difficult to determine what the impli-cations of love are and how to realize them once they are discovered. The most we can hope for is to approximate a justice which would extend the same opportunities to all; even this is inadequate, since people need not so much strictly equal opportunity as freedom to realize their own unique capacities. Justice can be the instrument of love, and as such is indispensable. But genuine Christian love is custom-made, not mass-produced, and as such requires more personal relationships than are possible in the complicated institutions of modern society.

6. A further complicating factor is the mixed complexion of most groups. Mention has already been made of the fact that Christians normally find themselves associated in various group enterprises with many persons whose religious persuasion is non-Christian, or who acknowledge no religious commitment at all. Even when ethical aims are similar—which often is not the case—sharing at the deepest level

of social concern is impossible when there is neither understanding of the Christian view of ultimate reality nor dedication to the God revealed in Jesus Christ. What can a secular humanist know of that trustful commitment to the forgiving grace of God which we have found so redemptive socially as well as individually? What can the sanctification of society mean to one who has no place in his vocabulary for any kind of holiness and no place in his life for the holy God? But Christians and Christian groups also differ widely among themselves, theologically and ethically, and frequently Christians working actively in social causes find closer bonds of understanding and purpose with non-Christian participants than with some members of their own church, who may actually oppose the goals sought.

Circumstances like those just considered make unmistakably plain that the task of social reconstruction is profoundly difficult, and indicate that the perfect accomplishment of God's goals for society is not to be expected within earthly history. However, they do not show that social redemption is impossible, or that Christian effort for a better society is useless.

Recent history contains so much of the chaotic that if we concentrated on this aspect alone we could easily surrender to despair. Human beings have shown themselves capable of sanctioning such brutalities as concentration camps, gas chambers, the shooting of hostages, obliteration bombing, and brain-washing. It is democratic, freedom-loving America which was responsible for the only instances in history of the use of atomic bombs on populated cities. At present the two most powerful nations in the world are engaged in the most intensive arms race of all time, seeking to surpass each other in the production of ever more deadly hydrogen bombs and intercontinental ballistic missiles.

Valuable cultural exchanges and reciprocal visits by top-level leaders reduce tensions and promote understanding, but do not conceal the persistent reality of bitter conflicts which could quickly erupt into a war that would mean the end of civilization on this planet. The unhealthiness of our state of mind is clearly revealed when relaxed tensions produce lower prices on the stock market and threaten what one columnist called a "peace scare." So abnormal are we that many dread a return to the normal, and fear the difficult economic adjustments which the end of the "Cold War" would bring.

241

The Christian must be willing to look at facts like these unflinchingly. However, true realism demands that he keep the positive factors in the picture along with the negative. Actually, history reveals many instances of social salvation in the sense in which we have defined it. Conditions which have cramped and blighted human life have been removed and replaced by others which have encouraged growth in personal wholeness and mutual concern. When the contemporary human situation is compared with what we know of primitive societies it is clear that considerable enrichment has occurred in the esthetic, intellectual, moral, social, and spiritual aspects of individual and group life. It is also true that during the Christian era such evils as child exposure, human sacrifice, the suppression of women, legalized slavery, duelling to kill, and the unrestricted exploitation of industrial workers have either disappeared from the civilized world or are under the condemnation of large sections of humanity.

Nor is the world of the mid-twentieth century lacking in evidences of social advance. Support of international organization as a means of preserving peace is well-nigh universal, and without doubt the United Nations has been instrumental in preventing or ending hostilities which apart from its good offices could easily have led to major wars. Amid all the tensions of our time, nations continue to seek at the conference table compromises of deep-seated differences which otherwise would almost certainly explode into full-scale armed conflict. Many scientists now labor responsibly to find ways of controlling internationally the stupendous power which their nuclear researches have unleashed. Colonialism is in the process of extinction, and peoples formerly exploited are now striding forward in self-rule, opening up new opportunities for their citizens and winning the respect and co-operation of other nations.

In the United States labor-management relations reveal not only deep-seated differences which periodically erupt in destructive nation-wide strikes, but also a mutual respect and a reliance on collective bargaining which were almost totally lacking a generation ago. Many of the goals of the original Social Creed have been won, and are now taken for granted. In spite of the bitterness which characterizes American race relations at many points, and the restrictions to which members of minority races are still subject, long steps have been taken in recent years in the direction of full equality of opportunity.

Despite the sinful proclivities of men, the findings of psychologist and social worker alike disclose an even more deep-seated characteristic of human nature—the need to love and to be loved. The successes of the resistance movement during the Nazi occupation of Norway were due not only to the moral stamina of the Norwegians, but also in no small measure to the low morale of the invading troops who, unwanted, resented, and far from their homeland, were assigned the unpalatable task of regimenting an unoffending and unco-operative people. Both the capacity of ordinary people for redemptive love and the power of such love, carefully disciplined, to break down intense opposition, have received telling demonstration in situations like the bus boycott in Montgomery, Alabama.

To the question whether through the centuries real social advance has occurred or not, no categorical answer can be given. Proof is not forthcoming either way. No man has historical grasp or perspective enough to draw up an objective balance sheet of good and evil events or to trace their long-range consequences. Whether we affirm or deny "progress" depends to a considerable degree on the presuppositions which we bring to our study of history. To the present writer, however, several things at least can be affirmed with confidence.

On the one hand, while taking in all seriousness man's need for bread, we must guard carefully against the temptation to equate material prosperity with the kingdom of God. There is an important distinction between making life easier and making it better, which ought to be clear to the sensitive Christian. A more comfortable society is not identical with a redeemed society.

On the other hand, a truly redemptive activity is at work in the world. We know that social redemption is possible because it has taken place again and again, making crooked ways straight and rough places plain, and changing human situations so that life is remolded more nearly in accord with the intention of God. We know, too, that dedicated persons who have made themselves willing channels of the power and love of God have played an indispensable role in making possible the changes that have occurred.

How much can be done for the removal of evil in human society God alone knows. But whether it be much or little, we who gratefully and obediently serve him are responsible for doing all that we can. God helping us, we can do no other. We are called to labor, in all the ways open to us, for renewal and transformation, leaving the outcome in his hands. This we can do in the assurance that what we do as an offering to God and in response to human need is significant, and will be used by him to advance his purposes.

When one Christian acts responsibly for social justice, already improvement has taken place. At least one person is now different in his social relations, and the obstacles in the path of change are not so great as they would be had he not acted. The same is true of corporate action carried out by the church or by other groups in which Christians seek to play a redemptive part. Those who act trustfully, intelligently, and decisively to right some social wrong reduce by at least their own number the weight of the opposition and thereby increase the likelihood of success. There are plainly some conflicts which will not be resolved unless we act and there are reconciliations which will be effected if we do.

The social needs of men and the fact that significant transformations have been wrought support the clear import of the gospel in summoning Christians to vigorous social action. A reassertion of faith in the positive possibilities of such action is profoundly needed today. Recent stress on the sinfulness of man and disillusionment with earlier optimistic extremes have encouraged many Christians to water down their personal ethical expectations and to accept social wrongs as inevitable and unchangeable. There is in Protestantism a real danger of a decline in moral sensitivity and social responsibility which is far from the intent of thinkers like Reinhold Niebuhr who have insisted most strongly on a "realistic" understanding of human nature.

Yet some of the conclusions drawn from realistic premises are not altogether surprising. Some writers now maintain that the kingdom of God means not the rule of God in a community of persons dedicated to his will, but the sovereignty of God which is exercised in spite of and is unaffected by the sin of man. In this context the expectation of "the kingdom of God on earth" is dismissed as a relic of outmoded liberalism; the kingdom, it is assumed, has no reference to the quality of human ethical and social relations in history. It is not strange that some Christians influenced by this view see little relation between their Christian faith and the proximate justice which its advocates uphold.

It is difficult to believe that either Jesus or the early church expected the coming of the kingdom in its fullness apart from the ethical response of those who were to compose it. The proclamation of the kingdom was combined with a call to repentance. The Sermon on the Mount portrays the character of the citizens of the kingdom. In the Lord's Prayer the petition, "Thy kingdom come," cannot soundly be separated from the one that follows and interprets it: "Thy will be done on earth as it is in heaven." Men are called to seek first the kingdom of God "and his righteousness" (Matt. 6:33). Certainly God does rule even when men flout his will and call forth his judgment, but the limitation of the kingdom to this meaning requires much more biblical and theological support than is thus far evident.

If the character of the King is essentially the holy love disclosed in Jesus Christ, then the fulfillment of his kingdom must involve the trustful, obedient love of those whom he calls to membership. A kingdom coercively established, without the free response of its participants, might be a smoothly meshing machine performing correctly the functions for which it was designed, but it would not be the kingdom of God. Nor would it be an extension of the covenant community portrayed in the New Testament accounts of the church.

By all means let us have realism in our view of men and society. However, let it be a realism which centers in the deepest reality of all—the redemptive grace of God offered to men in the gospel of Jesus Christ. That grace is an enabling as well as a forgiving grace. In response to it and supported by it, the Christian is invited to begin a new life within a new community, and thus to prepare for the coming of a new age. Moreover, he is summoned to take actual steps forward in obedience to one who is the Way and the Life as well as the Truth, and the covenant community is called to be a holy community, exercising a ministry of reconciling love, devoted service, and transforming power in the world.

Significantly, Reinhold Niebuhr himself, premier prophet of realism, combines with his sober view of man an essentially perfectionist norm for the Christian ethical life. Out of the believer's assurance of pardon and reconciliation, he writes, "There must come all the fruits of the love of God and neighbor by men who know that they are not good and that they cannot fool God by their strenuous virtues (or appearance of virtue), but who feel themselves committed to a life of responsibility which has no norms short of the love of Christ." [2]

We are living in a revolutionary era. But the Christian gospel is a revolutionary gospel. According to it, by the power of God men are redeemable, and God alone knows the limits of what he can accomplish in and through persons who have been turned around and recentered in him. Such persons will humbly but expectantly place themselves at his disposal, witnessing redemptively to his purpose and power as they share responsibly in the movements of their time which seek a better society. "It is the task of Christians and the church so to participate in the social revolution that they are instruments of God's revolution." [3]

As Christians thus express their love of God and neighbor, their deepest resource is faith in the final fulfillment of human life and history in the kingdom of God. Amid the perplexities and imperfections which mark even their best earthly endeavors, they look in confidence toward the ultimate consummation of his redemptive purpose. They are never sure of success at any point, but they are sustained by the abiding presence of the Holy Spirit, by the assurance that their committed efforts are not in vain, and by the promise that God's kingdom will finally and fully come and his will at last prevail.

The concrete meaning of such grounds for hope is well conveyed in the Report of the Advisory Commission on the Main Theme of the Evanston Assembly:

We can hope for and expect the success of concrete plans for the good of our fellow-men. We have no right to set limits to what God may be pleased to do within this present age. Indeed, such hopeful and expectant action for the doing of God's will in the world, in the face of apparently overwhelming odds, is an essential part of our full witness to the present reign of God. All our action will be but humble, grateful, and obedient acknowledgment that God has redeemed the world, and that in it we are called to participate in His ministry of reconciliation. We can therefore live and work as those who know that God reigns, undaunted by all the arrogant

[2] "The Gospel in Future America," The Christian Century, 75 (1958), 713.
[3] From an unofficial staff paper prepared as background for discussion at the Fifth Annual Assembly of the Division of Christian Life and Work of the National Council of Churches held in Cleveland, Ohio, October 31, 1955. Quoted by permission.

pretensions of evil, ready to face situations that seem hopeless and yet to act in them as men whose hope is indestructible.[4]

B. The Basis of Christian Decisions

Once Christians are committed to a ministry of reconciliation and renewal in society, and are sustained by the Spirit of God and faith in the ultimate triumph of his kingdom, how do they proceed? How do they discover the meaning of their redemptive role in concrete situations? Having moved from Eph. 2 to Eph. 4-6,[5] how do they move from Eph. 4-6 to West Berlin, nuclear testing, civil rights legislation, or a steel strike? In short, where do Christians find specific ethical guidance? On what basis do they form moral decisions in particular social contexts?

1. The Question of Guiding Principles

Since the ethical life of the Christian in society is a living response to the creative and redemptive action of a personal God, it cannot be adequately interpreted as conformity to a moral code or a rigid system of abstract laws. Broad ethical principles may be derived from, but are not as such revealed in man's transforming encounter with his Redeemer. For Christian faith revelation is not the transmission of a body of truth, but a series of acts by which God seeks to draw men to himself. As A. G. Hogg wrote in his essay for the Madras Conference, "God reveals Himself; He does not reveal ready-made truths about Himself." [6] The Christian ethical life, therefore, is obedience to the will of God as disclosed to men in a continuing, dynamic, personal relationship.

Against the background of this conception, J. H. Oldham advocates what he describes as an "ethic of inspiration," as over against an ethic of ends. Such an ethic is concerned primarily not with the goal to be attained, but with "the source of action in a living fellowship with God." In the living present a free and sovereign God "makes known his will to those who humbly seek to know it." Oldham is therefore suspicious of fixed norms and codes. Right decisions "cannot be made

[4] New York: Harper and Brothers, 1954, p. 47.
[5] See above, pp. 245-46, 252.
[6] "The Christian Attitude to Non-Christian Faith," *The Authority of the Faith*, Madras Series, I (New York and London: International Missionary Council, 1939), 99-100.

in advance by a careful balancing of principles and considerations," but "only in the moment of decision itself." [7] However, Oldham affirms the importance of previous reflection based on a man's settled convictions and all that he has learned from experience, and he insists that every situation is "shot through with laws, connections, meanings" which must be carefully taken into account.[8]

A number of contemporary Christian moralists go much farther, denying that general principles or universals of any kind can play any part in guiding the Christian's ethical decisions. According to Emil Brunner, for example, no principle can help us to decide "beforehand" what God's command to love our neighbor requires in a given situation. If we open ourselves to the claims of our neighbors and listen for the voice of God we shall learn what is expected of us in that situation. Principles previously arrived at would be an impersonal barrier between our neighbor and ourselves, while also dulling our sensitivity to the unique command of God for that particular relationship.[9]

Similarly, Paul Lehmann places Christian "contextual ethics" over against "absolutistic" ethics which attempts to apply general principles to specific situations in the manner of Aristotle or the Stoics. The question, "What am I to do?" cannot be supplied by a standard of conduct, whether an idea, an ideal, a value, or a law, "which can and must be applied to all people, in all situations, in exactly the same way." Instead, the answer is to be sought in "the concrete complex of the actual situation out of which the ethical problem arises." [10]

Albert T. Rasmussen protests that the Christian ethic is not "a directory of ethical rules that are unambiguously applicable in concrete situations," nor is love an imperative or a principle providing in advance a "categorical prescription for human behavior." Love is rather "a kind of self-forgetting response to others and an identification with them." What love-in-community means must be decided afresh in each concrete situation—though not without the values and perspectives of the whole self, or the "resources conserved in memory

---

[7] Ibid., p. 230.

[8] W. A. Visser 't Hooft and J. H. Oldham, The Church and Its Function in Society (Chicago and New York: Willett, Clark & Co., 1937), pp. 219-220, 232-33.

[9] The Divine Imperative, pp. 111-113, 117.

[10] "The Foundation and Pattern of Christian Behavior." John A. Hutchison (ed.), Christian Faith and Social Action, pp. 104-05.

or in the community of faith." "Every decision must be a unique confrontation of God in a particular situation." [11]

Alexander Miller rejects principles as a rationalistic, idolatrous substitute for God. The God of biblical faith is not a rational principle; he alone is good, and "no rational formula, no legalistic principle, can be idolatrously elevated to His place." "The absolute is an absolute loyalty and not an absolute principle." Instead of offering men principles, Christianity "binds life in a matrix of obligation, which is a very different matter." [12]

In the judgment of Clyde A. Holbrook, the quest for the universal and absolute reflects a spirit of ethical detachment, neutrality, and objectivity which interferes with the commitment of personal and social choices in concrete situations. Moreover, the effort to apply universals to particular problems easily degenerates into legalism and moralism, which confine and narrow the human spirit, producing frustration, guilt, hypocrisy, and self-righteousness. There is a place for the "ought" in Christian ethics, but not for laws.

"There must ever remain the concrete personal demand (not law) of God, which is absolute, yet not universal." [13]

One major emphasis of these writers can hardly fail to commend itself to alert Protestants. Christian ethical decisions must address themselves directly and concretely to the specific human situations which call them forth. The right judgment can never be reached by attempting to force the actual needs, wants, and conflicts of living persons into a rigid, abstract mold. The effort to determine mechanically, by reference to a previously constructed list, which acts are good and which bad can miss the deepest import of the ethical life and open the way to legalism at its worst. Most importantly, the Christian's ethical choices should always be an aspect of his personal relation to God, and reflect what he has learned of God's will for his life in each new context.

But it is not apparent why the preservation of these insights demands the scuttling of principles, norms, standards, or even laws. Why must ethical principles be regarded as inseparable from "ration-

[11] *Christian Social Ethics; Exerting Christian Influence* (Englewood Cliffs, N. J.: Prentice-Hall, 1956), pp. 155, 167, 164, 168-70.
[12] *The Renewal of Man*, pp. 90, 101, 94, 123.
[13] *Faith and Community; a Christian Existential Approach*, pp. 84-95.

alism," legalism, casuistry, and inflexible, unambiguous applicability? Why must they be assumed to be out of all relation to concrete situations? May they not actually have grown out of earlier very similar situations, and therefore have real relevance to the particular problems now faced? Why must they rule out living fellowship with God? May they not even root in the meetings with God experienced by sensitive persons? As interpretations of the word of God heard in those meetings, they would then provide important background and guidance for new encounters in new situations. Why must concern for ends be at variance with a living response to God? Does not God himself have "ends" for man—the mind of Christ, eternal life, a community of love? To questions like these the writers mentioned offer no clear answers.

Moreover, the situational ethic has its own serious weaknesses, four of which may be briefly mentioned.

1. It easily becomes subjectivistic and intuitional, opening the door to improvisation and even fanaticism. If reason is subject to distortion, as it is, for the sake of the justification of our private wants, still more is reliance on the illumination of the moment, if completely separated from critical thought, susceptible to the sinful identification of our own watered-down version of our duty with the will of God. Even though we transcend our individual perspective by utilizing "the resources of a cumulative inheritance," [14] unless we weigh the rightness of previous choices, we may fall victim to an uncritical traditionalism.

2. Contextual ethics cuts itself off from resources which are needed for intelligent choice. In many situations we confront conflicting claims of many different persons. To say that in such a situation we need only to open ourselves to these claims and listen for the voice of God is greatly to oversimplify the problem. As George F. Thomas points out, we need principles to help us to decide which claims are primary and how they may be reconciled when they differ. Such principles "must be derived from an analysis of the various kinds of human needs and relationships and the best methods of dealing with them." [15] In this connection valuable knowledge may be gained from

[14] Alexander Miller, The Renewal of Man, p. 96.
[15] Christian Ethics and Moral Philosophy (New York: Charles Scribner's Sons, 1955), p. 387.

anthropology, psychology, philosophical ethics, and social philosophy. If the Christian really wants to love his neighbor, and if this means ministering to his neighbor's needs, will he not welcome all the guidance he can get as to how this can best be done?

3. In spite of its emphasis on concreteness, this ethic actually offers little concrete guidance for the making of decisions. If universals and principles are taboo, how does the Christian, when he encounters God in the new situation, relate to it his previous convictions and those of the Christian community? Does he rely on God to do this for him? When Alexander Miller comes to this question from the standpoint of "justification ethics," he urges the necessity of joining faith with facts. Though this counsel wisely stresses the need for securing accurate data from all sources, it does not tell us how to relate the facts to the faith. Where there is no more guidance than this, what happens all too easily in practice is that the facts submerge the faith, which is compromised in deference to the demands of present existence.

4. Contextual ethics seems to overlook the fact that the God whom I met in Jesus Christ is the God of all men. Certainly his will, to be meaningful, must be his will for me, taken to heart and acted upon by me. But his will for me is not utterly different from his will for others. He created all men, acted to redeem all men, and seeks to lead all men into a community of love. I should therefore be helped in answering the question, "What am I to do?" by broadening the context to ask also, "What are men—especially redeemed men—to do?" This requires a reference to something approaching universal norms.

2. GUIDANCE OFFERED BY A SOCIAL THEOLOGY OF REDEMPTION

Like contextual ethics, the social theology of salvation which we have proposed centers in the response of the Christian and the Christian community to the creating, saving, and renewing work of God. However, unlike the situational ethic, this theology of society regards ethical principles as important and necessary guides in the formation of decisions.

What is a principle as used in ethics? The Latin root, *principium*, means simply beginning or foundation. Obviously both of these are present in every ethical choice. As the term is used in mathematics, deductive logic, some metaphysical systems (e.g., Descartes, Spinoza, absolute idealism), and the natural sciences, a principle is, as one definition given by Webster indicates, "a comprehensive law or doctrine, from which others are derived, or on which others are founded." But when moralists use the term they have in mind another meaning also listed by Webster; here a principle is simply "a governing law of conduct; an opinion, attitude, or belief which exercises a directing influence on the life and behavior." In this conception there is nothing suggesting necessary rigidity of application, abstraction, or absence of relatedness to concrete situations.

As we are using the word, a principle indicates the general direction which conduct should follow, but it does not and cannot prescribe the specific highway to be taken. It says, "Go west"; it does not order, "Take the New York Thruway to Buffalo, then follow Canadian Route 3 through Ontario." It leaves the choice among particular routes to be determined when the trip is taken, in relation to road conditions then prevailing and the particular needs and interests of the traveler at the time. *Both* a general direction and specific roads must be followed if we are to reach our destination. Neither excludes the other.

We may now turn directly to the question: What kind of help may the Christian rightly expect from a social theology of redemption as he confronts particular ethico-social decisions? Such a theology offers two main types of guidance.

1. In its three major emphases—social repentance, faith, and social sanctification—it provides important background orientation for the effective facing and making of decisions.

a. Awareness of the reality of and Christian involvement in social evil, leading to remorseful changes in attitude and commitment to action harmonious with the divine will, sensitizes the consciences of those who repent and fosters alertness to the ethical aspects of issues which call for decision. The very spirit of contrition encourages sensitivity to the needs and rights of others over against us, and prompts us to weigh such needs and rights as we make our choices.

b. The conviction that we are justified by grace through faith provides powerful motivation for decisions based on love for God and neighbor, and strengthens the Christian for making and carrying out hard choices in reliance on the divine grace. Released from concern for proving his own righteousness, he is free to seek the welfare of others. Knowing his own sinfulness and the reality of God's forgiveness, he is also less likely to evade responsible decisions because he fears making a mistake.

c. Concern for the fulfillment of God's will in all phases of the life of man deepens as well as broadens the base of the Christian's ethical decisions. Feeling called to incarnate the redemptive love of God in human society, he is prompted to give his utmost and to seek the closest possible approximation to the divine purpose. Moreover, he is conscious in all his efforts of the empowering presence of the Holy Spirit. Since the holiness which he believes God wants in men and society includes such goals as righteousness, love, mutual responsibility in community, and character befitting citizens of God's kingdom, he has general guidance for his specific choices. Further, since his reason is one of the God-given capacities which he is moved to place at God's disposal, he uses it reverently and critically in trying to relate the alternatives open in each situation to the general directions to which he is committed.

2. As the Christian faces actual decisions, he may find in a social theology of salvation broad ethical principles which provide constructive guidance in many different types of situations. Since these spring from his basic religious faith, they provide in advance of each decision a perspective from which he can judge the issues which arise. However, they do not contain neat, precise answers, and in no sense do they contain legal prescriptions concerning what course should be followed. Their meaning must be discovered and applied anew in each situation.

The ten principles to be listed here are by no means complete, but it is hoped that they are representative and suggestive. They are stated concisely and without comment, since they grow naturally out of the preceding discussion (especially Chapter Eight). Though no sharp line of distinction is possible, the first five are more formal in nature, while the second five are more material. However, they neither pretend nor aim to form a system.

Formal standards relevant to Christian decision include the following:

1. Since the entire ethical life of the Christian is a response to the redemptive activity of God, he should make all his decisions in an

awareness of the presence of God and relate them to the expectations, judgment, love, and power of God.

2. The Christian should always act in society not only in the light of the convictions which he derives from human ethical insight in general, but as a Christian relating his decisions specifically to the realities—both indicative and imperative—of his religious faith.

3. Since the acts of God to redeem mankind come to a focus in the life, teaching, death, and resurrection of Jesus Christ, the ethical teachings related to the earthly ministry of Jesus and called forth by the fellowship of the early church with the living Christ are particularly normative for Christians.

4. As a sinner who falls far short of the glory of God, the Christian is called upon to reach his decisions in humility, aware that self-interest and a limited perspective may warp his judgment, yet with faith that God can use his dedicated thought and action to advance divine ends.

5. Since both persons and situations are unique, decisions should always be concretely related to the specific needs of persons in the particular situations confronting them.[16]

To these may be added five other Christian ethical standards which involve more definite content.

6. Since God in love has created man and in love redeems him, those human attitudes and actions are most right which proceed from and best express love toward God and man.

7. Since God in creating and redeeming man has imparted to all persons immeasurable worth, Christians should respect this worth by seeking always the fullest welfare of other persons, without regard to race, national origin, or economic or social status.

8. Since God in Christ seeks a community of persons reconciled to him and harmoniously related to each other through him, Christians should support those social provisions which most effectively reduce hindrances to reciprocal love among persons and groups of persons and most constructively advance such love.

9. Since the full realization of the unique potentialities of persons in community requires a social order in which basic rights, freedoms,

---

[16] Is not this principle at least actually implicit in the thought of those Christian moralists who reject principles on the ground that their application to new, specific, concrete situations inevitably involves rigidity and distortion?

and responsibilities apply equally to all, Christians should seek at all times the spread of justice under law and the removal of injustice.

10. Since Christians and the Christian community are called to a ministry of reconciliation, they are responsible for making those decisions which will best witness to God's reconciling love and make most clear God's redemptive purpose for the persons and groups concerned. A decisive question in every choice is: Will what I now contemplate doing be a real ministry to those involved—an act of reconciliation? [17]

Principles like these are admittedly—and purposely—general. They must be intelligently and critically applied in particular situations involving specific issues and the lives of flesh-and-blood people. They do not tell us how to vote in a national election, whether the high schools in Middletown should be integrated in September 1960, whether to recognize the People's Republic of China, or how to solve the problems of the Arab refugees in the Middle East. If they did prescribe answers to such questions, they could be rightly dismissed as legalistic. Yet Christians still need a bridge from the broad ethical standards rooted in their faith to the everyday issues which demand decision.

Such a bridge is extremely difficult to build. Not only are there wide differences of opinion in the population as a whole on economic, political, and social questions, but Christians seriously disagree among themselves in these areas—in spite of the fact that they are in almost complete agreement on general Christian principles. We have noted convincing evidence of this in the MESTA questionnaire. Moreover, where the welfare of many persons is involved whose needs and capacities vary widely and whose personal interests conflict, it becomes impossible for finite minds, however well-intentioned, to determine

[17] Charles C. West writes of a group of East German students who were trying to determine their Christian responsibility as they faced Communist pressure demanding ideological conformity. "Should they argue and think for themselves in the required courses in Marx-Leninism? Should they write the truth and not the line required in their examinations? What attitude should they take to the 'Free German Youth' of which they were all perforce members? False steps at any of these points might lead to expulsion from the university and possible arrest. But the concern of the students was not to avoid these two fates, if such were the price of Christian action. It was rather that their action be a witness to the lordship of Christ and thus a ministry to the Communist, not merely an act of enmity and resistance" (*Communism and the Theologians*, pp. 10-11).

unambiguously what course will in the circumstances best conserve the good of all.

Further, the application of one principle may sometimes hinder the fulfillment of another. The justice sought in the decision of a labor union to strike may be inconsistent with love for the minority of members who oppose the walk-out because they cannot afford the loss of income, or with full regard for the personalities of the strikers' children who suffer through lack of needed medical care. In such situations no decision can perfectly fulfill the demands of Christian ethics. The closest possible approximation to such fulfillment is the right course in the circumstances, and therefore what might be called the circumstantial will of God. But Christians still face the problem of determining what that closest possible approximation is.

A helpful approach to this problem is found in the "middle axioms" first proposed by J. H. Oldham in 1937 in the essay previously cited. According to Oldham, these

are attempts to define the directions in which, in a particular state of society, Christian faith must express itself. They are not binding for all time, but are provisional definitions of the type of behavior required of Christians at a given period and in given circumstances.[18]

Such axioms stand midway between purely general ethical statements and particular courses of action in concrete situations. In the words of John C. Bennett, "a 'middle axiom' is more concrete than a universal ethical principle and less specific than a program that includes legislation and political strategy." [19]

Good examples of middle axioms relating to international relations are provided by the Six Political Propositions or "Pillars of Peace" formulated in 1943 by the Commission of the Federal Council of Churches to Study the Bases of a Just and Durable Peace. The fourth of these affirms: "The peace must proclaim the goal of autonomy for subject peoples, and it must establish international organization to assure and to supervise the realization of that end." This connects a general political principle with the proposal of an organiza-

[18] W. A. Visser 't Hooft and J. H. Oldham, *The Church and Its Function in Society*, p. 194.
[19] *Christian Ethics and Social Policy*, p. 77.

tion to implement it, without actually specifying the program to be worked out.

In the area of race relations, typical examples of middle axioms are found in the statement on "The Churches and Segregation" adopted by the General Board of the National Council of Churches on June 11, 1952. This statement urged the churches to "renounce the pattern of segregation based on race, color, or national origin," and to "work steadily and progressively toward a non-segregated church." It then offered six principles for the guidance of churches toward this goal, dealing with membership, fellowship, worship, ministerial outreach, educational and welfare services, and employment. The first of these asserts: "All persons who accept Christ as Lord and Master and the doctrinal standards of the communion ought to be invited and welcomed into membership of our communion's parish churches." These statements apply the principle of nonsegregation to specific areas of church practice, but they make no attempt to prescribe legislation for the communions or to tell local congregations what steps they should follow.

A similar approach to economic problems appears in the statement on "Christian Principles and Assumptions for Economic Life," adopted by the National Council's General Board on September 15, 1954. Following a very general declaration of fundamental religious and ethical assumptions, the statement offered thirteen ethical norms for the guidance of Christians. The fourth of these is as follows: "Economic institutions should be judged also by their impact upon the family—which involves standards of living, hours of labor, stability of employment, provision for housing, and the planning of cities, especially in relation to their industrial development and the elimination of blighted areas." It will be noted that the statement does not specify what living standards or hours of labor are desirable or how the norms listed are to be put into effect.

Many of the provisions of the Methodist Social Creed have the character of middle axioms. Two examples may be cited, dealing with intoxicants and narcotics and with civil rights: "We seek to protect the individual, the home, and society from the social, economic, and moral waste of any traffic in intoxicants and habit-forming drugs." "We stand for the recognition and maintenance of the rights and responsibilities of free speech, free assembly, and a free press, and for the encouragement of free communication of ideas essential to the discovery of truth." [20]

The working out of such positions by churches, smaller groups of Christians, and individuals definitely advances the process of discovering the concrete implications of general ethical principles. Obviously there are more than three positions on the continuum from universality to specificity; middle axioms themselves represent various degrees of particularity. Moreover, they seldom command unanimous support. However, agreement is much more likely at this level than at the point of specific legislation or programs of action.

The process of making our day-by-day ethical decisions as Christians is definitely advanced if we can come to them not only with a general commitment to love and justice and a redemptive concern for persons, but with principles previously thought through which relate these broad goals to specific areas of social responsibility. We are then called upon to determine the bearing of these norms on each new situation as it arises. This cannot be done in advance, and no one can do it for us. Utilizing knowledge gained from all available sources, in consultation with other persons, and especially with minds open to fresh illumination from God, we must explore and weigh the alternatives and decide which course of action in the situation at hand best accords with Christian goals.

A concrete problem may serve to illustrate the procedure which the Christian might follow in reaching an ethical decision. In towns and cities all over the country many people find it difficult or impossible, because of their race, religion, or national origin, to secure adequate housing. When neighborhoods previously homogeneous in these respects feel threatened by change, tension and conflict arise.

Let us suppose that in my community a nearby home owner, about to move away, wishes to sell his house. He has a good offer from a family of good character of another race, and is seriously considering its acceptance. Learning of the prospective sale, some of his neighbors are deeply concerned, and are circulating a petition asking him not to consummate the sale and thus change the racial complexion of the neighborhood. My wife and I are asked to sign the petition, and to attend a meeting which would consider ways of preventing the

---

[20] 1956 *Discipline*, par. 2020, pp. 705, 707.

sale and plan requests to real estate agents not to show houses to prospective buyers who are racially "undesirable." How do we decide what to do? How do we determine the will of God for us in this instance?

We might well begin by reminding ourselves of our involvement in the social situations which deny to many people the comforts we have enjoyed; by seeking in the grace of God both forgiveness for past indifference and strength for the right choice now; and by committing ourselves to search for the closest possible approximation of the divine purpose.[21] Then we shall want to remember our special vocation as *Christians,* and our responsibility for seeking the course most in harmony with the deepest convictions of our faith and the ethical teachings of the New Testament. This will lead us to relate the particular problem to ethical principles like those discussed above,[22] asking such questions as: Will joining the protest be the best way to manifest respect for the worth of the persons involved—our present as well as our potential neighbors? Which course will best express love toward the persons and families involved and encourage them to seek each other's fullest welfare? Which action on our part will be most genuinely a ministry of reconcilation in a tense situation?

Since Christians have already devoted much thought to questions of this kind, "middle axioms" are available which should help us as we try to relate these principles to our particular problem. As we have seen, both the National Council of Churches and The Methodist Church have on various occasions asserted that discrimination and segregation based on race are contrary to Christian ethical teaching.[23] The Methodist Conference on Human Relations, meeting in Dallas in September 1959, came still closer to our problem when it declared: "In the field of housing, we should provide open occupancy. Discrimination in selling or renting homes because of race violates Christian principles." [24] My wife and I will not regard these statements as binding our consciences; nevertheless, since they represent the considered judgment of a large number of responsible Christians we shall give them great weight. In particular, we shall relate them care-

[21] See above, pp. 214-15.
[22] See above, pp. 252-55.
[23] See above, pp. 183-86.
[24] See above, pp. 258-59.

fully to our own conscientious examination of the relevant Christian principles. We may feel that they overlook important considerations and hence we disagree with their main conclusions. Or we may find that they either express or helpfully correct our own interpretations, and accept as our own the policies they favor. In either case we shall need to go much farther in relating the position we have reached to the petition and the protest meeting.

Let us assume, however, that we agree with the "middle axioms." We then have a host of specific questions to ask ourselves. Would joining the protest constitute a form of discrimination or segregation? If so, do we really oppose these practices when they touch our own neighborhood? Suppose the house for sale were next door; would that make any difference? Would we be willing to have children of a different race as playmates and schoolmates for our children? Are we ready to have the family join our church if they desire? Is there anything about their race that would make them undesirable neighbors? Is it possible that families of our own race, to whom no objection would be raised, might be less desirable neighbors? What are the basic qualifications of a desirable neighbor? What about the fear of some petition-signers that property values would go down? Has this actually happened in communities like ours which have become racially mixed? What are the facts? What about the human values involved? Will it hinder or advance the growth of personality, impoverish or enrich life, to have one family—and possibly more—of the other race in our community?

Let us suppose that this kind of reflection and discussion leads to the conclusion that we would not object to the proposed sale, or would positively favor it. We can then politely decline to sign the petition and stay away from the meeting. Or we may see in the meeting an opportunity to bear a Christian witness and introduce into the situation a badly needed spirit of reconciliation. By attending, listening to our neighbors, and sharing with them the convictions we have reached, we may be able to reduce tension, promote understanding, deepen insight, and contribute toward a much better solution than would otherwise have been possible.

Many conscientious and thoughtful readers, disagreeing with the "middle axioms," or giving to the later questions different answers from those implied in the above conclusion, may reach a different decision. However, the questions raised are of the kind that are relevant to any search for a Christian answer to the problem. Some such procedure as this may be followed in connection with other ethical and social questions.

Many of the decisions we reach will inevitably involve compromise, and all will fall short of God's ideal will. However, a compromise which represents the fullest possible embodiment of a clearly held norm is likely to be closer to the absolute will of God than one which is reached without such a perspective, with no awareness even of what is being compromised. The procedure suggested will guard us from ethical relativism and easy-going latitudinarianism, and demand that we keep always in the center the intention of God rather than the vagaries of men who easily mistake the pragmatic pressures of the moment for the purpose of the Eternal. Much depends on where the emphasis is laid—on the ambiguities of the situation and the necessity of compromise or on the creative and redemptive purpose of God as revealed in Jesus Christ.

The words of Georgia Harkness offer a lucid summary:

Taken as a whole, the message of Jesus does not tell us to choose the lesser of two evils. It does tell us, with a realistic awareness of the range of these evils, to choose the greater good. This is more than a verbal difference, for the one takes the world's evil as its base line, the other takes God's goodness as it has been manifest in Jesus. The greater good is that course of action which, in a given circumstance, is relatively the fullest embodiment of faith and love with God at the center in the act of decision.[25]

C. The Ministry of the Laity in Society

The Christian social action which ultimately counts most is not the "actions" contained in pronouncements by ecclesiastical bodies, but the deeds of Christian individuals and groups which witness to God's reconciling love where people live and work. Likewise, if the decisions of Christians on social questions are to be instruments of God in the salvation of society, they must be made in the midst of the life which God seeks to redeem. This means that they must be made chiefly by Christian laymen who are conscious of the church's

[25] Christian Ethics—Sources of the Living Tradition, edited by Waldo Beach and H. Richard Niebuhr. Copyright 1955, The Ronald Press Company, p. 66.

place in God's redemptive purpose, and of their responsibility in the church.

Highly important for Christian social thought and action, therefore, is the new understanding of the ministry of the laity which is now rapidly spreading, deepened by the work of various Christian lay centers and encouraged by the World Council of Churches. Methodists are peculiarly equipped by their heritage to contribute constructively to and participate creatively in this movement—though it involves much more than the use of lay preachers or upholding the rights of laymen in church government. What should be the basic role of the laity?

The church originated in the experience of those who, confronted by God's forgiving love and transforming power in Jesus Christ, were called out of sin into a new relation to God and their fellows (Eph. 4:1; II Tim. 1:9). God's *klesis* (call) resulted in his *ekkletoi* (those called out), who in turn became the *ekklesia* (called assembly or congregation). Obedience to God's call was thus not merely an individual matter. Christians were summoned to membership in the *laos tou theou*, the people or laity of God. Significantly, the *laos* of God in the New Testament refers not to nonministers, but to the whole church. Within this *laos* each person had his *diakonia* (ministry), whether he was called to be an apostle, a prophet, a teacher, a healer, or something else better fitted to his God-given talents.

Thus everyone who responded to the call of God was both a layman —one of the people of God, and a minister—one of those summoned to service. Some were designated bishops, presbyters, or deacons and were given special pastoral oversight, teaching responsibility, or leadership in worship. Others accepted different responsibilities fitted to their capacities. But all had a ministry, and all were expected to discharge their functions as members of one body, one people of God. In a profound sense all were evangelists, called to witness daily for Christ and to devote themselves wholly to God.

The stirring commission in I Peter 2:9 is addressed not to ordained clergy but to the whole church, to a fellowship of people brought together by a common life and driven forward together by a common mission. The New Testament in general recognizes among Christians different offices and functions, but it knows nothing of a sharp distinction between professional and amateur Christians, between wholly dedicated clergy and laymen who are less active in furthering the gospel.

This false separation can be overcome if we recognize, with the Methodists of New Zealand, that both ministry and laity "are of the esse of the church, and both share its universal ministry." [26] The former is called upon to exercise the ministry of the Word and the Sacraments; the latter, a large variety of other gifts and offices. All are called to witness and evangelize. The church is neither a priesthood ministering to the laity, nor a lay body appointing a ministry to full-time service in the performance of special functions. It is the whole people of God united in his work.

Yet many Christians continue to think of the church, if not as a building, as the congregation which assembles in a building and carries on there certain activities, or as the sum total of such congregations. Certainly this is partly what the church is. The worship, education, fellowship, and service which center in our church edifices are the indispensable core of the church's life, and the devoted labors of those who make these activities possible are an incalculably important ministry. But just as certainly the church and its lay ministry extend far beyond this. The church is wherever the people of God live, work, think, play, pray, serve, and struggle for divine ends.

Truly seen, the church is present not only when the worshiping congregation rises in praise on Sunday morning, but equally on Tuesday night when some of its members stand intelligently and courageously for Christian goals in the P.T.A., the hospital board, the labor union, or the Chamber of Commerce. It is functioning on Thursday afternoon when one of its number, because he is a Christian, advertises his wares honestly or charges a fair price for a careful job of repairing a car. It is active in those who, supported by their sense of belonging to a redemptive fellowship, uphold the rights of racial and other minorities, and work for reconciliation among nations. It is present whenever and wherever its members see in other people children of God for whom Christ died, sense the burdens they bear and the struggles they face, and in spirit, word, and deed mediate the love of God.

In wide circles laymen are still viewed largely as assistant pastors,

---

[26] *Towards the One Church*, p. 26.

whose chief purpose is to help the minister perform the activities of particular concern to him. The MESTA questionnaire indicates that three out of five laymen of The Methodist Church hold this conception of their role. Might it not be sounder to think of the pastor as an assistant layman? Especially is this true in relation to the church's social task. As J. H. Oldham has written: "A church aflame with social passion should recognize that the largest contribution of the Christian ministry to social transformation is an indirect one, and that the awaking, educating, and spiritual encouragement of those who bear the varied responsibilities of the corporate life is the highest and most rewarding strategy." [27]

As one of the *laos* of God, the minister has the sacred function of leading people into the presence of God in worship. He is commissioned to help acquaint them with the roots and resources of their faith and relate these to the world in which they live; to deepen their sense of fellowship with each other and with Christ; and to send them out thus equipped for the ministry which they alone can perform. Periodically they return to their physical headquarters for worship, spiritual renewal, mutual strengthening through shared experiences, and deepened understanding of their common task. Then they go out again to be the church in home and school, farm and factory, store and office, court and legislative hall, hospital and hotel, on land and sea and in air—wherever men need to know the power and love of God. So related, pastor and people together make up the laity of God. He and they alike are ministers of Christ, discharging together the ministry of reconciliation to which the church is called.

[27] W. A. Visser 't Hooft and J. H. Oldham, *The Church and Its Function in Society*, p. 186.

Appendixes

Appendix A

Social Characteristics of Methodism, 1959

Sources of Information. TWO TYPES OF SOURCES HAVE BEEN utilized in an analysis of the social characteristics of Methodism. First, there has been a utilization of Methodist resource materials, both from official publications of the church and also from supplementary research studies. Official publications include: *The Methodist Fact Book, 1957,* the most recent issue at the time the study was made; and *The General Minutes of the Methodist Church, 1958.* An additional resource book used was *The Emerging Patterns in Town and Country Methodism, 1959.* Especially helpful have been the MESTA Inquiry on "The Beliefs of Methodists" [1] and the tabulated summaries from the project studies of *Church Surveys* of Boston University School of Theology. The MESTA Inquiry has been based on a representative sample of 5,020 Methodists. The *Church Surveys* studies have provided cumulative data and tabulated summaries from individual survey cards filled out for more than 600,000 Methodists within the past three years.

The second type of reference, the basis for comparison, has been summary data concerning the total U. S. population. The official reference for this has been *The Statistical Abstract, 1958.* Considerable use has been made of the monthly Current Population reports—Series P-20, No. 77, U. S. Bureau of the Census, Department of Commerce.

Sociological Definition of a Methodist. The point of reference will be the Methodist "parishioner" rather than "member" in order to have comparable data. Full members[2] of The Methodist Church would include only persons approximately twelve years of age and over, for the most part. Most U. S. Census data include reference to persons of all ages. A study based on Methodist parishioners rather than members obviates the difficulty.

A parishioner is defined as any person who is a part of the household

---

[1] See Appendix B.
[2] All persons responding to the MESTA Inquiry were members.

of a member family. A member family is a family which has at least one adult member of the church as a part of its household. Parishioners then would include not only all full members of the church in such a family, but also all unbaptized children, all children who have been baptized and who are preparatory members of The Methodist Church if they have been baptized as Methodists, and also any other person in a member household. The members of non-Methodist churches in such a household would be offset statistically by Methodist constituents who have not yet joined the church, and who are part of non-member households.

Median age of Methodists. The median age of Methodists is approximately 34.5 years, based on cumulative survey reports, with one-half the parishioners above this age and one-half below. A median age of 34.5 years is 15 per cent higher than the total U. S. population which had a median age of 30.2 years in 1950. The median age varies from state to state, with a low of 24 years for New Mexico and a high of 33.7 years for New York State. The median rural farm population age is 26.3 years. The median age has been increasing steadily in the nation from 22.9 years in 1900 to a high of 20.3 years as reported in Current Population Survey reports, 1956, U. S. Bureau of the Census.

Sex Ratio. Eleven out of twenty Methodists are females. There are more females than males in the U. S. population at the present time, according to U. S. Census estimates, but the proportion of females is higher in The Methodist Church than in the total population. There are only 90 males per 100 females in The Methodist Church, as compared to 99.2 males per 100 females in the U. S. population as reported in the 1950 census. The ratio of males per 100 females has been gradually lowering since 1910, at which time there were 106 males per 100 females in the U. S. population. The decline in ratio of males has been attributed to various causes including wars, the employment of men in hazardous industries, and the general improvement in health and longevity for women.

Marital Status. Eight out of ten Methodists 25 years of age and over are married, according to an adjusted report of the MESTA Inquiry, approximately the same ratio as to be found in the total U. S. population. A total of 80.1 per cent of the Methodists 25 years of age and over are married as compared to 78.3 per cent in the same age group for the total population.

One in ten Methodists is single, approximately the same ratio as found in the total U. S. population among persons 25 years of age and over. Only one Methodist in one hundred is divorced as compared to more than two per one hundred reported in the total population. However, in view of the opinion of census takers that a large number of divorced persons reported themselves to be "single," there is a possibility that the divorce rate for Methodists is comparatively lower than the given figures would indicate. A greater degree of honesty would be expected for parishioners than for persons not affiliated with a church. Nine Methodists out of one hundred are widows or widowers among those 25 years of age and over.

Family Size. The average size of the Methodist family is 3.6 persons, identical with the U. S. average reported in the 1950 Census. The size of the Methodist family was obtained from the MESTA Inquiry, and compares favorably with the cumulative project studies of *Church Surveys, Boston University.*

The average size of the Methodist household, however, is only 3.1 as obtained from the cumulative reports of *Church Surveys* to date, compared to the average household size of 3.34 as reported in the Bureau of the Census estimate of March 1957. In The Methodist Church a large number of widows, widowers, and single persons have their own household. Many of these are elderly persons, as reflected in the higher median age for Methodists than for non-Methodists.

There is some evidence that Methodists may have a higher longevity record than the total U. S. population, due to a correlation of higher median age with an average family size. The percentage of Methodists 75 years of age and over is 40 per cent higher than the percentage of the total U. S. population in the age grouping, according to cumulative reports from the Church Surveys studies.

Education. The average Methodist replying has graduated from high school and has completed one semester of work in college. The median of educational attainment for Methodists is 12.4 years of schooling beyond kindergarten, with one-half of the Methodists having less education, and one-half more. This is somewhat higher than the median educational attainment of 10.8 years for the total population 25 years of age and over, from various reports of the U. S. Bureau of the Census studies as of March 1957. The educational attainment of Methodists has been obtained from the MESTA Inquiry.

The chance of a son or daughter graduating from college is at least three times as high if he or she comes from a Methodist family. More than one-third of the Methodists 25 years of age and over have graduated from college. As a denomination, Methodists have the highest percentage of students in the State Colleges and Universities of the U. S. in addition to having the largest number of church-related colleges and universities of all the Protestant groups.

Family Income. Methodists have a median family income of $5,329 per year, according to the MESTA studies, with one-half of the families receiving more income and one-half of the families receiving less. This is higher than the median family income of $4,687 for the U. S. total population of males aged 35-54 as reported in Current Population Reports, March 1957, U. S. Bureau of the Census.

This is especially significant in view of the large rural farm population in The Methodist Church. In a bulletin published June 1958, the Census Bureau reported the median money income of urban and rural nonfarm families in the United States to be $5,232 for the preceding year, as compared with the median money income of rural farm families at $2,490 for the preceding year.

Size of Community. Three out of four Methodist congregations are located in communities of less than 2,500 population, according to studies published in The Emerging Patterns in Town and Country Methodism, 1959. Six out of ten Methodists live in the "town and country," or rural areas of the United States, according to the definition of such areas as places of less than 10,000 population, as defined in the 1956 Discipline of The Methodist Church. Approximately 33.3 per cent more Methodists live in rural areas than the proportion of the general U. S. population.

More Methodists were reared in small communities than live in them at the present time, according to the MESTA Inquiry. A total of 51.2 per cent more Methodists were reared in communities of less than 2,500 than live in them at the present time. And conversely there are more Methodists living in large cities than were reared in them. There are 66.7 per cent more Methodists living in cities of 10,000 to 99,999 than were reared in them. There are 23.8 per cent more Methodists living in cities of 100,000 and over than were reared in them.

Size of Church. One out of every five Methodists is affiliated with a church of less than 250 members. Nearly one-half of the Methodists are in churches of less than 500 members.

Twice as many Methodists were reared in small churches as are affiliated with the smaller churches at the present time. According to the MESTA Inquiry slightly over one-half of the Methodists were reared in churches of less than 250 members. And conversely the percentage of Methodists who are now affiliated with larger churches is much higher than the percentage reared in them. A total of 76 per cent more Methodists are now in churches of 1,000 or more members than were reared in them.

Denominational Background. Two out of three Methodists were reared in The Methodist Church. Of those reared in other churches, two-thirds came from one or another of these backgrounds: Presbyterian, Congregational, Baptist, Lutheran, or Episcopal. Less than two per cent of all Methodists were reared in a Roman Catholic background. Less than one out of ten Methodists was reared in any background other than those which have been named.

Length of Membership. One out of four Methodists has been affiliated with the church twelve years or less. The percentage of newcomers in The Methodist Church is low, however. A total of 14.5 per cent have been members of the church six years or less. From length of residence studies it has been estimated that a church needs to have 17.5 per cent of its membership composed of newcomers who have lived in the community six years or less, or who have been members of the church six years or less. The median goal of 17.5 per cent has been set for a normal church to keep pace with population growth. The Methodist Church is not keeping pace with total U. S. population growth.

Evangelistic Ratio. During the year 1958 one new member for every twenty-six members was added to the church on profession of faith. The evangelistic ratio is the number of full members of the church required to win one person to Christ and to membership in the church on profession of faith. The Board of Evangelism has estimated that one person should be received on profession of faith for every fourteen members. As a result of hardly more than 50 per cent efficiency in attaining the evangelistic ratio goal, The Methodist Church is growing slightly over half as fast as the total U. S. population. From 1950 to 1958 The Methodist Church has increased in membership from a total of 8,935,647 members in 1950 to a total of 9,691,916 members in 1958, a net gain of 756,269, or 8.5 per cent. From 1950 to 1958 the U. S. population has increased from a total of 150,697,361 persons in 1950 to an estimated total of 174,060,000 on July 1, 1958, according to Robert W. Burgess, Director, Bureau of the Census, Department of Commerce. This represents a gain of 23,362,639, or 15.5 per cent.

Correlation studies on the family size of Methodists and the net gain in membership would indicate that the church is not retaining its own constituency, and is not retaining its share of the total population. Most of the net losses are due to Methodists on the move, whose church membership has not moved to the new places of residence. One out of five Americans aged one year and over changes his place of residence each year, according to the results of a sample survey conducted by the Bureau of the Census from April 1956 to April 1957. The average American would be moving once every five years.

Church School. For every hundred members of The Methodist Church, there are seventy-four members of a Methodist Church School. Approximately one out of five members of a Methodist Church School is not a parishioner of the church, and is not affiliated with the church in any

271

other way than through a relationship to the church school. They are not in church member families or households.

Methodist Church Schools are becoming expanding frontiers of evangelistic opportunity. Some are located in areas not now served by a Methodist Church. Some church schools, formerly closed, have been reopened. From 1956 to 1958 Methodist Church Schools have increased from 37,923 to 38,350, a net gain of 427. During the same period of time Methodist Churches, or "preaching places," have decreased from 39,845 to 39,317, a net loss of 528.

Race. Less than one out of twenty members of The Methodist Church is nonwhite, but more than one out of ten persons in the total U. S. population is nonwhite. The Bureau of the Census reported a total of 11.5 per cent of the U. S. population as nonwhite in 1950. One out of twenty-five Methodists (3.9 per cent of the total) is a member of the Central Jurisdiction which consists almost entirely of Negroes. An estimated .7 per cent of the members of the other Jurisdictions are American, Indian, Japanese, Chinese, or Negro, mostly the latter.

Nearly one fourth of the members of all Methodist bodies are Negroes, however, and are members of the following four more or less segregated groups: African Methodist Episcopal Church, African Methodist Episcopal Zion Church, the Colored Methodist Episcopal Church, and the Central Jurisdiction of The Methodist Church.

More than four out of ten Negroes will be living outside the South in 1960, according to estimate reported in The Methodist Fact Book, 1957. The evangelistic ratio of the Central Jurisdiction is low at the present time. There has been an assimilation of six congregations over scattered areas from the Conferences of the Central Jurisdiction to the Conferences in various other Jurisdictions of The Methodist Church. In 1958 one person was received on profession of faith for every thirty-one members of the Central Jurisdiction. For the most part, Negroes are not being reached efficiently by the Central Jurisdiction.

Occupation. The occupational profile of Methodists shows a preponderance of professional men and women and managers, as compared to the total U. S. population, 1958 estimate from the Bureau of the Census. Conversely, the proportion of operatives, service workers, and laborers is very low compared to the total population.

Generally speaking, Methodists have a much higher percentage of persons in the professional, managerial, and so-called "white collar" occupations in urban life. Methodists have about the same percentage in the so-called "blue collar" occupations, meaning primarily the craftsmen.

The percentage of professional men and women in The Methodist Church is over three times as high as the percentage of professional men and women in the total population. This is correlated with the fact that the percentage of college graduates in The Methodist Church is three times as high as the percentage of college graduates in the total population.

The percentage of farm operators and various types of managers is approximately 6 per cent higher than the percentage of managers and farm operators in the total population.

The percentage of sales workers in The Methodist Church is less than one per cent higher than the percentage of sales workers in the total population.

The percentage of clerical workers in The Methodist Church is approximately 2 per cent higher than the percentage of sales workers in the total U. S. population.

The percentage of craftsmen in The Methodist Church is approximately 3 per cent lower than the percentage of craftsmen in the total population.

The percentage of operatives in The Methodist Church is 12.6 per cent lower than the percentage of operatives in the total U. S. population.

The percentage of service workers and laborers is 14.3 per cent lower than the percentage of service workers and laborers in the total U. S. population.

The percentage of private household workers in The Methodist Church is 2.9 per cent lower than the percentage of private household workers and domestic service employees in the total U. S. population.

Summary. In general it can be said that Methodists have characteristics similar to the total population in respect to family size. The median age is slightly higher than for the total population. The sex ratio of males per 100 females is slightly lower for Methodists than for the total population.

Characteristics which pertain to attainment find the Methodists far ahead. Methodism, then, reflects socially the configuration of the total population of the United States. In family stability, educational attainment, longevity, and occupational status, Methodism is exceptional. Its families stay together, its members are well educated and long-lived. In all other ways studied, the Methodists of the various census regions are truly representative of the general populace.

The Methodist Church is of service to persons in all occupational groupings, though not wholly adequate in serving the manually employed. There is sparse evidence that other denominations have been more effective here, but there is little comfort in this.

Perhaps the most dramatic social trend noted here is the migration of

273

Methodists from rural to urban areas. The sample clearly evidenced the earlier rural training of members who are now urban residents. The large number of urban Methodists in the next generation will constitute a major challenge.[3]

[3] This survey reveals the paucity of presently available information about the social characteristics of Methodists. Thus, for example, there are no data in Conference Journals which are comparable with Federal Census data classifications. Similarly, the Conference Minutes fail to indicate the physical location of Methodist properties, churches, and so forth. If such geographical (township, county, etc.) identification could be obtained, it would be possible to establish far more profitable correlations between census data and Methodist data.

Appendix B

An Inquiry on the Beliefs of Methodists

IN THIS VOLUME REFERENCES ARE REPEATEDLY MADE TO THE IN-
quiry on "The Beliefs of Methodists." The committee realized at an early
stage that its documentary research needed to be supplemented with an
investigation of the actual religious beliefs and social attitudes to be found
in American Methodism today. In the summer of 1958 the committee, assisted for sometime by a public opinion research specialist, William
Cascini, developed a questionnaire which, after numerous pretestings, was
mailed out in January 1959. The office of the Division of National Missions of The Methodist Church in Philadelphia provided valuable assistance in the preparation of the punch cards. A portion of these data
was used in conjunction with the fourth Town and Country Convoca-
tion of The Methodist Church at Wichita, Kansas, July 1959.

The following account briefly explains the structure and form of the
questionnaire; reproduces the questionnaire itself with the responses received in percentages by jurisdiction; and discusses the methodology of
the inquiry and the representativeness of the responses.[1]

Structure and Form of Questionnaire

The questionnaire consists of four parts, covering respectively religious
beliefs (questions 1-25), ethical and social beliefs (26-44), social action
(45-58), and social background (59-78). Questions 1-20 and 26-44 offer a
choice among four or five statements ranged on a continuum between
poles. However, in the questionnaire as distributed the actual continuum
was concealed by sequential rotation in order to avoid stereotyping of
answers. Thus in question 1 the first statement represented position 1;
in question 2 the first statement represented position 2, followed by positions 3, 4, 5, and 1; in question 3 the first statement represented position
3, followed by 4, 1, and 2; in question 4 the first statement represented
position 4, followed by 1, 2, and 3; and in question 5 the order returned

---

[1] A comprehensive account of this inquiry and its results will be published separately
in a technical monograph.

to that in question 1. This pattern continued throughout the questions listed. In answering questions 1-20 and 26-44 the respondent was asked to check under each heading the one statement which seemed to him to correspond *most closely* to his own belief, expressing better than any other what he regarded as centrally important. If he found no statement satisfactory, he was invited to write his own in the space provided.

In Part I on religious beliefs, questions 1-10 represent more or less a common continuum ranging broadly from orthodoxy or conservatism to humanism. Position 1 reflects belief, for example, in the absolute power, sovereignty, and grace of God and the sinfulness and helplessness of man, while the other extreme stresses the freedom, ability, and potential goodness of man and, consequently, the central importance of human effort and achievement. The one pole is God-centered, the other man-centered; the one relies on the supernatural, the other on the natural.

Questions 11 and 12 deal with two historic Methodist emphases, the witness of the Spirit and sanctification or perfection. Question 11 therefore reflects the degree of certainty believed possible in religious experience; question 12, the degree to which holiness of life is regarded as normative for individuals and society.

Questions 13-20 attempt in various ways to relate theology and life. They have in common the fact that each indicates the degree to which the individual responding regards a particular reality, concern, belief, or action as relevant to his Christian responsibility or that of the church. Each of these questions has its own continuum from relevance to irrelevance, but they are too diverse in subject matter to scale meaningfully.

In Part II on ethical and social beliefs (26-44) each question presents a range of possibilities more or less evenly spaced between poles or a spectrum of the views most commonly held. The subjects are so diverse that no unified scaling is possible.

The last five questions (21-25) of Part I deal with the extent of the guidance which Christians receive from their religious beliefs with respect to certain social problems. Four possibilities are offered on a Likert scale, ranging from direct guidance to no guidance. Part III on social action (questions 45-58) seeks information on the nature and extent of expressions of social responsibility anl sources of guidance and leadership in areas of social concern. Likert scaling is used here also, with choice of four positions ranging from "Regularly" to "Never" or "Much" to "None."

Part IV (questions 59-78) provides for a variety of information about the social background of the respondents, including such items as age, sex, education, occupation, income, size of church and community, church activities and contributions, and the like.

Questionnaire With Responses

THE FOREWORD TO THE PARTICIPANTS*

The Board of Social and Economic Relations of The Methodist Church has asked the faculty of the Boston University School of Theology to make a comprehensive study of The Methodist Church in Social Thought and Action. The significance of such an enquiry at the present time is evident. Methodism has all through its history been noted for its intense social concern. Along with other Christian communions, The Methodist Church today faces the imperative task of rethinking and vitalizing its witness in a rapidly changing culture. It needs to ponder the lessons of its own heritage, to redefine its social motivations and ideals, to assess its present activities and resources, and to evolve creative strategies adequate for new advance in an increasingly complex society.

Your co-operation in completing this questionnaire and returning it to your pastor in a sealed envelope will aid Methodism in knowing for the first time the thinking of its total constituency on basic issues.

Under each of the following headings, please check the one (only one) statement which seems to you to correspond most closely to your own belief. By checking one statement you mean that it expresses better than any other what you regard as centrally important.

If no statement is satisfactory, write your own in the space provided.

* This and the following pages represent a reproduction of the MR-2 questionnaire, with the results given in percentage form.

I. RELIGIOUS BELIEFS

1. The Bible

	Total	C	NC	NE	SC	SE	W
Every word is true because it came directly from God	8.4	7.5	8.2	7.8	10.6	9.7	5.7
The Bible is the inspired Word of God, but not all parts are of equal spiritual value	32.0	33.4	30.7	30.0	33.6	36.0	30.8
As the unique historical record of God's revelation to inspired men, the Bible contains the word of God	49.7	48.4	51.7	51.2	48.7	45.3	49.2
The Bible is one of several records of man's religious search	7.0	7.6	6.7	8.2	4.9	5.1	11.9
Write-in	2.2	3.1	2.0	2.1	1.2	3.2	2.0
No report	.7	.0	.7	.7	1.0	.7	.4

2. God Is

	Total	C	NC	NE	SC	SE	W
the awesome being, wholly other than man and the world, whom we encounter only in Jesus Christ	10.0	4.5	10.7	10.9	10.8	7.7	9.7
the omnipotent Lord who exists eternally in three persons and whose righteous will rules his whole creation	60.1	62.1	61.3	57.1	62.5	64.0	50.9
the supremely personal Spirit who works in nature and history to realize his purposes	11.4	13.6	11.1	12.1	9.6	12.0	12.7
the creative, perfecting power in nature and history which supports and makes possible the realization of values	11.3	10.6	10.2	12.6	10.8	8.4	18.0
the name given to our highest human aspirations	3.0	6.2	3.3	3.2	2.5	2.3	3.5
Write-in	2.6	1.5	1.9	2.4	2.7	3.9	2.8
No report	1.6	1.5	1.5	1.7	1.1	1.7	2.4

Total Percentage

3. Man Is

a creature of God who in sinful pride has rejected his Creator and deified himself	3.9	7.6	3.4	3.9	3.8	4.7	3.4
a being who has blurred and distorted the divine image in which God has created him	4.0	6.0	4.0	3.8	3.4	5.6	2.6
a rational being capable of knowing God and entering into fellowship with Him	78.2	81.8	79.3	75.4	81.5	77.3	77.0
a product of nature whose innate powers for achieving goodness, truth, and beauty are almost unlimited	10.5	3.0	10.3	12.9	8.1	8.1	14.6
Write-in	2.0	.0	1.6	2.3	1.3	3.4	2.0
No report	1.4	1.6	1.4	1.7	1.9	.9	.4

4. Sin Is

a corruption of man's nature inherited from Adam, and rebellious acts resulting from this condition	17.1	28.8	15.7	17.5	14.4	24.6	9.5
a condition of self-centeredness and pride which distorts the wills of men and affects even their best choices	21.5	25.7	20.0	18.3	21.3	26.4	24.5
voluntary attitudes and actions, partially due to our involvement in society, which are contrary to God's will	50.8	33.4	54.2	52.7	52.6	39.0	55.5
antisocial conduct caused by ignorance or bad environment	5.0	4.5	5.4	6.4	4.8	2.5	5.3
Write-in	2.8	3.0	2.2	2.4	3.2	4.1	3.0
No report	2.8	4.6	2.5	2.7	3.7	3.4	2.2

I. RELIGIOUS BELIEFS

Total Percentage

5. Salvation Means

		C	NC	NE	SC	SE	W
going to heaven and escaping hell	2.1	1.0	2.8	1.2	1.4	2.6	1.1
peace and joy with God through His forgiveness of our sins	41.4	28.7	44.9	43.2	40.2	36.2	38.2
power to live a new life in fellowship with God and man	50.0	65.2	46.9	49.2	51.6	53.3	52.9
the integration and highest fulfillment of the self in harmonious social relations	2.3	1.5	2.0	2.4	2.0	2.1	3.8
Write-in	2.7	.0	1.7	2.2	3.5	4.6	3.0
No report	1.5	4.6	1.7	1.8	1.3	1.2	1.0

6. Jesus Christ Is

		C	NC	NE	SC	SE	W
God Himself, not subject to human limitations	13.7	10.6	14.4	11.9	13.6	13.3	12.4
both divine and human	37.5	53.0	34.3	36.4	35.7	47.3	29.8
a man uniquely endowed and called by God to reveal Him to man	36.4	22.7	38.7	37.2	39.6	26.6	43.3
one of the world's great spiritual teachers	6.6	4.6	7.6	8.5	5.4	5.5	9.3
Write-in	3.9	6.0	3.1	3.6	3.6	5.2	4.2
No report	1.8	3.1	1.9	2.4	2.1	2.1	1.0

7. The Christian Church Is

the custodian of the authority and grace committed by God to the apostles and their successors	6.3	6.1	6.9	7.0	6.3	4.3	6.5
the faithful congregation in which the pure Word of God is preached and the sacraments rightly administered	23.7	21.3	24.9	27.8	22.0	21.0	18.0
the community of those who have been renewed through Jesus Christ and empowered by the Holy Spirit	34.6	56.0	31.2	30.0	36.2	47.1	29.0
a society of those who have joined together in their quest for the religious life	30.4	10.6	32.5	30.7	28.6	22.3	41.5
Write-in	2.5	3.0	2.2	1.7	3.3	3.7	2.8
No report	2.5	3.0	2.3	2.8	3.6	1.6	2.2

8. Men Are Saved

entirely by divine grace	3.9	4.6	4.4	3.7	4.2	3.3	3.0
by believing that Jesus Christ is the Son of God	10.6	7.5	9.0	9.6	9.6	16.4	9.8
by divine grace when they respond in repentance and trustful obedience	54.3	66.7	55.5	50.4	55.0	55.6	52.4
by belief in Jesus Christ and upright living	24.6	15.1	25.0	28.8	25.0	18.2	26.8
by their upright character	1.5	1.5	1.5	1.9	.5	.8	3.2
Write-in	3.4	3.0	2.6	3.9	4.4	4.4	3.4
No report	1.7	1.6	2.0	1.7	1.3	1.3	1.4

I. RELIGIOUS BELIEFS

9. The Chief Aim of Missions Should Be

		Total Percentage					
		C	NC	NE	SC	SE	W
to save those who know not Christ, and who will be lost unless he is made known to them	19.9	21.2	21.1	19.2	21.3	21.2	12.3
to bring individuals to accept and live by the good news of the redemptive love of God revealed in Jesus Christ	42.9	37.9	44.2	43.7	44.5	38.9	43.0
to release in both individuals and society the redemptive power of God disclosed in Jesus Christ, so that all human life may be made whole	23.3	31.8	21.6	19.7	22.2	30.9	23.3
to improve the well-being of people by giving them new and improved methods of agriculture, industry, education, and health	8.5	1.5	8.5	11.5	7.1	3.6	14.2
Write-in	3.4	3.0	3.1	2.8	3.1	3.2	5.6
No report	2.0	4.6	1.5	3.1	1.8	2.2	1.6

10. The Kingdom of God Is

		C	NC	NE	SC	SE	W
the supernatural reign of God to be established wholly by divine action	12.7	12.1	13.8	12.7	10.0	11.8	14.2
the righteous rule of God which depends mainly on God's initiative, but requires man's co-operation	26.4	30.4	25.7	21.4	25.0	35.3	24.2
the fulfillment of God's purposes which depends mainly on the efforts of men aided by God	52.8	39.3	53.6	56.7	57.2	43.8	54.1
a name for the ideal social order to be built wholly by human wisdom and effort	1.8	7.5	1.6	2.1	1.2	1.4	2.5
Write-in	2.4	4.6	2.1	2.6	2.8	3.1	1.8
No report	3.9	6.1	3.2	4.5	3.8	4.6	3.2

11. Religious Experience

We cannot be sure whether our sins are forgiven; God alone knows	3.9	.0	4.8	4.6	3.7	1.4	4.7
By the inner witness of the Spirit, every Christian can have a sure trust that through the sacrificial love of Christ his sins are forgiven and he is reconciled to God	46.1	53.0	43.6	45.1	48.3	53.4	39.7
Christians may personally experience the presence and power of God in their lives	41.5	31.8	43.1	41.9	40.7	38.0	44.1
God revealed himself vividly to great souls in the past, but does so only infrequently to men today	.4	1.5	.5	.0	.2	.2	.6
We experience religion whenever we co-operate with our fellows in high ethical endeavors	4.0	6.1	4.2	4.4	2.8	2.6	6.9
Write-in	2.5	3.0	1.9	1.9	3.5	3.1	3.2
No report	1.6	4.6	1.9	2.1	.8	1.3	.8

12. Growth in Grace

Life is so complex and sin so powerful that advance in human righteousness cannot be expected in this life	1.0	3.0	.9	.8	1.9	.7	1.4
Only Christians who receive a second work of grace can live without sin	1.9	3.0	1.9	2.4	1.0	3.0	.3
Christians should expect through the power of God to attain perfect love in this life	11.3	13.6	9.3	10.1	10.7	18.8	7.0
With God's help both individuals and society may progress toward the fulfillment of his purposes	81.9	69.8	84.4	81.9	82.3	73.7	89.1
Write-in	1.6	3.0	1.2	1.8	1.7	1.7	1.4
No report	2.3	7.6	2.3	3.0	2.4	2.1	.8

I. RELIGIOUS BELIEFS

	Total	C	NC	NE	SC	SE	W
13. Belief and Conduct							
What one believes is all-important, because it determines conduct	43.3	40.9	44.6	38.7	46.3	44.7	41.3
Our actions are affected by our basic beliefs more than by anything else	37.2	39.4	37.9	36.0	34.5	36.2	42.2
Though some beliefs are essential, right conduct is much more important than correct beliefs	7.2	3.0	6.3	8.2	7.2	8.5	7.6
It doesn't matter what one believes—it's how he lives that counts	8.0	9.1	7.4	11.9	7.6	6.2	5.5
Write-in	1.7	3.0	1.4	1.8	1.7	2.0	1.2
No report	2.6	4.6	2.4	3.4	2.7	2.4	2.2
14. A Christian Should Live a Good Life Mainly Because							
it will win an eternal reward, and failure to do so will bring everlasting punishment	11.1	9.1	11.1	12.1	11.5	12.8	6.9
it is the will of God	36.6	28.7	37.7	34.9	37.4	38.7	32.6
all Christians should follow the example of Jesus	31.4	42.5	31.7	32.2	33.1	25.0	36.1
it works better than any other way, bringing more satisfactory results	14.9	12.1	14.7	15.7	12.5	14.1	18.4
Write-in	4.2	1.5	3.4	2.9	3.7	7.2	4.8
No report	1.8	6.1	1.4	2.2	1.8	2.2	1.2

Total Percentage

15. The Ethical Teachings of Jesus

were suitable for a time in the first century for those expecting the end of the world, but have limited application to us	.5	1.5	.4	.6	.3	.8	.6
set up general goals for Christians, but cannot be achieved in this world	1.3	.0	.6	3.1	1.2	1.3	.6
provide basic principles which are just as valid now as when first uttered	80.4	81.8	80.3	78.4	80.0	81.9	82.6
are the most practical basis for human conduct	14.6	10.6	15.8	14.7	14.2	12.8	13.8
Write-in	1.1	1.5	.9	.7	1.9	1.6	.8
No report	2.1	4.6	2.0	2.5	2.4	1.6	1.6

X 16. Laymen Are

those who are ministered to by the clergy who are the true church	4.9	1.5	4.9	7.8	4.1	4.1	9.1
people in part-time Christian service	5.2	1.6	5.3	6.0	5.5	4.2	5.0
nonordained Christians whose function is to help the clergy do the work of the church	60.4	57.6	63.3	59.7	61.7	53.7	56.3
members of the people of God called to a total ministry of witness and service in the world	24.9	33.3	22.5	21.4	23.3	32.6	26.2
Write-in	2.5	3.0	2.0	2.6	3.0	3.8	1.2
No report	2.1	3.0	2.0	2.5	2.4	1.6	2.2

I. RELIGIOUS BELIEFS

			Total Percentage				
	Total	C	NC	NE	SC	SE	W
17. Social Change							
is no responsibility of the church, since if individuals are soundly converted social problems will take care of themselves	7.6	15.1	7.2	6.0	7.9	9.7	10.8
is a partial responsibility of the church, but secondary to the transformation of individuals	40.5	16.7	39.7	38.2	40.5	46.4	36.4
is of equal importance with individual transformation	25.5	30.3	25.7	26.8	22.2	22.4	27.8
is even more important than individual conversion, since social conditions greatly affect individuals	9.0	7.5	10.1	9.9	9.6	6.0	11.7
is the all-important task of the church	11.7	22.8	11.9	12.2	13.0	9.5	9.1
Write-in	1.5	3.0	1.4	2.8	3.5	2.2	1.6
No report	4.2	4.6	4.0	4.1	3.3	3.8	2.6
18. A More Christian Society Will Come Mainly Through							
the conversion of individuals to Jesus Christ	44.1	39.4	44.5	41.9	47.9	53.0	34.0
the efforts of individual Christians for social betterment	23.1	16.6	22.4	22.3	22.4	19.9	29.6
the leadership of organized churches in advocating measures for social betterment	18.2	27.3	18.7	18.8	17.5	15.3	20.0
the co-operative efforts of socially minded persons and organizations in securing legislation to advance human welfare	8.8	12.1	9.6	11.4	4.6	4.6	11.2
Write-in	3.0	1.5	2.3	2.8	3.2	4.1	3.0
No report	2.8	3.1	2.5	2.8	4.4	3.1	2.2

19. Life After Death

Concern with life after death cuts the nerve of social responsibility	.9	1.5	1.2	.7	1.3	.6	.6
Concern with life after death weakens one's sense of social responsibility	2.0	6.1	1.5	2.1	1.4	2.9	2.6
Belief in life after death enhances one's sense of social responsibility	47.4	48.4	47.0	43.4	50.3	49.2	49.8
Belief in life after death is one of the strongest motivations for social responsibility	38.7	36.4	40.4	41.6	36.3	35.7	34.9
Write-in	3.8	1.5	3.5	4.0	4.4	4.3	3.4
No report	7.2	6.1	6.4	8.2	6.3	7.3	8.7

20. Human Rights Should Be Safeguarded Because

man is ultimately responsible to God alone, and must be free to fulfill his responsibility	27.0	12.1	28.3	27.1	27.9	25.8	25.5
people should have unlimited opportunity to develop their capacities as children of God	42.3	51.5	43.3	41.1	43.1	40.1	42.9
man by nature is a being of inherent dignity and worth	14.3	19.7	12.8	13.8	11.3	19.4	14.2
their recognition will lead to a happier society	11.3	12.1	11.7	12.9	10.8	8.0	12.8
Write-in	1.4	1.5	.8	1.1	1.5	3.2	1.4
No report	3.7	3.1	3.1	4.0	5.4	3.5	3.2

I, AS A CHRISTIAN, GET GUIDANCE FROM MY RELIGIOUS BELIEFS AS FOLLOWS:

	DIRECT GUIDANCE FOR MY OWN CONDUCT.	NO DIRECT GUIDANCE, BUT FIND MORAL PRINCIPLES TO GUIDE MY CONDUCT AND SOCIAL POLICY.	INDIRECT GUIDANCE FOR MY CONDUCT AND SOCIAL POLICY.	NO GUIDANCE BUT MAKE DECISIONS ON BASIS OF TASTE AND PRACTICALITY.	NR
21. Whether to drink intoxicants	42.9	36.3	6.3	4.9	9.6
22. What to do about segregation.	33.5	38.7	8.1	6.9	12.8
23. Whether to give economic and technical aid to other countries.	24.4	36.7	12.2	12.3	14.4
24. What the regulation of marriage and divorce should be.	42.2	33.7	7.0	4.1	13.0
25. Whether to participate in war.	28.4	37.4	10.2	9.0	15.0

II. ETHICAL AND SOCIAL BELIEFS

			Total Percentage				
		C	NC	NE	SC	SE	W
26. Temperance: I, As a Christian,							
may drink without reference to religious scruples	1.2	.0	.9	1.3	2.3	.8	1.1
may drink at social gatherings to avoid offending my host	1.0	1.5	4.6	1.0	.6	1.3	1.0
may use alcoholic beverages as long as I do so temperately and within reason	26.5	15.1	31.4	35.0	18.7	17.8	32.4
should totally abstain from alcoholic beverages	56.8	65.2	49.5	49.9	61.1	64.2	51.8
should work for prohibition	8.8	10.6	8.8	7.7	10.4	9.8	7.9
Write-in	3.9	3.0	3.4	2.9	5.6	4.6	4.2
No report	1.8	4.6	1.4	2.2	1.3	1.5	1.6
27. War: I, As a Christian Citizen,							
am obligated to support my country in war when its continued existence is at stake, apart from considerations of justice	47.2	50.0	47.7	51.3	48.1	40.7	47.2
can support or participate in war only for the preservation of justice	41.3	37.8	41.6	36.7	41.3	47.4	39.3
cannot support or participate in war in the nuclear age, since war can no longer serve the interests of justice	3.2	3.2	3.5	2.6	3.8	2.6	3.7
can under no circumstances support or participate in war	2.5	6.0	1.9	3.1	1.4	2.9	3.4
Write-in	2.6	1.5	1.9	2.4	2.4	3.2	4.6
No report	3.2	1.5	3.4	3.9	3.0	3.2	1.8

II. ETHICAL AND SOCIAL BELIEFS

28. Race

	Total	C	NC	NE	SC	SE	W
Some races are inherently inferior, and are not entitled to equal rights and privileges with those of superior capacity.	.6	.0	2.6	.7	1.2	2.9	.4
Members of all races should have equal opportunities, but segregation is desirable to preserve racial purity	24.3	1.5	17.7	19.8	26.5	41.2	12.1
Members of all races should have the same opportunities, but present patterns must be changed gradually	52.6	16.6	56.3	55.7	50.0	40.6	59.4
All discrimination and enforced segregation based on race should be abolished	18.6	80.4	20.2	19.7	18.3	8.4	24.9
Write-in	2.0	1.5	1.8	1.9	1.9	4.5	1.4
No report	1.9	.0	1.4	2.2	2.1	2.4	1.8

29. Race in the Organization of The Methodist Church

	Total	C	NC	NE	SC	SE	W
All jurisdictions, conferences, and churches should follow racial lines	14.5	1.5	10.2	9.1	15.5	34.1	6.4
The future status of the all-Negro jurisdiction and segregated Annual Conferences and local churches should be determined under permissive legislation	19.0	7.6	16.2	15.6	17.6	31.9	15.2
The all-Negro jurisdiction should now be abolished, and segregated Annual Conferences and local churches should be gradually eliminated by permissive legislation	20.4	16.6	22.1	23.7	23.8	9.3	24.7
Racial segregation should be abolished at all levels	33.2	72.7	39.1	39.5	28.0	10.1	42.0
Write-in	3.6	1.6	2.2	3.4	4.7	6.5	3.0
No report	9.3	.0	10.2	8.7	10.4	8.1	8.7

30. Politics

is of no concern to the Christian, whose citizenship is not of this world	.6	4.5	.2	1.1	.0	2.8	5.9
is a necessary evil, and Christians should be careful not to be contaminated by participating in it beyond necessity	2.4	13.6	2.1	2.2	2.8	2.1	1.8
should call forth the serious and intelligent concern of the conscientious Christian	64.4	50.0	63.4	64.1	63.6	65.0	62.0
is an area which Christians should regard as a special responsibility	29.4	30.3	31.4	28.7	29.6	26.8	27.9
Write-in	1.5	1.6	1.3	1.4	2.1	1.4	1.8
No report	1.7	.0	1.6	2.5	1.9	1.9	.6

31. A School Teacher Should

join no "cause" organizations	2.1	1.5	1.6	2.2	1.9	2.7	2.5
join only those organizations approved by the institution employing him	8.6	3.0	6.5	5.2	11.1	16.9	5.3
be free to join any "cause" organization (such as the League of Women Voters, National Association for the Advancement of Colored People, Citizens Council, Americans for Democratic Action, American Legion) so long as his membership does not interfere with his effectiveness in teaching	70.4	81.8	75.3	72.9	68.5	56.5	73.7
be able to join any "cause" organization	12.1	6.1	12.1	11.9	11.7	13.3	12.1
Write-in	2.9	4.5	1.7	3.3	2.7	5.0	3.2
No report	3.9	3.1	2.8	4.5	4.1	5.6	3.2

II. ETHICAL AND SOCIAL BELIEFS

Total Percentage

		C	NC	NE	SC	SE	W
32. A Methodist Minister Should							
not speak on controversial social issues	1.6	1.5	1.5	1.3	1.4	1.7	2.2
speak only on issues on which there is agreement in his local church	1.8	1.5	1.5	2.1	1.5	2.2	2.4
be free to take a position on controversial issues if it is in accord with the Social Creed	9.7	21.2	9.6	12.7	8.7	7.2	8.3
be free to take a position on controversial issues as long as this does not interfere with his parish ministry	14.4	12.2	14.5	16.2	12.4	12.7	16.4
be free to take, on controversial issues, any position which he regards as Christian	68.4	60.6	69.1	64.2	72.0	70.0	67.9
Write-in	2.2	1.5	2.0	1.5	2.5	3.1	2.2
No report	1.9	1.5	1.8	2.0	1.5	3.1	.6
33. The Family							
should seek to reclaim the whole range of functions once performed by the family	7.1	13.6	6.8	8.0	6.0	7.9	5.9
may share some functions with other institutions, but should retain primary responsibility for moral and religious education	60.1	48.5	62.9	57.1	63.0	53.9	64.7
should share with other institutions the responsibility for all of the functions	23.8	31.8	22.1	23.6	23.5	27.6	22.9
should accept the more limited range of functions left to it as other institutions now care for education, recreation, moral instruction, security for the aged, etc.	3.8	3.0	3.0	5.8	3.2	3.9	3.3

Write-in	1.0	3.1	1.0	1.3	.6	1.5	.2
No report	4.2	.0	4.2	4.2	3.7	5.2	3.0

34. Public Power Projects Like TVA

are a threat to our free enterprise economy	9.4	1.5	9.9	10.4	9.2	6.8	11.4
are questionable because they tax all our citizens to provide cheap electricity for a few	13.5	13.6	13.0	18.9	12.7	10.5	10.9
greatly improve the total economic welfare of the nation	41.0	48.5	41.2	35.5	39.3	48.3	38.9
provide worthy experiments in the extension of democracy	18.7	19.7	18.6	18.5	17.1	20.2	19.4
Write-in	3.0	4.5	2.6	2.7	2.7	3.9	3.9
No report	14.4	12.2	14.7	14.0	19.0	10.3	15.5

35. Economic and Technical Aid to Other Countries Should

await our caring for our own needs and interests	3.4	4.5	2.9	3.4	3.9	2.7	3.2
be granted only if it will advance our military objectives and economic interests	1.3	1.5	1.0	2.8	.9	4.9	.9
consider the welfare of the peoples involved as well as American interests	45.6	41.0	44.1	46.6	45.9	44.8	42.1
be allocated on the basis of the needs of humanity as a whole	45.1	50.0	47.5	42.5	43.9	42.7	49.8
Write-in	1.1	1.5	.8	.6	1.6	1.7	1.2
No report	3.5	1.5	3.7	4.1	3.8	3.2	2.8

36. United Nations

World organization involves dangerous infringement on national sovereignty; hence each nation should pursue its own course, making only such temporary alliances as serve its ends	2.7	3.0	2.5	2.2	8.9	5.1	2.2

II. ETHICAL AND SOCIAL BELIEFS

Total Percentage

		C	NC	NE	SC	SE	W
The UN deserves support as our best political hope for world peace	80.4	75.8	80.6	82.3	74.0	78.2	80.4
The UN deserves full support, but should be superseded as soon as possible by real world government	8.6	15.1	8.4	7.7	8.9	7.3	10.6
Full world government, abolishing national sovereignty, is the world's best political hope	1.5	1.5	1.6	1.6	1.1	1.0	1.4
Write-in	2.3	1.5	2.1	2.1	3.6	3.1	1.2
No report	4.5	3.1	4.8	4.1	3.5	5.3	4.2

37. The Main Purpose of a Prison Should Be

		C	NC	NE	SC	SE	W
the punishment of the enemies of society	1.2	.0	1.4	1.5	.5	1.5	1.2
the confinement of criminals whose freedom would endanger society	18.4	7.6	17.9	19.3	18.7	17.2	21.8
the cure of sick and maladjusted persons	4.7	3.0	4.3	5.6	5.9	4.9	2.5
the rehabilitation of offenders and their restoration to normal life in society	69.7	84.8	71.5	67.9	68.1	69.2	67.1
Write-in	3.6	3.0	3.1	3.3	3.8	4.1	5.2
No report	2.4	1.6	1.8	2.4	3.0	3.1	2.2

38. Occupations Should Be Chosen Mainly in Terms of

		C	NC	NE	SC	SE	W
income and social status	.7	1.5	.9	.6	.3	.6	.7
security in job and residence	4.8	3.0	5.1	5.9	4.4	2.8	5.8
personal satisfaction and meaning in work	37.0	27.3	40.1	39.2	35.5	26.9	42.9
use of personal capacities in the service of mankind	14.6	12.1	16.9	13.6	14.1	9.9	18.1

use of personal capacities on the basis of stewardship to

God	36.0	53.0	30.1	33.3	38.8	52.9	25.9
Write-in	3.2	3.1	2.9	2.9	4.7	3.0	3.4
No report	3.7	.0	4.0	4.5	2.2	3.9	3.2

39. Status of Men and Women

Woman's place is in the home	6.9	9.1	6.7	7.4	6.2	8.4	5.1
Men and women have complementary but different roles to play	23.7	18.1	23.3	21.5	24.1	27.2	23.3
The principle of full equality must be modified by woman's responsibility to home and children	30.6	27.3	30.8	31.4	31.0	28.5	32.0
Men and women should have equal and identical rights in employment and education in both church and society	34.1	45.5	34.3	35.2	33.9	30.5	36.2
Write-in	2.2	.0	2.5	1.9	2.4	2.3	1.4
No report	2.5	.0	2.4	2.6	2.4	3.1	2.0

40. The Methodist Church

has the true gospel and should not jeopardize its witness by joint activities with other denominations	1.5	3.1	1.1	3.2	1.1	2.3	.6
should co-operate with other Christian bodies in activities that can be done together better than separately	63.4	63.6	65.3	59.6	67.1	64.4	64.6
should, while co-operating with non-Methodist Christian bodies, seek full union with other Methodist bodies	7.9	6.0	7.6	7.0	8.6	7.8	6.3
should seek full union with all Christian bodies willing to explore the possibility	22.9	22.7	22.1	25.6	18.9	20.7	24.9
Write-in	1.6	1.5	1.5	1.9	1.7	2.2	1.4
No report	2.7	3.1	2.4	2.7	2.6	2.6	2.2

II. ETHICAL AND SOCIAL BELIEFS

	Total Percentage						
		C	NC	NE	SC	SE	W
41. Public Education Should Receive Federal Aid							
only if complete control remains with the states	21.6	9.0	21.1	16.7	24.2	29.3	18.4
only if parochial and private schools are specifically excluded	12.0	6.1	10.6	15.6	9.7	10.4	16.0
if parochial and private schools receive no direct subsidy but only such indirect aid as bus transportation	3.4	.0	3.6	4.0	3.4	2.5	3.4
on the basis of need	53.5	80.3	56.3	54.1	50.4	47.4	53.3
Write-in	4.5	1.5	4.0	4.9	5.5	5.1	4.1
No report	5.0	3.1	4.4	4.7	6.8	5.3	4.8
42. Health							
Socialized medicine would kill the individual initiative of doctors and the self-reliance of their patients	20.4	7.5	23.1	20.3	23.0	17.2	15.6
Health insurance is the best way for people to meet the costs of illness	54.0	59.1	52.2	53.5	53.4	56.5	56.5
The co-operative employment of physicians by voluntary health associations would provide adequate care at lowest cost	15.0	25.8	14.9	15.3	11.8	15.1	17.6
The government should provide free medical and dental care for all the people	1.8	.0	1.6	2.3	1.6	2.1	2.1
Write-in	3.9	4.5	3.9	4.0	3.4	3.8	4.6
No report	4.8	3.1	4.3	4.6	6.8	5.3	3.6

43. In Labor Legislation the Federal Government Should

pass "right to work" laws and curb the power of labor unions	29.3	16.7	29.6	29.3	33.5	28.3	26.7
aim primarily at controlling unethical labor practices and racketeering	44.3	51.5	44.0	44.4	43.2	42.5	49.0
protect labor's right to a union shop but limit the right to strike in the public interest	14.2	21.2	14.2	14.2	10.2	16.1	14.6
protect labor unions in provision for union shop, collective bargaining, etc.	3.4	6.0	4.0	3.0	1.6	3.1	4.3
Write-in	2.6	1.5	2.6	3.0	2.2	2.6	2.4
No report	6.2	3.1	5.6	6.1	9.3	7.4	3.0

44. The Federal Government Should

let the farmer care for himself and his soil	9.0	1.5	12.1	8.4	9.4	5.3	6.2
concern itself only with soil conservation	9.2	3.1	10.9	8.2	9.1	7.4	9.8
concern itself with control of agricultural surpluses and with soil conservation, but not with price support	24.4	18.1	24.8	26.8	22.1	21.0	28.4
act to stabilize farm prices, control surpluses, and conserve the soil	47.5	69.7	43.1	47.8	47.1	54.4	47.4
Write-in	2.9	4.5	2.8	2.2	4.4	2.7	2.2
No report	7.0	3.1	6.3	6.6	7.9	9.2	6.0

III. SOCIAL ACTION

HOW DO YOU EXPRESS YOUR SOCIAL RESPONSIBILITY?

	REGULARLY	FAIRLY OFTEN	SELDOM	NEVER	NR
45. By voting in national elections.	83.5	4.1	1.2	2.9	8.3
46. By voting in state elections.	79.6	6.9	1.3	3.3	8.9
47. By voting in local elections.	75.5	10.2	2.1	3.2	9.0

By participation in nonchurch organizations concerned with social problems:

	REGULARLY	FAIRLY OFTEN	SELDOM	NEVER	NR
48. On the national level.	16.7	17.2	21.8	18.0	26.3
49. On the local community level.	33.0	27.3	16.1	8.2	15.4

In writing letters expressing your concern:

	REGULARLY	FAIRLY OFTEN	SELDOM	NEVER	NR
50. To members of Congress.	3.5	11.3	29.4	41.0	14.8
51. To the editors of newspapers.	2.1	5.6	23.3	50.1	18.9

52. In the above areas, do you consider your action to be aimed in general at:
    - a. Seeking social change? 34.1
    - b. Conserving present traditions? 20.4
    - c. No report 45.5

DO YOU LOOK FOR GUIDANCE AND LEADERSHIP IN AREAS OF SOCIAL RESPONSIBILITY FROM:

	MUCH	SOME	LITTLE	NONE	NR
53. Your minister?	33.5	36.8	8.4	6.0	15.3
54. Your local church commission?	10.8	29.7	16.3	18.1	25.1
55. General church boards and publications?	14.6	32.5	15.7	13.9	23.3
56. General Conference pronouncements?	10.1	22.9	19.3	20.1	27.6
57. National Council of Churches?	9.0	20.8	18.7	22.9	28.6
58. National publications other than Methodist, such as *Christian Century, Christian Herald?*	8.1	22.2	14.7	27.0	28.0

IV. GENERAL BACKGROUND

59. Age
    10-24   8.1
    25-44   40.4
    45 up   48.0
    NR   3.5

60. Sex
    Male   45.6
    Female   46.8
    NR   7.6

61. Marital Status
    Married   77.5
    Single   10.7
    Widow or widower 7.1
    Divorced   1.2
    NR   3.5

62. Education
    a. Elementary School:
       ATTENDED   3.2
       COMPLETED   5.4
    b. High School:
       ATTENDED   10.8
       COMPLETED   24.6
    c. College:
       ATTENDED   19.1
       COMPLETED   13.9
    d. Graduate School:
       ATTENDED   6.2
       COMPLETED   13.0
    e. NR   3.8

63. State Your Racial Background
    a. White   81.8
    b. Non-white   1.5
    c. NR   16.7

299

64. State Your Exact Occupation

1. Professional   15.3
2. Farm Operators & Managers   9.4
3. Clerical Workers   6.8
4. Sales Workers   3.3
5. Craftsmen, Foremen & Kindred Workers   4.7
6. Operatives   2.3
7. Domestic Services   .2
8. Services Workers   1.0
9. Farm Laborers & Laborers   .9
10. Housewives, Retired, Student, & Unemployed   37.9
11. Ministers   9.5
12. NR   8.7

65. Family Income Per Year

1. Under $2,500   10.4
2. $2,500-4,999   28.7
3. $5,000-9,999   41.3
4. $10,000 up   11.1
5. NR   8.5

66-67. Size of Community in Which You Were Reared and Now Reside

	WERE REARED	NOW RESIDE
1. 0-2,499	56.9	37.4
2. 2,500-9,999	13.0	16.7
3. 10,000-99,999	13.5	22.5
4. 100,000 up	10.5	13.0
5. NR	6.1	10.4

68. In What Church Were You Reared?

1. Methodist   66.6
2. Presbyterian, Congregational, Baptist, Lutheran, Episcopal   19.5
3. Roman Catholic   1.8
4. Other   8.4
5. NR   3.7

69.-70. Size of Church in Which You Were Reared and Now Belong

	WERE REARED	NOW BELONG
1. 0-249 members	52.0	26.0
2. 250-499 members	18.6	23.9
3. 500-999 members	10.3	17.6
4. 1,000 up	7.5	20.7
5. NR	11.6	11.8

71. How Long Ago Did You Join the Methodist Church?

1. 0-6 years	14.5
2. 7-12 years	11.8
3. 13 up	61.6
4. NR	12.1

72.-73. Estimate the Number of Sundays Attended During the Past Year.

	WORSHIP	SUNDAY SCHOOL
1. 1-4	7.6	5.1
2. 5-12	7.7	4.9
3. 13-24	24.8	6.3
4. 25-36	12.0	12.4
5. 36 up	39.2	45.3
6. NR	8.6	25.9

at least 50% a Sunday   49% a Sunday

74. How Much Does Your Family Contribute Weekly to Your Church?

1. $ .00- 1.00	10.3	*5*
2. $ 1.01- 2.00	13.3	*20*
3. $ 2.01- 3.00	11.7	*29*
4. $ 3.01- 4.00	10.6	*37*
5. $ 4.01- 5.00	16.5	*74*
6. $ 5.01-10.00	13.8	*96*
7. $10.01 up	5.9	*60 min.*
8. NR	17.8	*# 321 per family (ave. 2 members per family)*

at least $76 per member a year

75.76. Are You Related to Any of the Following Church Organizations?

	MEMBER	OFFICER
1. WSCS	1756	595
2. Methodist Men	793	111
3. MYF	325	168
4. Official Board	1520	464
5. Choir	605	65
6. Church-school Teacher	808	296
7. Other	1155	700
8. None	528	717
9. NR	398	2023

77. Check Your Political Preference

1. Republican	49.4
2. Democrat	33.1
3. Independent	11.4
4. Other	1.0
5. NR	5.1

78. Number of Persons in Household

1. One	6.5
2. Two	25.5
3. Three	18.7
4. Four	21.6
5. Five	14.2
6. Six up	9.5
7. NR	4.0

301

METHODOLOGY AND REPRESENTATIVENESS OF THE INQUIRY

To make possible a fair sampling of the total membership of The Methodist Church, every sixtieth church was selected electronically from an alphabetical list of charges. The pastors of these churches were asked if they would be willing to co-operate. Since the distribution of the favorable responses changed somewhat the character of the sample, replacements were sought according to the known control categories of (1) size of church, (2) size of community, and (3) jurisdiction. The co-operation of the resident bishops of the episcopal areas involved was also enlisted. Thus every effort was made to establish a sample which would represent the different sizes of churches and communities approximately in the proportion in which these sizes actually occur in each jurisdiction.

Altogether a total of 357 pastors agreed to co-operate. Each was requested to select alphabetically, without regard to age, sex, education, intelligence, social or religious attitudes, degree of church interest and activity, or similar factors, every tenth member of his church, asking him to complete the questionnaire and return it unsigned to the pastor in a sealed envelope. Questionnaires numbering 5,020 were finally returned from a total of 267 Charges. Since 12,000 schedules were mailed out, this represents a return of about 41.8 per cent.

At the minimum, these data represent adequately the 150,340 members of the co-operating churches. At most, they may be said to be the best possible sample of the entire church. Generalizations as to the beliefs of all of Methodism are safely supported by the tests and comparisons demonstrated below.

Table 1

Distribution of 22,435 Methodist Churches by Jurisdiction Compared with 267 Responding [1]

		JURISDICTIONS					
	Total	C	NC	NE	SC	SE	W
ALL CHARGES	100%	7.3	22.3	20.8	19.3	23.4	6.9
CHARGES SAMPLED	100%	3.3	27.7	31.5	12.4	16.1	9.0

[1] *Source Book of Town and Country Methodism* ed. by Roy A. Sturm (Philadelphia: Division of National Missions of the Board of Missions of The Methodist Church, 1955), p. 147. Section quoted was by Herbert E. Stotts. The alphabetical symbols designate respectively the Central, North Central, Northeastern, South Central, Southeastern, and Western Jurisdictions.

Table 2
*Distribution of 9,691,916 Methodists by Jurisdiction
Compared to 5,020 MESTA Respondents.[2]*

	JURISDICTIONS						
	Total	C	NC	NE	SC	SE	W
ALL METH-ODISTS	100%	3.7	23.3	19.8	19.6	27.3	6.3
SAMPLE	100%	1.3	37.1	20.4	12.7	18.4	10.1

Table 3
*Distribution of 6,165,353 Methodists by Size of Community
Compared to 5,020 MESTA Respondents.[3]*

	SIZE OF COMMUNITY					
	Total	0-2,499	2,500-9,999	10,000-99,999	100,000 up	NR
ALL METH-ODISTS	100%	39.3	17.8	20.9	16.3	5.7
MESTA SAMPLE	100%	37.4	16.7	22.5	13.0	10.4

Table 4
*Distribution of 9,691,916 Methodists by Size of Church
Compared to 5,020 Persons Responding [4]*

	SIZE OF CHURCH					
	Total	0-249	250-499	500-999	1,000 up	NR
ALL METH-ODISTS	100%	19.7	24.5	30.2	24.4	1.2
MESTA SAMPLE	100%	26.0	23.9	17.6	20.7	11.8

[2] *General Minutes of the Annual Conferences of the Methodist Church*, 1958.

[3] *Source Book of Town and Country Methodism*, p. 126. Data on distribution by size of community are not available for the other members of The Methodist Church. NR designates no response.

[4] *Ibid.*, p. 127.

303

The judgment that these distributions are adequately representative is confirmed by Chi Square calculations made on representative questions as succeeding waves of schedules were returned and tabulated. A Chi Square of .05 means that each succeeding wave could be expected to provide the same distribution of answers in 95 per cent of the cases. Such patterns appeared at the .05 level, for example, on questions 6, 26, 32, 38, and 44, indicating that any number of additional returns would have yielded substantially the same results.

Table 5

Comparison of 121,188,924 Persons Aged 10 and over
in the U.S. Population with the 5,020 Respondents [5]

Age Groups	U. S. Population	MESTA Sample
10-24 yrs.	27.6	8.2
25-44 yrs.	37.5	39.7
45 and over	34.9	48.6
No report		3.5

Surveys made in 1959 of the Methodist churches of five widely scattered districts[6] show that members aged 10-24 comprise an average of 21 per cent of the total membership of those districts. Thus the number of Methodist church members in this age-group is proportionately smaller and the number above 24 is proportionately greater than the numbers in these brackets in the general population. Many persons do not join the church until they reach adulthood. Yet the percentage of young people in these districts is still considerably higher than the percentage in this category in the MESTA sample.

Although pretesting showed that teen-agers were capable of answering the questionnaire under controlled conditions, it appears that Methodist youth did not respond in proportion to their probable numbers in the church. The research committee considered the possibility of removing from the total sample the 422 questionnaires returned by persons aged 10-24. However, though these are not adequate in number, they are probably not unrepresentative in character, and it is clearly desirable that Meth-

[5] U. S. Census, 1950, Vol. I.
[6] Fort Wayne, Bloomington, Fort Worth, Geneva, and Sunbury, located respectively in the North Indiana, Indiana, Central Texas, Central New York, and Central Pennsylvania Annual Conferences. These studies were made by the Department of Church Surveys of Boston University.

odist youth be represented. It therefore seems best to include them, while discounting the results accordingly.

Table 6

Marital Status of 111,703,400 U.S. Residents
14 Years of Age and over
Compared to 5,020 Methodist Respondents [7]

MARITAL STATUS	U. S.	MESTA
Total	100%	100%
Married	66.6	77.5
Single	23.1	10.7
Widowed	8.0	7.1
Divorced	2.3	1.2
No Response		3.5

The comparison of Methodists with the total population by marital status is in conformity with the experience and expectation of the research team.

The smaller percentage of divorced persons is probably a fair reflection of a lower divorce rate among Methodist church members than in the total population.

Among the Methodists surveyed are 479 ministers, 212 more than the number of pastors of co-operating charges. Sample comparisons make plain that the inclusion of these questionnaires does not produce distortion, and they provide valuable augmentation of the returns from this jurisdiction.

The following table illustrates that, with two exceptions, in each question sampled the position with the highest score (the "model category") for the clergy is the same as that for the total number of respondents. Furthermore, with one exception the second rank in each case follows the same pattern of co-variance.

[7] U. S. Census, 1950, Vol. I.

Table 7

Modal and Second Rank Categories
Compared for 479 Ministers and 5,020 National Methodist Scores
* M designates ministers; T, the total group.

QUESTION					
Position No.	7 Christian Church	9 Religious Experience	13 Belief and Conduct	16 Laymen	18 Christian Society
1 M*			47.5		43.7
T			43.3		44.8
2 M	19.2	63.6	41.0		21.9
T	23.7	46.1	37.2		22.6
3 M	61.1	32.2		30.5	
T	34.6	41.5		59.9	
4 M	13.6			62.6	
T	30.4			24.8	
5 M					
T					

QUESTION					
Position No.	28 Race	32 Ministerial Freedom	38 Occupational Choice	40 Ecumenical Co-operation	67 Size of Community
1 M*					40.5
T					37.4
2 M				55.1	
T				64.2	
3 M	48.8		11.7		19.8
T	52.3		36.6		22.5

QUESTION					
Position No.	28 Race	32 Ministerial Freedom	38 Occupational Choice	40 Ecumenical Co-operation	67 Size of Community
4 M	28.4	8.0		33.0	
T	18.9	14.4		22.4	
5 M		78.7	78.5		
T		68.4	33.2		

The two exceptions are questions 16 on the role of the laity and 38 on occupational choice, and in each case the divergence is what one would expect. Of the total number of replies 59.9 per cent view laymen as "non-ordained Christians whose function is to help the clergy do the work of the church," while only 30.5 per cent of the clergy themselves and 34.5 per cent of the southeastern clergy take this position. In contrast, 62.6 per cent of the ministers and 60.1 per cent of the ministers in the southeast, but only 24.8 per cent of the total sample, regard laymen as "members of the people of God called to a total ministry of witness and service in the world." Comparably, 78.5 per cent of the clergy and 77.3 per cent of the southeastern clergy maintain that occupations "should be chosen mainly in terms of the use of personal capacities in stewardship to God," while only 36 per cent of the total group make this answer. Of the total number of respondents, 37 per cent think that occupations should be selected chiefly in terms of "personal satisfaction and meaning in work," while only 11.7 per cent of the ministers and 13.1 per cent of those in the southeast hold this view. It is noteworthy that in each of these deviations the ministers of the Southeastern Jurisdiction are closer to the position of the total sample than are the ministers as a whole.

Although in question 7 on the church the modal category is the same for ministers and laymen, the percentages differ widely, and the second-rank positions also are different. Many more ministers (61.1 per cent) than laymen (34.6 per cent) view the church as "the community of those who have been renewed by the Holy Spirit," and many more laymen (30.4 per cent) than ministers (13.6 per cent) think of the church simply as "the society of those who have joined together in their quest for the religious life."

On the other questions of theology and socio-ethical belief the replies of the ministers do not deviate sufficiently to justify removing them from the total sample. The divergences noted reflect differences which one would expect to find between clergy and laity in the particular areas concerned. They do inevitably change somewhat the character of the total results for those questions. However, even in these instances the removal of the 212 polled in the special study would change the score for any one position by less than two per cent.[8]

Further light is shed on the universe studied by the replies to questions 72 and 75 on frequency of attendance at Sunday worship and membership in church organizations. Of the total number of respondents, 55.5 per cent attended 37 Sundays or more during the preceding year, 18 per cent attended from 25 to 36 Sundays, and only 10 per cent attended 12 Sundays or less. The respondents also included 1756 members of the Woman's Society of Christian Service, 793 Methodist Men, 325 members of the Methodist Youth Fellowship, 1520 members of official boards, 808 church school teachers, and 605 choir members. In spite of the presence of overlapping memberships, these figures on church attendance and activity strongly suggest that the questionnaires returned represent the most loyal, interested, and active members of our churches, and therefore those most likely to have opinions which they are able and willing to articulate on questions related to Christian and church responsibility. It seems highly doubtful whether any other type of approach would have won a much more affirmative response from the nominal Christians who are so numerous in the average congregation.

When all factors are weighed, it can be said with considerable assurance that the results of the questionnaire represent adequately the views of the 150,340 members of the congregations sampled, with the possible exception of those aged 10-24. The tests and samples cited also indicate that generalizations may safely be drawn respecting the views of the membership of The Methodist Church as a whole.

[8] For example, in question 16, where the most extreme variation occurs, if the 212 ministers were omitted the percentage of the total sample for position 3 would rise from 59.9 to 61.2, while that for position 4 would drop from 24.8 to 23.1.

Bibliography

Anderson, William K. (ed.). *Methodism*. New York and Nashville: The Methodist Publishing House, 1947.

Arndt, Elmer J. F. (ed.). *The Heritage of the Reformation*. New York: R. R. Smith, 1950.

Baker, Eric. *The Faith of a Methodist*. London: The Epworth Press, 1958.

Beach, Waldo and H. Richard Niebuhr. *Christian Ethics: Sources of the Living Tradition*. New York: Ronald Press, 1955.

Bennett, John C. *Christian Ethics and Social Policy*. New York: Charles Scribner's Sons, 1946.

————. *Christians and the State*. New York: Charles Scribner's Sons, 1958.

————. *Social Salvation*. New York: Charles Scribner's Sons, 1935.

Boulding, Kenneth E. *Religious Perspectives of College Teaching in Economics*. New Haven: Edward W. Hazen Foundation, n.d.

Bowne, Bordon Parker. *Personalism*. Boston: Houghton Mifflin Co., 1908.

Brooks, Phillips. *Lectures on Preaching*. London: Griffith, Farrar, Okeden, and Welsh, 1886.

Brunner, Emil. *The Divine Imperative: A Study in Christian Ethics*. Translated by Olive Wyon. New York: The Macmillan Company, 1937.

Cannon, William Ragsdale. *The Theology of John Wesley*. Nashville: Abingdon Press, 1946.

Carter, Paul A. *The Decline and Revival of the Social Gospel: Social and Political Liberalism in American Protestant Churches, 1920-1942*. Ithaca: Cornell University Press, 1956.

Chalmers, Allan Knight. *High Wind at Noon*, New York: Charles Scribner's Sons, 1948.

Childs, Marquis W. and Douglass Cater. *Ethics in a Business Society*. New York: New American Library of World Literature, 1954.

Clark, Elmer T. and E. Benson Perkins (eds.). *Proceedings of the Ninth World Methodist Conference, Lake Junaluska, North Carolina, U.S.A., August 27-September 12, 1956*. Nashville: The Methodist Publishing House, 1957.

Culver, Dwight W. *Negro Segregation in the Methodist Church*. New Haven: Yale University Press, 1953.

DeWolf, L. Harold. *The Case for Theology in Liberal Perspective*. Philadelphia: Westminster Press, 1959.

————. Harold. *A Theology of the Living Church*. New York: Harper and Brothers, 1953.

Flew, R. Newton (ed.). *The Nature of the Church*. London: S.C.M. Press, 1952.

Harkness, Georgia. *Christian Ethics*. Nashville: Abingdon Press, 1957.
———. *The Modern Rival of Christian Faith: An Analysis of Secularism*. Nashville: Abingdon Press, 1952.
———. *Understanding the Christian Faith*. New York and Nashville: Abingdon-Cokesbury Press, 1950.
Holbrook, Clyde A. *Faith and Community*. New York: Harper and Brothers, 1959.
Hutchison, John A. (ed.) *Christian Faith and Social Action*. New York: Charles Scribner's Sons, 1953.
Kennedy, Gerald. *I Believe*. Nashville: Abingdon Press, 1958.
Kern, Paul B. *The Basic Beliefs of Jesus*. Nashville: Cokesbury Press, 1935.
———. *Methodism Has a Message!* Nashville: Abingdon Press, 1941.
Leibrecht, Walter (ed.). *Religion and Culture: Essays in Honor of Paul Tillich*. New York: Harper and Brothers, 1959.
Lewis, Edwin. *The Creator and the Adversary*. Nashville: Abingdon Press, 1948.
Liggett, Frank M. (ed.). *The Book of the Sesqui-Centennial of American Methodism*. Baltimore: Frank M. Liggett, 1935.
Lindström, Harold. *Wesley and Sanctification*. Stockholm: Nya Bokförlags Aktiebolaget, 1946.
McConnell, Francis J. *By the Way: An Autobiography*, Nashville: Abingdon Press, 1952.
MacLeod, George Fielden. *We Shall Rebuild*. Glasgow: Iona Community Publishing Department, 1944.
Micklem, Nathaniel. *The Theology of Politics*. London: Oxford University Press, 1941.
Miller, Alexander. *The Renewal of Man*. Garden City, N.Y.: Doubleday and Company, 1955.
Miller, Robert Moats. *American Protestantism and Social Issues, 1919-1939*. Chapel Hill: University of North Carolina Press, 1958.
Muelder, Walter G. *Foundations of the Responsible Society*. Nashville: Abingdon Press, 1959.
———. *Religion and Economic Responsibility*. New York: Charles Scribner's Sons, 1953.
The Nature of the Christian Church According to the Teaching of the Methodists. London: Methodist Publishing House, 1937.
Nelson, J. Robert. *The Realm of Redemption*. London: The Epworth Press, 1951.
Niebuhr, H. Richard. *Christ and Culture*. New York: Harper and Brothers, 1951.
———. *The Kingdom of God in America*. Chicago: Willett, Clark and Company, 1937.
Niebuhr, Reinhold. *An Interpretation of Christian Ethics*. New York: Harper and Brothers, 1935.
———. *Moral Man and Immoral Society*. New York: Charles Scribner's Sons, 1932.
Outler, Albert C. *The Christian Tradition and the Unity We Seek*. New York: Oxford University Press, 1957.
———. *Psychotherapy and the Christian Message*. New York: Harper and Brothers, 1954.

Oxnam, G. Bromley. A *Testament of Faith*. Boston: Little, Brown and Company, 1958.

Peters, John Leland. *Christian Perfection and American Methodism*. Nashville: Abingdon Press, 1956.

Rall, Harris F. *Religion as Salvation*. Nashville: Abingdon Press, 1953.

Ramsey, Paul. *Basic Christian Ethics*. New York: Charles Scribner's Sons, 1950.

———. (ed.). *Faith and Ethics: The Theology of H. Richard Niebuhr*. New York: Harper and Brothers, 1957.

Rasmussen, Albert Terrill. *Christian Social Ethics: Exerting Christian Influence*. Englewood Cliffs, New Jersey: Prentice-Hall, Inc., 1956.

Rauschenbusch, Walter. *A Theology for the Social Gospel*. New York: The Macmillan Company, 1918.

Richardson, Alan and Schweitzer, Wolfgang (eds.). *Biblical Authority for Today*. Philadelphia: Westminster Press, 1951.

Spann, J. Richard (ed.). *The Church and Social Responsibility*. Nashville: Abingdon Press, 1953.

Straughn, James H. *Inside Methodist Union*. Nashville: The Methodist Publishing House, 1958.

Symons, C. T. *Our Fathers' Faith and Ours: A Manual of Membership of the Church of New Zealand*. Auckland: Board of Publications of the Methodist Church of New Zealand, n.d.

Thomas, George F. *Christian Ethics and Moral Philosophy*. New York: Charles Scribner's Sons, 1955.

Towards the One Church. Christchurch, New Zealand: National Council of Churches of New Zealand, 1954.

Visser 't Hooft, W. A. and J. H. Oldham. *The Church and Its Function in Society*. Chicago and New York: Willett, Clark and Company, 1937.

Welch, Claude. *The Reality of the Church*. New York: Charles Scribner's Sons, 1958.

Wesley, John. *Explanatory Notes upon the New Testament*. London: William Bowyer, 1818.

———. *The Works of John Wesley*. Reprint of 1872 Edition. Grand Rapids, Michigan: Zondervan Publishing House, [1958-59].

———. *The Journal of the Rev. John Wesley, A.M.* Edited by Nehemiah Curnock. 8 vols. New York: Eaton and Mains, n.d.

———. *The Letters of the Rev. John Wesley, A.M.* Edited by John Telford. 8 vols. London: The Epworth Press, 1931.

———. *Wesley's Standard Sermons*. Edited by Edward H. Sugden. 2 vols. London: The Epworth Press, 1921.

Wesley, John and Charles. *The Poetical Works of John and Charles Wesley*. Edited by George Osborn. 13 vols. London: Wesleyan-Methodist Conference Office, 1868-1872.

West, Charles C. *Communism and the Theologians*. London: S.C.M. Press, 1958.

Yinger, J. Milton. *Religion in the Struggle for Power*. Durham, North Carolina: Duke University Press, 1946.

General Index

313

Index of Persons

317